RAINFOREST RELATIONS

RAINFOREST RELATIONS

Gender and Resource Use among the
Mende of Gola, Sierra Leone

MELISSA LEACH

SMITHSONIAN INSTITUTION PRESS
Washington, D.C.

This book is dedicated to the villagers living around Sierra Leone's Gola reserves, and to their hopes for a peaceful forest future.

Published in the United States of America by
Smithsonian Institution Press

ISBN 1–56098–500–3 (cased)

Library of Congress Catalog Number
available from the publisher

First published in Great Britain by
Edinburgh University Press Ltd

Typeset in Linotronic Plantin
by Speedspools, Edinburgh
Printed and bound in Great Britain by
The University Press, Cambridge

CONTENTS

LIST OF FIGURES, PLATES AND TABLES

FIGURES

PLATES

TABLES

PREFACE

The Gola forest reserves of Sierra Leone were, until recently, in a region of peace and political stability in which long-term conservation planning seemed both feasible and desirable. This was the context in which this book was researched, and which its arguments address. However, in early 1991 the area was brought sharply and shockingly into the war and conflict which had afflicted Liberia over the preceding year and which now spilled into the border zones of Sierra Leone. Many of the Mende villagers living around the Gola reserves, who had hosted large numbers of refugees from the Liberian civil war throughout 1990, became refugees themselves; others remained in the forest area under appalling rebel-occupied conditions. At the time of writing, the war continues and the full extent of its complex causes and consequences are still unclear. Conflict of this kind provides a very different context for conservation. This book does not try to address it, although it does make some reference to the effects of the 1990 refugee-host relations on the use of forest resources (see also Leach, 1992a).

ACKNOWLEDGEMENTS

This book is the product of several stages of research involving different sets of colleagues, and my numerous debts of gratitude reflect this. My thanks are due first and foremost to the people of Madina and Malema chiefdom, for their warmth, friendship, cooperation and insight during the time that I lived with them. The original research for this book was funded by the Economic and Social Research Council (ESRC, award no. A00428624040), with additional fieldwork support from the Central Research Fund of the University of London. The MacArthur Foundation funded a subsequent period of fieldwork on which this book draws, under the auspices of the Institute of Development Studies 'Securities' project. I am grateful to all these funders.

In Sierra Leone, I should especially like to thank my research assistant, Mary Konima Williams, and Adama Idriss and family who continually provided a friendly alternative home for me in Bo. I was affiliated to the Institute of African Studies, Fourah Bay College, and the Department of Environmental Studies and Geography, Njala University College of the University of Sierra Leone. My thanks are due to Professor Magbaily Fyle of the former, and Dr Osman Bah, Dr Serrie Kamara, Dr Bob Kandeh and Esther Mokuwa of the latter, for the academic and material support they provided. At Njala, my thanks are also due to Dr Sillah of the Department of Biological Sciences who kindly helped me with the identification of fish species, and B. M. S. Turay and Mr Boboh of the National Herbarium who assisted with plant identification. Invaluable information and assistance was provided by staff of the Forestry Division of the Ministry of Agriculture, Natural Resources and Forestry, especially the late David Gabba, and by staff of the Royal Society for the Protection of Birds and the Conservation Society of Sierra Leone, especially Peter Wood. Collaborative links with the University College London Gola Project provided an important context for this research. I am grateful for the encouragement, support and opportunity to share ideas offered by Paul Richards, Glyn Davies and others connected with the project.

This book draws on my doctoral dissertation, completed in the Department of Anthropology, School of Oriental and African Studies, London (SOAS), and was itself written while I was a Fellow of the Institute of Development Studies at the University of Sussex. Numerous London and Sussex colleagues provided invaluable academic and personal encouragement, including Elisabeth Croll, Richard Fardon, Philip Gatter, Robin Mearns, David Parkin and Paul Richards. I have had the opportunity to present a number of chapters at seminars and conferences. Chapter 2 formed the introduction to the 1991 seminar series on 'Women and Environment' at the Centre for Cross-cultural Research on Women, Queen Elizabeth House, Oxford, and was presented again at a SIDA workshop in Stockholm and in the social anthropology department at Sussex University. Earlier versions of Chapter 3 were discussed at the EIDOS conference on Cultural Understandings of the Environment at SOAS, 1989 and at the American Anthropological Association annual meeting 1991. Chapter 7 was presented to the University College London Biological Anthropology seminar, and parts of Chapters 1 and 6 were discussed in the IDS seminar series on 'Environmental Change, Development Challenges' and at the Centre of African Studies in Edinburgh. I am grateful to the organisers and participants in these seminars for the opportunity to air the material and for their helpful comments. Special thanks are due to Gerald and Penelope Leach for their support and inspiration. It is their back-up, and the kind efficiency of the International African Institute and Edinburgh University Press, which saw this book through to publication despite my absence on further West African fieldwork. Above all, thanks to James Fairhead, my colleague and partner. None of the people mentioned here are in any way responsible for the conclusions, judgements and errors in this book; these are mine alone.

Melissa Leach
1994

NOTES AND ACRONYMS

LINGUISTIC CONVENTIONS

Mende words and phrases are italicised in the text. Mende citations follow the orthographic conventions of Innes' *A Mende-English dictionary* (1969) and *A practical introduction to Mende* (1971). The symbols ɔ, ε and ŋ in written Mende are pronounced as follows:

ε like the 'e' in English 'pet'
ɔ like the 'o' in English 'pot'
ŋ sometimes as a consonant similar to English 'ng' as in 'sing', and sometimes to add nasality to the preceding vowel.

Words which do not occur as part of sentences are usually given in the indefinite singular form, but I have occasionally used plurals (formed with the addition of *nga* [indefinite] or *isia* [definite]). Although most of the Mende words are translated each time they occur, some common terms are defined only once and subsequently used without translation. For the reader's reference, I have included all of these in the glossary. The Mende language has four functional tones; these are not marked in the text, but are given in the glossary.

MONEY

The unit of currency in Sierra Leone is the leone. At the time of fieldwork in 1987–8 the official exchange rate was approximately 60 leones = £1. As an indication of relative value, the official salary of a government clerk or primary schoolteacher was about 700 leones per month at this time. Since then currency values have been considerably altered by inflation, devaluation and currency flotation. In late 1993 the exchange rate was approximately 850 leones = £1.

UNITS OF MEASUREMENT

I have indicated quantities of produce, etc. with the volumetric units most familiar to Mende villagers. The main units for solids (e.g. rice and coffee) are the bag, the bushel, the thruppence pan and the butter cup.

1 bag = approximately 3 bushels
1 bushel = approximately 21 thruppence pans
1 thruppence pan = approximately 5 butter cups

One bushel contains approximately 38 kg of clean rice, 38 kg of coffee, and 29 kg of cocoa.

The main units for liquids (e.g. palm oil) are the 4 gallon kerosene tin and the 'pint'. The Sierra Leonean pint is gauged on a standard local beer bottle, which is 16 fl oz instead of the usual 20 fl oz.

ACRONYMS

The following acronyms appear in the text:

EIADP	Eastern Integrated Agricultural Development Project
FAO	Food and Agriculture Organisation
ILCA	International Livestock Centre for Africa
ILO	International Labour Organisation
IUCN	International Union for the Conservation of Nature
SIDA	Swedish International Development Authority
WID	Women in Development
WWF	World Wide Fund for Nature

INTRODUCTION

This book is about gender relations and rainforests in West Africa. It looks at how local communities in rainforest areas view and use forest resources amid changing socio-economic conditions, and at different women's and men's experiences in this respect. Its concern is two-fold: to illuminate the place of forest ecology and resources in local social life, and to show why rainforest resource use cannot be understood without a concern for gender.

Rainforests occupy a prominent place in current debates about environmental change, and there is a growing concern to understand the various factors affecting their changing quality and extent. Policy-makers and donor agencies alike anxiously seek effective means to conserve the world's dwindling tropical forests and – increasingly – to involve local people in those efforts. A rather different strand of environmental debate, concerned with gender and the environment, highlights women's links with natural resources, their experience of environmental change and their roles in environmental improvement. This book shows that these twin policy concerns need to be considered together. Yet neither local rainforest resource management and use, nor its gender dimensions, are well understood in West Africa. Policies therefore run the risk of failing to address local interests in general, women's interests in particular, and ultimately environmental goals as well.

This book suggests that if conservation approaches are to respond sensitively to local concerns then more attention must be paid to the local social context of rainforest life. Account must be taken of how different local people, including women and men, value and use forest resources; their changing access to and control over them; and the terms in which they themselves consider the changing relationship between forests and society. Thus the prime concern of this book is with local people's own perspectives on issues which preoccupy conservationists and environment and development planners.

The local perspectives given prominence in this book are those of Mende-speaking people living around the Gola forest reserves in eastern Sierra

Leone. The Gola reserves form one of the last remaining areas of tropical forest in this part of the West African zone, and have attracted considerable national and international conservation interest. In the late 1980s this concern motivated an interdisciplinary research programme in the broad-based anthropology department of University College London (UCL) to examine relationships between local communities and the Gola forests, as a basis for assessing conservation policy options (Davies and Richards, 1991).[1] The study which forms the basis of this book was conceived in the context of a convergence between the UCL department's interests and my own in pursuing a doctoral study in social anthropology focusing on gender relations and natural resources (Leach, 1990). This book draws on the results of my anthropological fieldwork in the Gola forest area to provide a detailed account of gendered forest resource use in everyday life. This shows the social context in which forest resources are managed, used and thought about, and reveals the plurality of local viewpoints and experiences. Such a local-level, gender-focused analysis of forest resource use provides a rare vantage point from which to reflect on current policy debates concerning conservation and rural development.

THE STRUCTURE AND ARGUMENTS OF THIS BOOK

This book's arguments develop through two sections. Part One looks at issues, approaches and debates concerning rainforest conservation and gender and the environment at a general level. Part Two examines gendered resource use in the Gola forest of Sierra Leone. A final conclusion reflects on issues and approaches raised in the first Part in the light of the Mende analysis.

In West Africa, as elsewhere, numerous interest groups bring contrasting agendas to bear in forestry resource use and conservation. Rainforests are integral to current concerns with 'global environmental change', largely expressed in Europe and North America. Commentators point to the ways that commercial logging and agriculture, small-scale cultivators and hunters degrade what has come to be regarded as a global commons, with internationally important consequences such as a reduced sink for greenhouse gases, declining global biological diversity, and the loss of scientifically and aesthetically valuable wildlife species and habitats (Gradwohl and Greenberg, 1988; Miller and Tangley, 1991; Myers, 1984). For national governments and large-scale commercial interests, rainforest areas offer different sorts of benefit, including revenues from timber extraction and large-scale plantation agriculture. National-level conservation concerns include balancing forest-based industrial development with the long-term sustainability of forests and downstream ecosystems, and with other uses such as maintaining urban fuelwood supplies (Poore, 1989; Winterbottom, 1990). For local people whose history, social relations and day-to-day lives are intimately entwined with the forest environment, resource use and conservation priorities are different again. Yet local lives and livelihoods are affected by wider political and economic processes, including those which structure the commercial uses of rainforests and conservation policies. The extent to which forest conservation supports or compromises local interests is the central issue addressed in Chapter 1.

Chapter 1 examines how West African forest conservation agendas have emerged and changed during and since the colonial period, and how they have addressed or affected local communities. These effects have often been negative. West African peoples have commonly been portrayed as agents of forest degradation and forest conservation has generally been oriented towards the exclusion of local activities from reserves intended to serve national or global objectives, undermining local livelihoods. These 'exclusionist' approaches are being reassessed in the context of 1980s discussions of 'sustainable development', as they are neither equitable nor, in many cases, feasible. A new generation of conservation approaches is emerging which aims to make rainforest conservation much more 'people-oriented', linking it with rural development activities. New questions arise about the scope for reconciling the different concerns of forest-based communities and conservationists by building on complementarities and overlaps between their objectives, and for devolving forest management to local communities. A range of specific interventions are already being considered or implemented in West Africa.

Working with, rather than against, local people necessitates an understanding of local perspectives and concerns. I examine strands of the growing literature on people–forest relations which focus respectively on socio-economic, tenurial, demographic and knowledge-related aspects of forest resource use. While each provides useful insights, I suggest that they provide an inadequate basis for 'people-oriented' conservation-planning unless we understand how they are integrated within the local social context of forest resource management, and in terms which make sense to local people themselves. Crucially, this means going beyond the level of 'the community' to understand how different people and groups – women and men, young and old, kin group heads, strangers – use and manage resources, and the diverse interests in conservation issues they acquire in consequence.

Chapter 2 addresses social differentiation in local resource use by focusing specifically on gender. Much recent literature shows that women's relationship with the environment is distinct from men's, and that gender differences crucially affect how natural resources (including forest resources) are managed and used. This is not just relevant to gender equity, but also to the feasibility of rainforest conservation-with-development. How gender is understood influences policy. When the attention is on women's current environmental interests and activities, especially in subsistence and day-to-day socio-economic life, supporting special women's programmes and projects seems sensible. Ecofeminist approaches, in contrast, justify women's necessarily central role in environmental protection and enhancement on the grounds that there are especially close links between women and 'nature'. A third approach to gender and resource use links gender issues with historical materialist analyses, suggesting that capitalist relations are responsible for detrimental impacts on both women and the environment and thus need to be addressed.

I show how these approaches each offer important insights, but why each is also a problematic basis for conservation-with-development policy. Chapter 2 thus builds up the approach used later to analyse gendered resource use in the Gola forest: an approach which highlights the ways that gender relations shape, and are themselves shaped by, women's and men's access, use and control of resources. As gender issues influence overall patterns of resource use and ecological change, they are central considerations for conservation as a whole. Crucially, gender is just as relevant even when the underlying causes of rainforest degradation can be traced to wider political-economic processes. National and international influences articulate with local social processes, and it is impossible to understand their manifestations – in both ecological and socio-economic terms – without taking account of the local social relations with which they interlock.

When discussing these issues and approaches, Chapters 1 and 2 draw on some Sierra Leonean and Mende examples. But it is in Part Two that Mende perspectives come to the fore. In the light of Part One's critique of analytical approaches, this presents an analysis of gendered resource use in one of the four Mende-speaking chiefdoms around Gola North forest reserve. The reserve was designated during the colonial period primarily for timber production but is now a favoured site for conservation-with-development. During fifteen months of fieldwork in Sierra Leone during 1987–88, and two subsequent one month visits in 1990 and 1991, I lived and worked in and around the village of Madina in Malema chiefdom. In aiming to understand how different Mende women and men gain access to, use, manage and think about forest resources, my research methods centred on detailed participant-observation, case studies, interviews, and informal conversations in numerous day-to-day resource-using contexts, as well as certain surveys. Elderly people's recollections, older ethnographic literature and selected colonial archives helped to explain the history of forest resource use amid the socio-economic changes of the last fifty years.[2]

While I was carrying out the Madina case study on the northern edge of Gola North reserve, Davies and Richards of the UCL Gola Project conducted research from a base at Lalehun in another Gola North chiefdom. This study was broader and more oriented to a 'community' level of analysis than the gender-oriented Madina research. Covering twelve villages and six ecological survey sites, it included the following aims: (a) to consider socio-economic trends in rural communities around Gola North, and how these might affect the future of the forest reserve; (b) to record and understand patterns of exploitation of forest resources and the part they play in local subsistence strategies, and (c) to

comprehend villagers' cultural attitudes to forest resources and forest management, with a view to fostering local involvement in and commitment to
future conservation schemes (Davies and Richards, 1991: 1). Constraints of
an institutional nature, as well as the difference in focus and aims, militated
against the development of a common methodological framework for the
Madina and Lalehun-based studies, although some joint work was carried
out (e.g. Davies and Leach, 1991). Davies and Richards' study combined
biological survey methods with approaches from the social sciences. Their
social science methods were more oriented towards the collection of quantitative information than those I used in Madina, and centred on a number
of surveys of community characteristics, income-generating and forest
resource using activities. Part Two of this book refers to Davies and Richards'
(1991) findings both for the complementary information they lend to the
qualitatively oriented Madina study, and to set this in a locally comparative
context.

Following an introduction to the area, the analysis of gendered resource
use builds up through five chapters. The first four address different aspects
of natural resource management and use, respectively, annual cropping on a
rotational bush fallow system (Chapter 4), the cultivation of tree cash crops
(Chapter 5), local timber and non-timber forest product use (Chapter 6) and
hunting and fishing (Chapter 7). The sixth chapter examines the gender-
differentiated money and food economy, in the context of the changes in
land and resource use on the forest edge which the earlier chapters reveal.

Part Two documents many changes in forest-resource management and
use, with gender-differentiated effects, but it also highlights persistent themes
in gender and people–environment relations. It shows the inseparability of
women's and men's use of resources from issues of access and control. And
it shows that resource-using processes themselves shape ideas and relations
concerning gender. In the conclusion, I discuss the importance of understanding people–environment relations in these terms for 'people-oriented' conservation. By reflecting on specific conservation and development interventions
in Sierra Leone, I suggest that this can help identify often unexpected
overlaps and divergences between conservationists', and varied local, concerns. More broadly, I show that rainforest conservation agendas are matters
for debate within rural communities, as well as between local communities
and conservation planners. 'People-oriented' conservation needs not only an
understanding of gender-differentiated forest-resource use, but also sensitivity
to gender-differentiated opinions concerning forest futures.

PART ONE

Conservation, gender and the environment

1

FOREST COMMUNITIES AND FOREST CONSERVATION

The loss of tropical forest in West Africa has concerned planners and policy-makers since the beginning of this century. There have, however, been significant changes in the sorts of activity thought to contribute to forest degradation, and in why such degradation was thought to matter. Conservation agendas have shifted from concerns to protect timber supplies, which dominated colonial forest policy, to the issues ranging from local livelihoods to global environmental change which occupy rainforest conservationists today.

This chapter looks at the history of deforestation in West Africa, and examines the various ways that outside agendas have affected local communities in rainforest areas. Local forest resource use here has always concerned conservationists, since it is rare to find large tracts of uninhabited or sparsely inhabited rainforest in West Africa. Furthermore, most West African 'forest peoples' cannot be likened to those forest-dwelling groups in parts of Central Africa and Latin America, whose hunter-gatherer-gardener lifestyles may appear to be harmoniously compatible with rainforest cover. The agriculturally based livelihoods typical of people in West African rainforest areas involve the conversion of high forest to managed farm and fallow environments on the forest edge, as well as the use of 'wild' products from it. It is thus not surprising that indigenous forest uses have generally been perceived as major agents of deforestation, leading to conservation policies which exclude people from carefully protected reserves. Such policies contrast with recent attempts to involve local communities in conservation in more positive ways: attempts to reconcile local with other conservation concerns and to link the goals of conservation with those of rural development. I trace the emergence of such 'people-oriented' conservation approaches, and review a spectrum of the potential measures under current consideration.

People-oriented conservation approaches are supported by studies which examine the logic of rainforest communities' resource-using activities. The second part of this chapter looks at dominant themes in these discussions, which examine economic aspects of forest resource use, tenure arrangements, local knowledge and demographic change respectively. Insights from these debates are helping to guide policy-oriented discussions towards an improved understanding of people-forest relations. Nevertheless, this chapter finds certain inadequacies, and that these themes need to be better integrated with an understanding of the social relations and processes through which people use and manage forest resources. Fundamentally, this means avoiding analysis at the level of 'the community', and paying more attention to the ways social and gender differentiation affects forest resource use. As subsequent chapters show, conservationists could usefully draw on the concepts and idioms in which people's changing interactions with their forest environment are locally debated, as these are sensitive to the plurality of local resource use interests. The book's conclusion, which reflects on 'people-oriented' conservation approaches in this light, shows how and why the terms in which this chapter considers them provide an inadequate basis for conservation planning.

DEFORESTATION IN WEST AFRICA

Closed canopy forest is believed once to have covered a much larger proportion of the West African forest zone than it does today. Many commentators consider deforestation to have accelerated rapidly during the latter part of this century, but there is considerable uncertainty as to the precise historical trajectory, speed and scale of deforestation in different areas.

In West Africa the rainforest belt stretches from Guinea Bissau to Cameroon[1] (Figure 1.1). Rainforest[2] is a general term for a range of tropical moist forest types, encompassing evergreen and semi-deciduous forests, and those mixed and those dominated by a single tree species (Martin, 1991). All are characterised by an unusually high diversity of plant and animal species. Two major West African forest formations are separated by a 300 km stretch of savanna. To the west, the forests of Sierra Leone, Liberia, Guinea, Côte d'Ivoire and Ghana belong to the Upper Guinea forest block; to the east, forest areas in Cameroon, Nigeria and Benin form part of the much larger Central African forest formation.[3]

Tropical moist forests generally require annual rainfall of at least 1,600 mm; coastal areas of Guinea, Liberia and Sierra Leone receive more than 3,000 mm. Evenly distributed rainfall is equally important, and rainforest normally occurs only where 100 mm of rain falls during at least nine months of the year. Western parts of the West African forest zone have a single dry season (between November and April); further east rain falls in two peaks separated by a longer and a shorter dry season.

Scientific assessments of the changing extent and quality of West African rainforests are fraught with uncertainty, not least because of difficulty in agreeing a common definition of what to measure. A common view of 'deforestation', accepted by the Food and Agriculture Organisation (FAO),

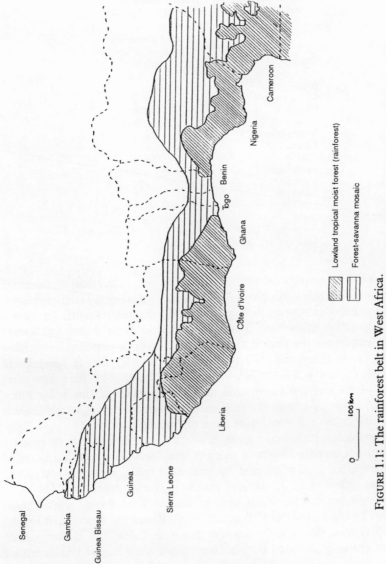

Lowland tropical moist forest (rainforest)

Forest-savanna mosaic

0   100 km

FIGURE 1.1: The rainforest belt in West Africa.

Source: After Martin (1991: 35), from UNESCO/AEFTAT/UNSO Vegetation Map of Africa.

TABLE 1.1: Distribution of closed broadleaved
forests in West Africa, 1980.

Country	Closed broadleaved forest (rainforest) ('000s ha)
Benin	47
Côte d'Ivoire	4,458
Ghana	1,718
Guinea	2,050
Guinea Bissau	660
Liberia	2,000
Nigeria	5,950
Sierra Leone	740
Togo	304
Cameroon	17,920
Total	35,847

Source: FAO, 1988.

considers it as 'a complete clearing of tree formations . . . and their replacement by non-forest land uses' (Singh *et al.*, 1990). In contrast, many environmentalists and conservation organisations, including the International Union for the Conservation of Nature (IUCN) and World Wide Fund for Nature (WWF) emphasise the degradation of 'entire forest ecosystems', involving reduced productivity and diversity, biomass stocks, wildlife species and gene pools (IUCN/WWF/UNEP, 1991; Myers, 1989). The latter view takes account of the differences between natural and modified (including forest regrowth) formations,[4] and of effects such as excessive logging which degrade forests without entirely converting them to other land uses.

The remaining high forest areas in West Africa comprise both primary and mature secondary forests of more or less degraded kinds. Surrounding and interspersed land is covered by cultivated fields, tree-crop plantations and bush fallow land in various stages of forest regrowth. The most reliable estimates of rainforest distribution in West Africa remain those compiled by the FAO/UNEP Tropical Forest Resources Assessment Project in 1980 (FAO, 1988), and these are given in Table 1.1. Unfortunately, they are not only outdated but also aggregated according to FAO's limited criteria.

Estimates of the rate of deforestation in West Africa vary widely. The scarcity and unreliability of baseline and current distributional data compound definitional problems. Rainforest degradation is often argued to have accelerated rapidly during the twentieth century, especially since the Second World War. One FAO study (Sommer, 1976), admittedly based on dubious figures, estimated that 680,000 km² of rainforest in West Africa (excluding Cameroon) at the beginning of the twentieth century had declined to 190,000 km², or 28 per cent of the original area, by 1959. FAO figures for 1980 not only showed considerable further decline in this area, they also showed that rainforest was being lost faster in West Africa than elsewhere in the world (Martin, 1991). Deforestation rates in Côte d'Ivoire for instance were estimated to have reached 7,600 km² per year during the late 1960s and early 1970s (Myers, 1989) although this rate subsequently declined along with the total reduction in forest area.

Preliminary results of FAO's 1990 assessment suggest that deforestation has accelerated over the last decade, estimating that across 15 countries in humid tropical Africa, rates of deforestation[5] have been 4,800 thousand hectares or −1.7 per cent per year during 1981–90 (FAO, 1990). Nigeria and Côte d'Ivoire are thought to be experiencing especially high deforestation rates; perhaps in excess of 14 per cent per year (Myers, 1989).

The historical record for Sierra Leone, while as inconclusive as elsewhere, suggests a rather older deforestation process. Climatic conditions would allow the country to support forest over about 60 per cent of its land area, whereas forest cover in 1976 was only 4–5 per cent (Gordon et al., 1979). Estimates of forest cover at the beginning of the twentieth century are as low as one per cent, however (Zon and Sparhawk, 1923). Commentators then noted the persistence of high forest on major ranges of hills and in large parts of the country's eastern and southern districts, but they also pointed to heavy forest exploitation either side of the railway and major navigable rivers, and produced pessimistic estimates of total forest cover on this basis (Unwin, 1909). There was also evidence of deforestation before the mid-nineteenth century, followed by forest regeneration. This was the case in Mende areas where nineteenth-century warfare (Malcolm, 1939) reduced agricultural activities, allowing the regrowth of high forest cover on previously farmed and bush-fallowed land. In the Gola area, warfare led to considerable depopulation in the 1850s and 1860s, and there had been extensive forest regeneration by the time Unwin visited the area in 1907 (Unwin, 1909).

The Sierra Leone case shows that deforestation cannot be assumed to be a steady, unilineal process; nor is it necessarily as recent as many commentators suggest. The Gola forest's history also illustrates the need to go beyond aggregate West African and national estimates to consider place-specific changes in rainforest status. Conservation policies have not always been based on these. Indeed, in the colonial period as well as today, conservation agendas have undoubtedly been shaped by imagined as well as by 'real' ecological changes. Equally, there have been shifting assessments of the significant causes and consequences of rainforest degradation. It is to these conservation and forest change processes, and the correspondingly varied roles attributed to forest communities in them, that we now turn.

DEFORESTATION, CONSERVATION AND EXCLUSION

Forest conservation became a concern of West African colonial governments in the early twentieth century.[6] The conservation policies which emerged encoded perceptions and valuations of much longer-established processes of forest resource use, involving both local communities and Europeans.

The forest areas of coastal West Africa have been affected by processes of agricultural settlement at least as far back as the fifteenth century. The Upper Guinean forest frontier appears to have been settled by farmers from two directions: from the east by root-crop-cultivating Akan-speaking groups, and from the north-west by grain-cultivating speakers of Mande and West Atlantic or Mel languages. For the most part, local agriculture involved the temporary clearance of forested land, often with the use of fire, and its subsequent management on a rotational bush fallow system. Areas of forest around settlements were therefore modified or converted to farmbush. Local communities also collected wild plant and animal products, mainly for local consumption but also for local and international trade.

Europeans had traded products such as cola nuts and ivory with coastal West Africa since at least the fifteenth century. European involvement intensified considerably during the nineteenth century, bringing new pressures on forest resources. First, there was an expansion of timber exports, although in many areas this took the form of a short-lived boom involving easily accessible forests, as interior forests could not be easily exploited with the prevailing technology. The first large-scale timber operations in Sierra Leone, around 1815, involved the felling of African oak (*Oldfieldia africana*) along navigable rivers to sell to the British for shipbuilding (Fyfe, 1962), but exports declined after the 1830s. Timber exports grew only slowly in West Africa until the Second World War, for these technical as well as market-related reasons. Second, exports of non-timber forest products expanded; in Ghana, for example, gum copal and rubber tapped from *Funtumia sp.* trees were exported by the late nineteenth century (Martin, 1991), while Sierra Leonean exports centred on camwood and wild rubber (*Landolphia heudelotii*). By 1900 these products had been surpassed by exports of oil palm products, largely from native wild palms. Third, West Africa became increasingly involved in commercial agricultural exports, especially of tree crops. For instance, rainforest areas were modified for cocoa plantations during the last quarter of the nineteenth century in Ghana and Nigeria and from 1890 in Sierra Leone (Are and Gwynne-Jones, 1974). Oil palm plantations began to be established around this time. Coffee was also cropped, but the establishment of plantations on a large scale awaited the late 1940s when the world market in coffee rapidly expanded. While some commercial tree-crop cultivation was carried out in large-scale plantations, it expanded most rapidly through 'spontaneous' spread among smallholders (Berry, 1975).

When colonial administrations began to formulate forestry policies in the early twentieth century, these were dominated by the need to protect commercial agricultural and forestry interests (Martin, 1991). In most countries a dual emphasis on forestry protection and plantation was adopted. From the early 1900s, for instance, plantations of commercially valuable timber trees were established in parts of Nigeria, Ghana and Togo. Forest reserves were established primarily to protect commercial timber supplies, and to conserve the ecosystem functions thought to assist good timber yields. The roles played by forests in conserving soil and water resources necessary for agriculture were also recognised. Watershed areas especially were given reserve status, while some administrations adopted regulations to restrict forest-damaging practices.

Local communities' activities were commonly perceived as incompatible with such conservation interests. Colonial administrations were especially concerned about the supposed environmentally damaging effects of shifting cultivation. Indeed, it was this particular concern which brought about the establishment of Sierra Leone's Forestry Department in 1911 (Millington, 1987). Shifting cultivation was seen as incompatible with timber protection, and also – given fears of impending population pressure on forest fallows – as a threat to the wild palms from which the colonial administration derived its main revenues. Efforts were made to dissuade farmers from shifting cultivation and to promote alternative agricultural systems, notably swamp rice cultivation, in its place (Richards, 1988).

The view that local and conservation activities were opposed was epitomised in the creation of forest reserves. Emphasis was placed on excluding local activities from areas subsequently to be controlled and policed by forestry authorities. For instance, in Ghana, forest reserve designation from 1911 stripped local people of all previous land use rights, and prohibited all cultivation, hunting and gathering (Martin, 1991). Forest reservation by French colonial governments, such as in Côte d'Ivoire from 1926, also tended to exclude local people entirely from forest-resource access. Unsurprisingly, these forest reservation programmes often proved locally unpopular. The Gola reserves in Sierra Leone were designated in 1926 and 1930 when interior Sierra Leone was a British Protectorate. Negotiations between the colonial authorities and local paramount chiefs acknowledged that the reserved lands still belonged to local communities, but gave the state custody of the reserves on the basis of an indefinite lease. Forest legislation did and still does exclude farming, although it does not extinguish all local rights to hunt and gather produce.

Along with these policies went a common perception of local populations as ignorant ecological villains, engaging indiscriminately in so-called 'destructive' practices. Such views supported the strong 'policing and patrolling' regulatory procedures often used to protect reserves. Especially in francophone West Africa, forest guards have been armed and equipped with draconian powers to fine people defined as 'poachers'. Such views also under-lay top-down approaches to conservation education, intended to instil 'better' values and urge people to amend their ways.

It would be wrong to portray colonial authorities as entirely uninterested in local livelihood concerns, however. For example the hostility which many colonial agricultural officers showed towards shifting cultivation was based, at least in part, on their view that it was an unproductive and unsustainable means of local food production, and was thus damaging to the long-term interests of local populations who practised it. Recognising that bush burning, although environmentally damaging, was necessary for agriculture, the Sierra Leone Forest Department had modified its aims by 1920 to conserve existing forests and restrict burning as much as possible, but to minimise conflicts with food crop-growers (Millington, 1987). By the 1930s some administrators in anglophone West Africa had come to appreciate the value of local resource-management practices, including bush burning, in producing crops amid the particular conditions and hazards of tropical environments. Some even sought to promote and build on them (Richards, 1988; Adams, 1990).

Early colonial wildlife protection policy in Sierra Leone also showed some responsiveness to local concerns. When in 1905 the Society for Preservation of the Wild Fauna of the Empire recommended the establishment of game reserves and asked for colonial governors' responses, Sierra Leone's four district commissioners all objected (Davies, pers. comm.). They claimed that there were no suitable areas in the densely populated country, that bushmeat was an important part of the local diet, and that most animals were killed in the course of necessary crop protection. Nonetheless, these instances of sensitivity to local concerns in early colonial agricultural and environmental policies began to be undermined as new pressures emerged in the late colonial and post-independence period.

The period following the Second World War saw the intensification of pressures on forest resources from non-local sources. These pressures in-creased further in the post-independence period to meet the revenue needs of newly independent governments. The expansion of commercial plantation agriculture led to the displacement of forest land for export crops such as rubber and palm oil and kernels (Martin, 1991). The impact of industrial timber production also increased as mechanisation allowed the increasing commercial exploitation of previously inaccessible interior rainforest areas. Nigeria and Côte d'Ivoire, especially, began to experience high annual deforestation rates attributable to the exploitation of high value saw and veneer logs (Gradwohl and Greenberg, 1988). Such large-scale commercial logging tends to be destructive not only because of the direct effects of tree removal on ecology and wildlife, but also because of the disturbing effects of heavy machinery.[7] Logging roads also attracted other resource-users, whether migrant farmers or commercial fuelwood cutters.

During the late colonial and post-colonial period there was also renewed hostility towards local resource use practices. In an effort to expand food production amid post-war commodity shortages, many West African governments pursued agricultural development policies based on large-scale mechanisation, focusing on the agro-ecologies offering the greatest potential productive gains. In this context many earlier gains in the appreciation of local practices were lost, and indigenous agricultural practices in forest areas were deemed inefficient and unproductive as well as ecologically destructive.

The rise of global environmentalism since the 1960s has added to the range of rainforest concerns.[8] Tropical moist forests were attributed a pivotal role in maintaining global climate and ecosystems, and animal, plant and habitat diversity, and these issues are now central to rainforest conservation agendas. Rainforests have become classified as belonging to a 'global commons', and their degradation is considered to carry transnationally shared costs, whether due to climate change or the decline of global biodiversity. Tropical forest degradation, for example, is thought to contribute to global warming through the reduced availability of a sink for 'greenhouse' gases (Miller and Tangley, 1991; Myers, 1989). Degradation of species-rich rainforests contributes to the loss of both valuable genetic resources and of rare wildlife and plant species and their habitats (Gradwohl and Greenberg, 1988; Flint, 1991). Sometimes ecological consequences are discussed in ethical terms turning on, for example, the survival rights of non-human species or intergenerational equity in the use of the world's biotic wealth (McNeely et al., 1990). Aesthetic concerns centring on the 'existence values' of rare animals or pristine 'wilderness' environments have undoubtedly played a major part in shaping public perceptions of rainforests, at least in industrialised northern countries (cf. Bell, 1987). Other commentators emphasise the economic costs to 'society' – global as well as national and local – implied by the loss of valuable resources, of stocks of natural capital, and of the 'option values' inherent in, for example, keeping open the future opportunity to use genetic resources for hitherto unforeseen drug manufacture (Pearce et al., 1990).

The incorporation of West African rainforests into global environmental change concerns provides a new set of arguments for restricting local communities' activities. As elsewhere, the needs, interests and values of forest-dwelling people have been marginalised and undermined by conservation approaches which aim to protect forest for global (or northern) climate, biodiversity and wildlife concerns. In Sierra Leone, for example, international consultants in the late 1960s and early 1970s reported that mammal populations were in need of urgent protection. This led to the establishment of a Wildlife Conservation Branch in 1967, a new Wildlife Conservation Act in 1972, the allocation of non-hunting status to four forest reserves and the

exclusion of local activities from game reserves established at Tiwai Island
and in the Outamba-Kilimi National Park.

PEOPLE-ORIENTED CONSERVATION

The extent to which local forest resource users have been denied access to
and control over their resources in the cause of 'the common good' has,
however, been mitigated by recent reorientations in rainforest conservation
approaches. Increasingly, it is argued that conservation must remain sensitive
to local livelihood concerns for reasons of both equity and feasibility.

The equity arguments for incorporating local interests into conservation
are part of broader debates concerning 'sustainable development' which
emerged in the 1980s, given impetus by the World Conservation Strategy
(IUCN/WWF/UNEP, 1980). These drew a firm link between environment
and development objectives, emphasising the social and economic, as well
as biological, aspects of conservation. Conservation came to be seen as part
of 'development which meets the needs of the present without compromising
the ability of future generations to meet their own needs' (WCED, 1987:
43) and 'improving the quality of life while living within the carrying capacity
of supporting ecosystems' (IUCN/WWF/UNEP, 1991).[9] The concept of
sustainable development itself contains no stipulation that the livelihood
needs of local communities should be taken into account. Indeed, colonial
administrations applied just such a concept most effectively to promote their
economic concerns over and above those of forest communities. However, for
equity reasons, local livelihood imperatives are now acknowledged as a prime
concern in sustainable development (Chambers, 1987; IUCN/WWF/UNEP,
1980; WCED, 1987).

The costs to local livelihoods of conservation oriented towards other goals
also provoke greater concern. Local people can become victims of forest-
protection policies when these diminish their access to resources on which
they depend for their livelihoods. Many of the supposed environment and
development benefits of rainforest protection accrue to other levels of society.
For example benefits from the preservation of global biodiversity and climatic
conditions accrue to a 'global' level. Wildlife conservation may provide
aesthetic satisfaction to people in other countries and regions. National
governments may acquire benefits such as revenues from tourism, and assess
the advantages and disadvantages of conservation in terms of the implications
for timber exploitation possibilities. Hence local inhabitants are often penal-
ised by forest-protection measures while receiving few benefits in return, so
that, in effect, a large part of the costs of conservation are being borne by
those least able to pay (Bell, 1987; Jeanrenaud, 1990).

The feasibility of forest conservation is closely linked to these equity
issues. Where forest reserves are established against local people's interests,
they often have little choice but to 'poach' and 'steal' resources from them

in order to survive. The greater the problems which exclusion poses for local people, the greater the pressure for 'illegal' incursions into parks and reserves (Jeanrenaud, 1990). Where 'policing and patrolling' policies have been enforced effectively, they have led to perpetual antagonism between local communities and conservation staff (Hough, 1988). In most of West Africa, they have proved unenforceable. State forestry services since Independence have usually been centralised, weakly staffed and underfunded, and thus ill-equipped to protect isolated forest areas effectively. The impossibility of guarding against local encroachments add to the difficulties already experienced by forestry administrations in controlling commercial and industrial pressures on forest reserves (Martin, 1991). Thus forest conservation programmes established against local interests rarely achieve their goals, however these are defined.

These equity and feasibility considerations are leading to new conservation approaches which attempt to work with, rather than against, local people. The Tropical Forestry Action Plan (TFAP) (FAO, 1985) now emphasises the need to include local community representatives within national TFAP planning processes, and includes improvements in local people's welfare among the evaluation criteria for the TFAP's longer-term results (Winterbottom, 1990). There is increasing debate within policy circles about ways to make conservation 'people-oriented', principally by linking conservation goals and activities with those of rural development. A number of conservation programmes in the West African forest zone now adopt a conservation-with-development perspective. Appraisals which take local livelihoods into the cost-benefit equation find that such projects compare favourably in economic terms with both 'exclusionary' conservation approaches and continued commercial forest exploitation (Ruitenbeek, 1990). The development and application of such approaches is evident, for example, in the Korup National Park in Cameroon (Republic of Cameroon, 1990) and plans for the adjoining park at Oban, Cross River State in Nigeria (WWF, 1990). Much of the discussion of people-oriented forest conservation is currently contained within research and planning documents for projects such as these (e.g. Jeanrenaud, 1990; Devitt, 1989). There is as yet no literature which examines and compares their experiences, except at a preliminary and general level (e.g. Gradwohl and Greenberg, 1988; Wells, Brandon and Hannah, 1992). Nevertheless, it is useful to review the spectrum of activities and approaches under consideration and to identify some important themes and areas of divergence.

Common to these approaches is that they extend conservation-programme involvement from forest reserves out to their surrounding areas. Most conservationists still consider it important to maintain some strictly protected areas in which vegetation and fauna are left undisturbed. But reserve protection is accompanied by attention to development needs and the productivity and sustainability of forest-resource use in the surrounding areas. Forest uses and management strategies may therefore be zoned. The UNESCO concept of biosphere reserves, first put forward as part of the 'Man and the Biosphere' Programme in 1979, created a complex model for multiple-use reserves in which a strictly preserved 'core area' is surrounded by concentric 'buffer zones', with progressively more intensive resource use – both by local communities and state/commercial interests, such as controlled logging – allowed in each. Recent rainforest conservation programmes have tended to adopt a simpler division into a core reserve surrounded by a support zone.

Some of the specific interventions considered for conservation-with-development focus on reserve management, others on the support zone. Where reserves are concerned, the emphasis is on acquiring and maintaining local support for reserve protection (Wells, Brandon and Hannah, 1992). This can involve ensuring that local people receive some economic benefit from protecting the reserve, either now or in the future. Immediate benefits can include local control of or shares in revenues generated from the reserve, such as from 'ecotourism' or scientific research fees. Long-term benefits from ensured future supplies of resources valued by local people could also encourage local interest, provided they are assured of real future access to these benefits. Participatory approaches to reserve protection can also involve working with indigenous institutions to regulate local access to resources in the reserved area, and to 'police' it against outside interests.

'Extractive reserves' receive much attention as a possible reserve or support-zone development (Gradwohl and Greenberg, 1988). These are based on the premise that local people will be more interested in conserving forest areas which contain resources of economic value to them. Local people are encouraged to harvest selected products which can be obtained on a sustainable basis, such as nuts, fruit and fibres. Attempts may also be made to enhance the income-generating potential of these extracted resources, such as through marketing schemes or improvements to road communications.

In the support zone, conservation-with-development interventions emphasise both enhancing local livelihoods and improving the productivity and sustainability of natural resource management (Munasinghe and Wells, 1992; Wells, Brandon and Hannah, 1992). On one hand, such interventions are intended to reduce pressure on the use of forest resources, including those protected within reserves. On the other hand, they aim to contribute directly to local development-oriented benefits from the conservation programme. Some natural resource-related measures focus on intensifying resource use in sustainable ways, so that support-zone environments can better support current and growing populations without necessitating encroachment on the reserve. Agricultural intensification is a particular concern, and the search for forms of permanent cultivation which provide stable alternatives to rotational bush fallow, a long-standing concern of agricultural research in the West African forest zone, has been lent added pertinence by current rainforest conservation concerns. Strong potential is thought to lie in agroforestry developments which combine food crops with leguminous trees. Other natural resource interventions focus on enhancing people's long-term access to much-used resources. Tree-planting on farmland and in community woodlots, and bushmeat farming are among the measures considered to enhance resource availability. Support to local institutional means to regulate the use of resources might help ensure that resources are managed on a sustainable basis.

Other interventions aim to reduce people's dependence on scarce or easily degraded forest resources by providing them with specific alternatives. For example, alternative supplies of animal protein may be developed to reduce the use of forest-dependent mammals as bushmeat. An extension of this is to promote more general employment and livelihood opportunities to widen people's range of choice, thus reducing their need to 'over-exploit' forest resources. Some of these choice-widening activities may involve the use of forest resources which can be exploited on a sustainable basis; for example, through the promotion of small industries which use non-scarce forest resources. Others aim at diversifying people's income-generating opportunities away from direct forest resource use, for example by increasing opportunities in trade.

Some conservation-with-development approaches recognise the scope for working with and building on local forest resource use knowledge rather than imposing 'solutions' derived elsewhere. Tree-planting and agroforestry developments on the forest edge could build on indigenous knowledge of species and tree-crop combinations, for example. Indigenous institutions sometimes provide the foundation for developing forest resource use controls and regulations, and for the local management of new rural development activities.

Rural development activities may also include enhancing access to local services, such as primary health care facilities, schools and local transport (e.g. Republic of Cameroon, 1990). On one hand, these may play an important role in improving local livelihood conditions on the forest edge. On the other hand, they are commonly proposed as measures to 'compensate' local communities for costs which the conservation programme entails for them.

Education is thought to have a place in 'people-oriented' conservation. But two important shifts of emphasis differentiate it from the top-down attempts to persuade people to amend their ways in line with conservation aims which often characterised earlier approaches. First, it is considered insufficient and inequitable to promote environmental education measures in isolation; they must be supported by real socio-economic benefits to participating populations. Second, there is more attempt to make conservation education a process of two-way dialogue. Rather than impose a set of preconceived outside ideas, some conservationists are trying to work from what local people know, the terms in which they think about forest resource use, and the socio-cultural attitudes they bring to bear on it. Rather than attempt to 'convert' local communities, some conservation education programmes now aim to promote local discussion and debate about conservation issues.

Many conservation-with-development approaches remain at the local level, focusing on people's interaction with the particular forest area in question. However, some also address the wider economic and political processes which affect local people's interactions with forests. This can include, for example, attempting to ensure that state forestry policies allow local communities an adequate share in royalty benefits from logging operations. It can also include altering fiscal policy and the climate of economic incentives which influence resource use, as emphasised in recent World Bank forest policy for example (Hazell and Magrath, 1992).

While 'people-oriented' conservation approaches share the view that conservation objectives should not prevail willy-nilly over local interests, they vary considerably in the nature and extent of local involvement in the decision-making process and in the way conflicts of objectives are resolved. Divergences between local and conservationists' forest resource use objectives are inevitable given the different agendas which shape their interests. Three kinds of response can be recognised. Sometimes the emphasis is on compensating local communities for the costs they incur as a result of the imposition of outside-derived conservation measures (cf. Bell, 1987). For example, early plans for the Korup Project in Cameroon recognised that: 'From the villagers' point of view conservation consists mainly of restrictions. One of the Project's main objectives is to offset these against new economic opportunities opened up through its development programme. Villagers' interest in participating in the Project depends largely on what they get . . . through cooperating with the project' (Devitt, 1989). Alternatively, the recognised need may be to reconcile local and outside forest resource use interests, primarily by identifying and building on complementarities between them. For instance, a bushmeat farming project might simultaneously meet local interests in increasing animal product supplies and conservation interests in reducing hunting pressure on forest-dependent mammals.

A third approach considers people-oriented conservation to mean enabling communities to make full use of their own organisations, knowledge and capabilities to manage the local environment in ways which satisfy their own perceived social and economic needs. This approach – recently endorsed in theory by major conservation agencies under the banner 'primary environmental care' (IUCN/WWF/UNEP, 1991; Pretty and Sandbrook, 1991) – goes further in calling for the devolution of authority, tenurial and administrative control towards forest communities. However, at least in a rainforest context, the potential for this approach is circumscribed by the persistence of external and global agendas driving conservation at the local level: local and conservationists' goals often fail to coincide. Specific interventions can be undertaken within each of these approaches, while many conservation-with-development programmes contain elements of all three.

PEOPLE–FOREST RELATIONS

Linked to these changed ideas about conservation approaches, there is a growing debate about local people's relationships with forests. Several dominant themes in this concern economic aspects of forest resource use, tenure arrangements, demographic change and local knowledge. These illuminate aspects of the logic behind local rainforest resource use and the ways it is changing.

First, discussion of the economic aspects of community-forest relations examines how economic incentives structure the management and use of forest resources. It considers how natural resource management and use is influenced by the availability and cost of the factors involved – including land, labour and capital – and by the prices received for the products (Barbier, 1990; Christophersen, Karch and Arnould, 1990; Pearce, Barbier and Markandya, 1989). Economic analysis shows conservationists how those resource uses which they consider destructive are, from a community viewpoint, logical choices. Extensive land-use systems, for example, such as shifting cultivation, are a logical economic response where supplies of labour are relatively low, but land fairly abundant; situations which still prevail in parts of the West African forest zone. Communities hunt and trap because they need animal protein but lack money to purchase it from livestock-rearing areas, and they hunt and trap in ways and places which provide optimum returns to labour. Relatively few studies attempt to establish the kind of econometric framework that puts a monetary price on all factors, resources and products (cf. Peters, Gentry and Mendelsohn, 1989; Pearce *et al.*, 1989), recognising that this can misrepresent the local worth of resources. Instead, they examine the local use values of certain resources, as indicated for instance by the frequency and magnitude of use of certain non-timber forest products or the labour time devoted to different activities (cf. Jeanrenaud, 1990).

Socio-economic pressures, such as material poverty and food insecurity, can force people into practices to meet immediate needs for food and income at the expense of the long-term status of the resource base (Chambers, 1987; Davies, Leach and David, 1991). Some conservation discussions consider poverty a major proximate cause of rainforest destruction, as, for example, forest dwellers are 'driven by poverty' to 'cut or burn the forest out of urgent need' (Serageldin, 1990), to over-exploit certain non-timber forest products or to invest in soil-damaging cash crops. From this perspective, poverty and natural resource degradation can become linked in synergistic downward spirals, as a progressively over-exploited and declining resource base contributes to further poverty (Durning, 1988; Leonard *et al.*, 1989). Poverty is only one of many interrelated factors affecting resource management, however, showing that the linkages are indirect (Leach and Mearns, 1991). Furthermore, poverty in rainforest areas evidently has many non-environmental, non-local causes. Both poverty and deforestation are partly attributable to economic and political processes operating at regional, national or international level, including discriminatory development policies and inappropriate commercial developments (Barraclough and Ghimire, 1990; Miller and Tangley, 1991; Repetto and Gillis, 1988).

Second, tenure arrangements are now recognised as a major influence on local forest resource management and use. Securely specified and defensible rights in natural resources are argued to be a necessary (if insufficient) precondition for people to take a long-term view in managing them. Insecure tenure rights can discourage investments in resource productivity and sustainability – especially those of a long-term kind such as tree-planting – since people cannot be confident of their ability to reap the eventual benefits (Bruce and Fortmann, 1989). The view arising from the 'tragedy of the commons' argument (Hardin, 1968) that only private or state property regimes give sufficient tenure security for sustainable resource management is now firmly discredited (Bromley and Cernea, 1989; National Research Council, 1986; Ostrom, 1990). A considerable body of research examines collective management arrangements for 'common property resources' (CPRs), showing how local institutions regulate and enforce how resources are used and by whom (Berkes, 1989; McCay and Acheson, 1987; Shepherd, 1990). In rainforest areas land resources, trees and wild plant and animal products are frequently managed as CPRs. Some conservation and forestry discussions accredit such local arrangements (which may not rest on notions of 'property' in a Western sense) with promoting effective and ecologically sustainable patterns of resource use, and recognise scope for building on them (Cernea, 1989; Little and Brokensha, 1987). By contrast, insecurities which lead to natural resource degradation can arise from the threat of privatisation, weakly enforced state property regimes, or the erosion of local institutional legitimacy.

A third strand of discussion highlights the demographic aspects of forest resource use (e.g. Cleaver, 1992). Population growth rates of two to four per cent per annum are common in tropical Africa. While by no means all rainforest areas are experiencing steady, unilineal population increase, there is considerable concern about the rising pressures on agricultural resources and non-timber forest products associated with demographic expansion. On the one hand, people may respond by extending resource use into previously little used forest areas, including, perhaps, encroaching on forest reserves. On the other, where limited forest availability or access fails to permit such extensification, intensification can lead to environmental degradation. For example, while rotational bush fallow is a sustainable system as long as sufficiently long fallows are maintained, rising population pressure can force farmers to shorten fallow periods so far that farmbush quality declines and savanna grasses begin to invade. These processes underlie policy concerns with technological and institutional means to intensify resource use in sustainable ways, including through support to indigenous intensification processes.

Immigration is often a significant component of population increase in rainforest areas. Migration to forests may be encouraged by adverse demographic, socio-economic or environmental conditions elsewhere. For example rainforest settlers have emigrated from areas of land shortage in parts of Nigeria, and from drought-stricken northern areas of Côte d'Ivoire and Guinea (Martin, 1991). Immigrants may be encouraged to forest areas by the availability of comparatively fertile land, by economic opportunities such as hunting, and by employment in logging schemes and plantation agriculture. In some areas, they have settled on the land previously opened up by commercial agricultural and timber operations. Conservation discussions commonly portray immigrants' resource use practices as distinct from those of 'traditional inhabitants', and in need of special policies (Barraclough and Ghimire, 1990; Serageldin, 1990). Immigrants may be especially poor and tenurially insecure, lacking the customary resource-use rights held by long-term residents, and thus especially likely to use forest resources in ways conservationists consider destructive. But while there is evidence to support these arguments, generalisations based on a strong distinction between migrants and traditional inhabitants overlook how immigrants' activities depend on their relationships with their hosts, and the ways these relationships have been shaped by place-specific historical experiences.

A fourth broad theme in the debates influencing conservation-with-development approaches concerns local knowledge and skills in natural resources management. Colonial administrators, foresters and anthropologists have long provided rich documentation of the range of forest products known, labelled and put to different uses by West African people (e.g. Dalziel, 1937; Deighton, 1957). While such early studies often consisted of catalogues of plant and animal species and their uses, recent studies of 'ethnoecology' and 'indigenous technical knowledge' examine local concepts concerning ecological processes and local resource-management skills. These draw attention, for instance, to the local knowledge underlying rotational bush fallow management and to the sophisticated ways farmers match cultivation techniques to micro-variations in agro-ecological conditions (Richards, 1985 and 1986). Local management skills are applied to trees, both separately and in ecologically and economically beneficial integration with crops (Mathias-Mundy et al., 1990), and to wild plant and animal resources. This literature shows conservationists the extent to which ecological issues are accounted for in local communities' forest-resource-use practices, and the importance of building upon them (cf. Chambers, Pacey and Thrupp, 1989).

Ecology and the relationship between society and the environment are central to local thought and culture in the West African forest zone, and are commonly addressed in local ritual and religious practices. That this bears relevance to conservation planning is recognised by major agencies such as IUCN within a growing literature on 'culture and conservation' (McNeely and Pitt, 1985). In some cases, these aspects of local belief concerning people–environment relations support practices which conserve natural resources. For example, forest groves and places which house spirits important to the maintenance of ecological productivity may be accorded special protection measures. The Akan-speaking Aouan in Côte d'Ivoire link the earth with a goddess who requires the bush to have regular rest-days and to be spared from forest-damaging forms of cultivation (Van den Breemer, 1989). Some discussions use such evidence to suggest a 'hands off' approach to conservation, on the grounds that local beliefs are the best guarantee of forest survival (Nowicki, 1985). Alternatively 'conservationist cultures' could be protected as part of the forest areas they inhabit, using reserve and support zone measures to exclude outside interference. From this viewpoint 'forest cultures', with their valuable ecological ethics, themselves become objects for conservation as part of a stable global cultural diversity (De Klemm, 1985; IUCN/WWF/UNEP, 1991).

As Persoon (1989) points out, however, it is misleading to translate forest communities' 'respect' for aspects of a culturally conceived environment into an all-encompassing, undifferentiating positive attitude towards nature in general (Persoon, 1989). Indeed, current idealisations of the ecological virtues of forest peoples ('green primitivism') can be seen as a modern environmentalist transformation of 'noble savage' views, saying more about Western ideology than about the reality of local people's lives (Ellen, 1986).[10] There is, in particular, no guarantee of local environmental 'respect' focusing on the issues which preoccupy conservationists, and this undermines the argument (e.g. of Clad, 1985) that forest dwellers are 'natural allies' of the conservation movement. Local resource-management ideas and practices are shaped by an historical and ongoing experience of forest life, and unsurprisingly give priority to those resources which hold key importance in local livelihoods and socio-culture. Mende, for example, treat their relationship with the bush as more precarious than harmonious, their socio-ecological ideas having been shaped by the historical struggle to create and sustain social life in hazardous conditions. Conservationists not only bring a range of external (including global) agendas to bear, implying interests in different resources, they also view local-level resource use issues from their own cultural perspectives. In this sense it is mistaken to speak of conflicts and complementarities between local people's and conservationists' values, because they are not directly comparable; they come from different places. This is not to deny that convergences can arise between local and conservationist interests with different origins and reasoned in different ways. For example, Mende value the white-necked Picathartes (*kpulɔkundi*, *Picathartes gymnocephalus*) and conserve its nesting sites in forested rocky caves because of its special importance to people's relationships with ancestral spirits. Conservationists also wish *Picathartes* protected, but as an internationally rare bird species of scientific interest. There is no reason why people-oriented conservation approaches should not usefully build on such 'fortuitous' overlaps of concern.

CONCLUSION

Discussions of local economy, tenure, demography and knowledge each usefully highlight different aspects of the logic behind forest communities' resource use. It seems banal to point out that these cannot be left unintegrated, and that useful policies cannot be constructed according to one analysis in isolation from the others. For instance, to assume that communities with 'conservationist' knowledge and beliefs have minimal or benign physical impacts on forest resources is to ignore the numerous socio-economic and tenurial issues which affect how resources are actually managed and used. Equally, before attributing particular practices to poverty, it is essential to consider how other issues – such as tenure arrangements, knowledge and demography – influence the activity in question. We are otherwise left with a persistent contradiction between the view that poverty directly causes natural resource degradation, and the considerable evidence of materially poor people who manage resources in sophisticated, sustainable ways.

This book adds a further, and crucial, dimension to the analysis. It argues that such theories of the conditions of local forest resource use remain inadequate, either separately or when integrated, unless coupled to an understanding of the local social dynamics of resource use and control. Local forest resource use, and hence local interests in conservation, simply cannot be analysed at the level of 'the community', because communities are made up of different people (women and men, young and old, rich and poor, strangers and hosts) who have different resource management concerns. Subsequent chapters show that forest resource use must be understood in terms of the varied interests and opportunities of these different social groups, and of people's changing relationships with each other. These social differences and intracommunity relationships mediate the environmental effects of such factors as demographic and external economic change. These social dynamics of resource control also influence local conceptions of people–environment relations, for these are shaped by day-to-day activities as well as by broad and seemingly timeless cultural considerations. In exploring everyday resource use and the ways in which it is locally conceptualised, then, this book shows that forest conservation-with-development agendas are matters for debate not only between communities and conservationists, but also within those communities.

This book gives priority to gender in the analysis of social differentiation. Examining gender helps us to understand how other forms of social difference influence rural environmental management, not just as 'proxy', but because other differences such as age, wealth or origins operate in gender-differentiated ways. Thus while other entry points to the analysis could have been chosen, gender could not have been ignored; equally in this gender-focused analysis, other types of difference have not been ignored. The gender focus in this book links with a growing literature and set of policy debates concerning gender and the environment, bringing rainforest conservation issues to them.

2

GENDER AND THE ENVIRONMENT

The growing debate on gender and the environment is developing partly in response to the need to move beyond an undifferentiated 'community' in thinking about rural environmental change. Importantly, it asks whether and how women's relationship with the environment and its resources is distinct from men's; and consequently, about women's roles and interests in environmental protection or improvement. These discussions are emerging largely in parallel with 'mainstream' work on rainforest conservation, notwithstanding a growing body of scholarship and experience of gender and forestry issues more generally. But gender issues have strong implications for rainforest-focused analysis and policy; indeed, as this book will show, local people's forest management and use cannot be understood without taking them into account.

This chapter looks at ways of thinking about gender and the environment. The first part examines three influential strands in current discussions.[1] First, I look at discussions of women's environmental roles, which have dominated policy-oriented perspectives over the last ten years. Second, I examine arguments about gender, nature and culture, especially as put forward by 'ecofeminists'. Third, I look briefly at feminist analyses of the effects of capitalist accumulation on women and the environment. Each approach illuminates gendered relationships with the environment and resources in different ways, offering useful insights but also, I suggest, certain problems. And each approach helps to construct different kinds of conservation-policy agenda. I examine the prevailing view that women's relationship with the environment is 'special', giving women a unique stake in natural resource-conservation initiatives. What are the grounds for this proposition, and is it helpful?

Considering these perspectives helps build up the approach later used to analyse Mende women's and men's use of forest resources. This looks at natural resource-management and use as part of dynamic gender relations, focusing on issues of resource access and control. I suggest that we need to take account of both the changing gender-differentiated activities, rights, claims and negotiations involved in day-to-day resource use, and of how these are conditioned by underlying social relations and ideas concerning gender.

WOMEN'S ENVIRONMENTAL ROLES

The last ten years have witnessed increasing discussion of women's relationship with the environment in conservation and development-policy circles, linking the burgeoning policy interest in the environment and 'sustainable development' in the 1980s with the concern for 'women in development' first popularised a decade earlier.

'Women in development' (WID) approaches began to pay explicit attention to environmental issues from the early 1980s, and discussions at the 1985 NGO Forum in Nairobi reflected this concern (Munyakho, 1985). They encouraged a growing body of further publications and meetings directed towards policy-makers and/or popular audiences (e.g. Dankelman and Davidson, 1988; OECD/DAC, 1989).[2] Environmental policy discussions have also shown increasing interest in women, not least in relation to forestry. A profusion of publications focusing on women's roles in forestry activity (e.g. Hoskins, 1983; FAO, 1987 and 1989; Molnar and Schreiber, 1989) have addressed issues integral to current rainforest policy debates, including land and tree management, tree planting, fuelwood, and the use of non-timber forest products. Some conservation agencies have also started special women's programmes. Following the recommendations of the 1986 conference on 'Conservation and Development: implementing the World Conservation Strategy', for example, a Women and Natural Resources Management programme was established within IUCN (Hannan-Andersson, 1990). In policy-oriented writings about rainforests, it is now commonplace to find a section devoted to the role of women (e.g. Serageldin, 1990: 13–14).

The starting point for most of these discussions is women's current roles. In emphasising women's involvement with the environment and its resources, they provide a valuable counter to the numerous environment and development discussions which remain entirely gender-blind. Several aspects of women's roles receive particular attention. First, it is pointed out that women's work involves them heavily in the use and management of natural resources. As hewers of fuelwood, haulers of water and involved participants in agricultural production, women characteristically perform tasks which involve them in close daily interaction with the environment, and for which they are directly dependent on natural resources. Second, women are said to have particular responsibilities which make them closely dependent on, and give them distinct interests in, natural resources, such as in providing for daily needs such as food and fuel. Third, women are said to have deep, extensive knowledge of natural resources, deriving mainly from their intimate daily experience of them.

Women's relationship with the environment, deriving from these current roles, has dual dimensions. On the one hand, women are users of natural resources and closely dependent on them. On the other, women are active, knowledgeable managers and caretakers of natural resources. Both aspects, it is argued, influence the links between women's status and the quality of the natural resource base. Natural resource degradation, including that induced by development processes, can undermine women's ability to perform roles such as food production, fuelwood or water collection, or mean they can fulfil them only with increasing costs in time and energy (Agarwal, 1989; Chimedza, 1989; Shiva, 1989). But women may play an important part in conserving natural resources, such as by planting trees and engaging in soil protection measures (Fortmann and Rocheleau, 1985; Hoeksema, 1989). If environmental policies fail to take account of women's roles, they risk both having negative impacts on the natural resources which women rely on, and failing to make use of women's important skills and knowledge (Dankelman and Davidson, 1988).

These insights – and, as Rocheleau (1990) points out, related popular images – have supported various policy approaches aimed at improving women's socio-economic position, the environment or both. But these have all too often picked up only selectively on aspects of women's roles, with negative results. First, women's close dependence on natural resources has often translated into an image of women as victims of environmental degradation, struggling, for instance, to find food and fuel from increasingly depleted land and treescapes. This implies that any outside intervention would be a help, and that women will willingly participate because they have no choice. Benefits to women and the environment will necessarily go hand in hand. However, social forestry projects motivated by such condescending concerns have often proved unsuccessful because they failed to recognise the opportunity costs on women's already overstretched time.

Second, women's roles in managing natural resources have led them to be portrayed as key assets to be 'harnessed' in resource conservation initiatives. This approach portrays women as 'fixers' of environmental problems. But it is increasingly recognised that it might have negative equity effects for women. It might simply add 'environment' to the already long list of women's caring roles. As Rocheleau (1990) notes, in social forestry women have sometimes been treated, in effect, as a source of cheap labour with little consideration given as to whether the project really served their interests. Thus it is now common to find emphasis laid on both women and the environment, as part of the positive notion of 'environment as opportunity'; that women can and should benefit from social forestry and conservation initiatives. This approach constructs the relationship between 'women and conservation' rather as the approaches considered in the last chapter construct the relationship between 'communities and conservation'. Similar suggestions are made as to policy approaches, this time of a women-targeted (as well as people-oriented) kind. It is suggested that projects should search out and build on complementarities between women's interests and environmental needs (Davidson, 1990), and that there are both environmental and equity advantages in enabling women to manage their environment within approaches such as 'primary environmental care'.

Identifying such complementarities clearly requires an understanding of women's interests and opportunities. But do 'women's role' approaches allow this? While discussions in this vein have importantly promoted awareness of women's environmental roles and of some of the possibilities and pitfalls they present for policy design, they commonly offer only a partial picture of women's interests and opportunities *vis-à-vis* natural resources. Two sets of problems recur, the first concerning the ways that they conceive of women's roles, and the second their narrow focus on women.

Understanding – and misunderstanding – women's roles

First, women's roles are often discussed in a highly generalised way. Women are portrayed as 'food producers', 'tree planters' and so on, with little consideration of precisely what this means in terms of activity, time, responsibility and knowledge. Without seeing more exactly what women do and the interactions between different aspects of their roles, it is hard to assess the trade-offs which might be implied by their involvement in environmental projects. Significant influences on natural resource management and use may be obscured if we fail to recognise, for instance, the constraints on women's tree-planting created by their heavy workloads in food-processing.

While a sufficiently detailed look at women's roles is clearly required, they must not be too narrowly conceived. A second problem in much 'women and environment' discussion lies in the equation of women's activities and interests with providing sustenance for family members through the productive and reproductive activities often thought of as part of a 'domestic' sphere. Thus women use natural resources in caring for their children, in 'survival tasks' (e.g. growing and processing food, providing water, gathering fuel, etc.), and 'household tasks' (e.g. cooking) (Dankelman and Davidson, 1988); activities which Shiva (1989) terms 'the production of sustenance'. Less often are women's important uses of natural resources to generate money given full attention. Little if any attention is paid to accumulative or asset-creating activities which women engage in, such as through trade involving natural resources and their products, or to the ways that natural resource use involves them in wider kinship and political spheres.

The tendency to equate women uncritically with a 'domestic' or 'subsistence' sphere has been particularly evident in relation to two issues: tree product use, and food and cash crops. Discussions of women and forestry in the early 1980s emphasised women's roles as providers of fuel and food.

When it came to tree-species choices for social forestry projects, women were assumed to be interested primarily in trees which would provide such products, whereas men would be more concerned with saleable tree products such as building poles. As Skutsch (1986) shows, projects that did not provide fuelwood were accused of marginalising women's interests, and fuelwood projects to meet them became the cornerstone of tree-planting schemes. Women's own responses to narrowly focused fuelwood projects have by now made clear that this does not capture the scope of their interests (e.g. Bradley, 1990 and 1991). But general recognition of women's broader interests in trees and their products is coming only slowly as part of a general broadening of approach to rural energy, land and tree management in Africa (Leach and Mearns, 1988). A similar equation is often made between women and food production, in contrast with men's presumed involvement with cash crops. A neat dichotomy between women and men, subsistence and commercial agriculture is often accepted and perpetuated uncritically, almost as if it were orthodoxy. However, accumulated evidence from case studies shows that crop divisions take widely varying forms. Where such dichotomies do appear, it is for diverse, historically specific reasons which need to be analysed (Moore, 1988).

Day-to-day sustenance responsibilities may indeed play a crucial role in shaping women's lives. But the view that women's work is connected with the sustenance and feeding of the family, while men are somehow associated with the 'public', non-domestic world is characteristic of Western ideologies. Assumed uncritically on to African societies, it may obscure major parts of the spectrum of women's activities and interests; aspects which may be both of crucial importance to women's social and economic status, and important in guiding any interest they may have in conservation. Policies conceived on this basis risk entrenching women in narrowly defined domestic roles, as colonial perceptions often did (Boserup, 1970).

The reasons why women perform certain tasks and have certain responsibilities and knowledges are rarely subjected to analysis. 'Women and environment' discussions often take women's current roles at face value, unquestioned. The implication is that they are natural and unquestionable – and so, it is implied, is the 'special relationship with the environment' which women acquire as a result. This partly arises from the association of women's roles with a domestic domain which, in Western thought, has often been assumed to be natural and unchanging, in contrast with the 'public' sphere of social life. It is also due to the ahistorical stance of much women and environment writing. The view is that we need look only at what women are doing now. But women's relationship with the environment is actually shaped by (and cannot be understood outside) specific historical factors and social, economic and political processes.

Changes in the character of women's work and responsibilities may have important consequences for their management and use of natural resources.

An important development within women and environment discussions is the attention now often paid to women's rights and control over decision-making (e.g. Rathgeber (ed.), 1989). This begins to reveal some of the bases for women's current roles; for instance, women may make heavy use of non-timber forest products from common land because they lack access to other income sources and gathering grounds. It also introduces a crucial set of issues into discussions of the relationship between women's socio-economic status and natural resource management. Declines in women's economic status may be triggered by a decline in their access to and control over certain resources, as well as a decline in overall resource quality and availability. Insecure tenure and insecure rights to products may limit women's incentives to invest in 'sound' environmental management. From this perspective, enhancing women's rights and control over resources might be an important prerequisite to overall improvements in natural resource management.

Nevertheless, women's access to and control over natural resources is often treated in terms of static and predetermined 'female domains'. The impression is that women operate within a fixed framework, their resource-management activities isolated from their relations with men and each other. But questions of rights and control, above all others, implicate the social relationships within which resources are managed and used.

Invisible men

This brings us to the second set of problems of 'women's role' perspectives: their narrow focus on women. Often, men are simply invisible. Although to an extent this rectifies a balance, since women are invisible in so much mainstream environmental writing, there is a danger that women's relationship with the environment may appear 'special' only because men's does not appear. Furthermore, focusing exclusively on women obscures their relations with men, implying that women's and men's resource-management activities proceed along isolated, parallel tracks. But this by-passes questions about how women's interests – in social life and politics as well as in relation to subsistence and family welfare – are shaped by their changing relationships with men and each other, which – as subsequent chapters will show – are crucial.

The focus on 'women' can also imply, misleadingly, that women are necessarily a distinct category when it comes to natural resource use and management; a distinct 'community'. Sometimes women are portrayed as a homogeneous group, ignoring critical differences related to age, kinship and socio-economic position. Even if women's heterogeneity is recognised, 'women' may still be thought of as a group in contradistinction to 'men', thus obscuring consideration of natural resource interest groups which form along age, kinship or socio-political lines, uniting members of both sexes.

Finally, an exclusive focus on women's relationship with the environment often translates practically into separate women's programmes and projects: women, environment and development (WED) components, like the women in development (WID) projects familiar to development practitioners. Extensive evidence from rural development more generally shows the frequent ineffectiveness of such approaches. Separate women's components are a poor vehicle to guarantee women access to needed resources or decision-making power. It is easy for 'women's projects' to become marginalised (or overtaken by powerful interests) relative to those that affect a whole community. And they are likely to be inadequate to address broader environmental concerns. Recognising this, some agencies involved with conservation and forestry development now stress the need for 'gender analysis' to underlie all programme design and implementation (e.g. SIDA, 1990); a concern which this book endorses and to which it attempts to contribute.

Notably, these policy-oriented discussions of gender and the environment, in as much as they identify women's development needs, focus on those arising directly from their current roles; what Moser (1991) terms 'practical needs'. The second and third approaches to gender and the environment which I consider in this chapter address the relationship at quite different levels, and call for very different kinds of change.

NATURE, CULTURE AND GENDER REVISITED: 'ECOFEMINISM'

Ecofeminism approaches women's relationship with the environment largely in conceptual and ideological, rather than material, terms, developing particular ideas about the relationship between women and nature.

Ecofeminism is a multi-stranded body of thought. Its positions, developing mainly in North America, have yet to be fully spelt out and reflect divergences within feminism itself.[3] Nevertheless, the broad argument can be summarised as follows (cf. Agarwal, 1991). Women are 'closer to nature'[4] at a conceptual level than men, who are associated with culture. 'Nature' is taken to encompass all things ecological in the environment, as well as natural (biological) human needs and capacities. In 'patriarchal' thought nature is seen as inferior to culture, and hence women are seen as inferior to men. The domination and oppression of women and the domination and oppression of nature have thus gone together. This gives women a particular stake in ending the domination of nature, so the feminist and environmental movements should work together.

Generalised policy discussions are starting to reproduce the view that a close link between women and nature can provide the basis for an ecologically sustainable future, endorsed by influential figures in 'women and environment' debates (OECD/DAC, 1989; Shiva, 1989). This view is sometimes linked with an argument raised in the last chapter about 'indigenous peoples'. 'Indigenous' societies, including those in rainforest areas, are often said to value the link between women and nature highly, within their supposedly harmonious overall conception of society-environment relations. Alternatively it is argued that such ideas about gender and nature once existed, but are being suppressed by inappropriate processes of development (Shiva, 1989). Thus 'indigenous principles' need to be recovered and built upon to orientate development in an environmentally sustainable and gender-egalitarian way.

These arguments are useful in drawing attention to the significance of ideological and cultural constructs in shaping gender status and people's relations with their environment, and in raising the possibility that these are linked. But what might ecofeminist arguments offer to (or detract from) a West African debate? In particular, on what is the 'special link between women and nature' supposed to be based? There are strong similarities between these recent perspectives and anthropological arguments about nature, culture and gender put forward in the 1970s (Ortner, 1974). It is essential to examine their assumptions, given criticisms applied to this earlier round of nature, culture and gender interest. Two rather different strands of ecofeminist thought must also be distinguished, although when policy-oriented discussions incorporate ecofeminist ideas they often mix them uncritically. I first consider those who treat the supposed association between women and nature as universal, derived from the specifics of female reproductive functions, and then those for whom it is an ideological construct which arose in particular places at particular times. While the first is highly problematic, the second is potentially useful.

Universal links between women and nature?

Some ecofeminists trace the connection between women and nature directly to female biology. They point to the female body as the source of experiences which situate women differently with respect to nature from men, and even give women different forms of consciousness (Salleh, 1984). The link is thus related to a notion of female essence, irreducible and unchangeable (Agarwal, 1991: 6). Anxious to avoid the problems in such essentialist notions[5] some anthropological writing has considered conceptual associations between women and nature as cultural constructs,[6] universally built upon the specifics of female biology but not reducible to it. At one level, a woman's physiology and specialised reproductive functions are said to make her appear closer to nature; they involve her more of the time with 'species life', and endow her with natural creative powers (Ortner, 1974: 77). Mies elaborates on this link, considering it as inherently cooperative:

> (Women) conceived of their own bodies as being productive and creative in the same way as they conceived of external nature as being productive and creative . . . Although they appropriate nature, this appropriation

does not constitute a relationship of dominance . . . They co-operate with their bodies and with the earth in order 'to let grow and make grow'. (1986: 56)

By contrast men are free to or forced to create artificially, i.e. through cultural and technological means. Male self-conception as human and productive is closely linked to the invention and control of technology. This means that men are associated with, and sustain, culture (Ortner, 1974).

At a second level, it is argued that women's biological functions lead them to be allocated social roles which are also seen as closer to nature. Here Ortner is referring to women's confinement within a domestic domain, where their social interactions revolve around fragmented mother-child groups and their work around the activities to sustain them such as childcare, procuring food, fuel and water, and cooking. These are, of course, the same 'domestic' roles on which the analyses discussed in the previous section often focus; some ecofeminists suggest that their association with women has a universal conceptual basis.

Because most of these viewpoints see a close link between women and nature as inevitable, they commonly see a more environmentally sustainable future to depend on celebrating it. Denigration of the woman-nature link is argued to have sanctioned both environmental degradation and female subordination. But closeness to nature now needs to be recast as a virtue.

The notion of a universally held association between women and nature proves highly problematic under cross-cultural scrutiny. Anthropological studies show the enormous variability in the meanings attributed to 'female' and 'male', and the ways they are linked with concepts such as 'nature' and 'culture' (MacCormack and Strathern (eds), 1980; Moore, 1988). A woman's procreative roles are by no means necessarily seen to place her closer to a universally conceived nature, and to exclude men from this relationship. Ortner (1974) has also been much criticised for assuming that all societies conceptualise a nature:culture divide. Anthropological studies have shown that even when other cultures appear to have similar concepts, such as of 'wild and tame', these rarely conform to Western ideas (Strathern, 1980). There is no reason to suppose that African societies consider people's relationship with the environment in terms of these binary categories; nor that they 'map on' to ideas about gender in the way universalist strands of ecofeminism suggest.

Of course people in rural West Africa, as anywhere else, categorise the world around them. Indeed, as we shall see, certain of the categories which Mende use can be seen as superficially similar to 'nature' and 'culture', as MacCormack (1980) has suggested for the neighbouring Sherbro; for example, the recurring distinction between 'bush' and 'village', and between 'proto-social' children and 'fully social' adults. But the complex Mende socio-cultural notions expressed through such categories are in no way captured by (or equivalent to) the 'nature:culture' construed by ecofeminist analysis.

Furthermore, for Mende, while such categories say a great deal about gender, they are not dichotomously linked with it. Both women and men engage with the bush and with the village in different circumstances, while lifestage transitions from child to 'fully cultural' adult occur in both men's and women's lives.

Nature, culture and gender as ideology

The second major strand of ecofeminist thought takes off, in effect, from the critique of essentialist and universalist positions. It argues that connections between women and nature, and the female:male::nature:culture dichotomies in which they are embedded, are ideological constructs that arose in particular societies at particular times.

Some ecofeminists suggest that such dualisms were present in Western classical thought. Others agree, but trace conceptualisations of woman–nature as inferior to the enlightenment period (Merchant, 1983). The scientific revolution and growth of a market-oriented culture in Western Europe in the sixteenth and seventeenth centuries brought about a fundamental shift in thinking about people–environment relations, undermining the image of an organic cosmos with a living female earth at its centre which had previously sanctioned both value to women and ecologically protective practices. Shiva (1989) powerfully argues that Western images of nature and culture, female and male as separate, the former to be dominated and subordinated by the latter, have been imposed on 'indigenous' societies in Asia and Africa through development processes during and since the colonial period. The pre-existing conceptions thereby undermined were often very different; people and 'nature' were frequently viewed as interdependent, and male-female relations were often non-hierarchical (Shiva, 1989).

This strand of ecofeminist thought is potentially very valuable. It raises questions about the social and historical construction of concepts relating to gender and the environment, and about the ways that different concepts interact during processes of developmental change. Furthermore, these strands of ecofeminist thought are able to call for changes which do not necessarily involve celebrating an immutable woman-nature link. Instead, they call for reconceptualisations of dichotomies between female and male, nature and culture so as to promote the free flow of human potential and more balanced relations between people and their environment; and for the recovery and rebuilding of marginalised modes of understanding in indigenous societies.

To address questions about the social and historical construction of gender and environment concepts adequately, however, we need to go beyond the treatments found in most ecofeminist formulations. First, this strand of ecofeminist thought can misleadingly imply, by implication and opposition, that 'indigenous' systems of thought are or were necessarily the opposite of

Western conceptual frameworks; in other words gender-egalitarian, and see-ing people and nature as inseparable (rather than separate) and people–environment relations as cooperative (rather than 'culture' dominant over nature). Shiva (1989) succumbs to this trap – and to an unwarranted extension of principles she associates with Hinduism[7] – when she suggests that all pre-colonial societies 'were based on an ontology of the feminine as the living principle' (Shiva, 1989: 42). But by offering only a single alternative and obscuring varied cultural conceptions, this can prove as misleading as (and ultimately only serves to reproduce) an ethnocentric nature, culture and gender framework.

Second, the discussions are reductionist. Ecofeminist formulations rarely move beyond a binary opposition between 'male' and 'female', thus ignoring conceptual distinctions between members of the same sex according to par-ticular social positions or lifestages (Moore, 1988: 19).[8] For instance Mende distinguish young women (nyapo) from mature women/wives (nyaha) from post-menopausal women (nyahamagbangɔe), attributing different character-istics and appropriate modes of interaction with the environment to each. Other distinctions which are significant for natural resource management such as between 'big person' (numu wa) and 'small person' (numu wulɔ), allude not to gender but to relative influence in patron–client relations. Furthermore, can all components and aspects of the environment be captured by a single concept such as 'nature'? Rural African societies typically have complex ideas about the physical and non-physical attributes of different micro-environments, ecological processes and the resources obtainable from them. By failing to disaggregate 'environment', ecofeminist formulations fail to ask whether different environmental categories are differently linked with ideas about gender.

Third, there are problems with the view that societies have a single, static set of concepts concerning issues such as nature, culture and gender. This leaves no room for the coexistence of several ideological strands, and for the possibility that different groups in society might see and experience things in different ways (Moore, 1988: 19). As Losche has pointed out:

> Oppositions form, not a hegemony of categories, but the subject of debate and questioning in other societies as well as 'our own'. (Losche (1984), in Strathern, 1987: 8)

Recent anthropological analyses of gender ideology rightly locate the ways in which certain ideas are produced, debated and entrenched within social and political processes, and in relation to particular groups and institutions. Just as indigenous concepts are not necessarily unified, there is no single 'Western model'. Merchant's (1983) revealing historical analysis of Western ideas about the domination of women and nature shows how several strands of thought developed and still coexist. As Strathern (1980: 177) points out, there is no single meaning to 'nature', 'culture', 'female' or 'male' in Western thought;

each term is polysemic, and each set offers a matrix of contrasts which might be differently drawn upon by different people at different times.

From this perspective, there are problems with the argument that Western thought systematically marginalises other cultures' views. The picture of one monolithic set of ideas wiping out another set is misleading at best and certainly cannot be upheld once we recognise that ideas are not so unified and clearcut. Instead, an analysis of changes in cultural constructs and ideologies means looking at the changing relationships between different ideological strands, and at how new views get entrenched, including the ways in which certain groups are able to bring about shifts in their favour. But with the exception of Merchant's (1983) analysis, these dimensions are missing from ecofeminism and the formulations of 'nature, culture and gender' which are influencing current debates about gender and the environment in Africa.

It is especially important in this respect to take account of people's material relationship with the environment and its resources. People's ideas concerning such issues as gender and the environment may not map in a one-to-one way on to their differential positions regarding resource access and control. As a large body of feminist scholarship now recognises, broad cultural representations of gender 'rarely accurately reflect male-female relations, men's and women's activities, and men's and women's (resource-related) contributions in any given society' (Ortner and Whitehead, 1981: 10; see also Rogers, 1975). But neither can ideological and resource control issues be understood independently, and this is an enquiry which any analysis couched in 'cultural' terms must embrace. Here ecofeminist analyses fail, as Agarwal's (1991) critique emphasises. Their arguments that close conceptual links between women and nature can provide the basis for an ecologically sustainable future thus run the risk of, in effect, giving women responsibility for 'saving the environment' without considering whether they have the material resources to do so.

There are, however, approaches to gender and the environment which do embrace material issues, from a historical angle.

PATRIARCHY AND CAPITALISM

The third analytical perspective I consider in this chapter is the feminist analysis of the role of patriarchy in capitalist accumulation, and its dual subjugation of both women and 'nature' (Shiva, 1989; Mies, 1986). From this perspective, capitalistic development is viewed as a masculine project which does violence to women and nature not only ideologically but also materially. These analyses go beyond ecofeminist formulations in addressing the material relations of property and power, and beyond the first perspective considered in this chapter in addressing processes of historical change. They help to construct environmental and gender policy agendas which would involve a major restructuring of gender relations and political economy. But at the same time as they are worth considering, these analyses present their own problems; and as for the previous two perspectives, critiques from feminist anthropology help to reveal them.

Such analyses often start from some presumed time in history when gender relations were egalitarian and people's relationships with the environment were cooperative and harmonious. But new material relations between men and women and between people and natural resources emerged, allowing new forms of female subordination and ecological destruction. Some arguments point to the rise of private property relations at some (unspecified) time, altering the implications of a pre-existing division of labour for gender relations and for the environment. To simplify, warrior-hunter men used their relative freedom from daily activities and their monopoly over arms and technology to exploit natural resources for the accumulation of private property, and to create relations of exploitation and domination between the sexes, assuming control over women whom they captured as wives and slaves. Female productivity and nature thus became slaves to male wealth and status, laying the basis for intensified forms of subordination under capitalism (Mies, 1986).

Others emphasise how gender and people–environment relations were restructured under capitalist development, implying that they were cooperative and egalitarian before this (Shiva, 1989). Shiva considers 'development' as a colonially derived masculine project which, in alliance with reductionist scientific paradigms, has systematically undermined women's natural resource-management roles and sources for 'staying alive'. Building on the well-documented struggles of women's environmental movements in India to protect trees for sustenance uses as against the interests of industrial logging firms, she describes how women have had to continue their sustenance roles under increasingly problematic and underresourced conditions. Masculine-oriented development sanctioned the ecological destruction of forests, soils and water and their removal from women's management and control; the privatisation of land eroded women's rights to gather forest products from commons, for example, and the expansion of cash-crop production undermined women's roles in food production.

Apart from introducing an explicit concern with ecology, these analyses share many features with interpretative frameworks which have been influential in anthropological studies of gender and rural economic change. Mies (1986) draws on Meillassoux's (1975) model of patriarchal relations and 'control over women' in marriage in structuring the articulation of capitalist and pre-capitalist modes of production. Boserup's (1970) influential analysis of the effects of colonialism and 'capitalist penetration' on subsistence agriculture produced arguments that resonate with Shiva's. The outline of Boserup's well-known thesis is that as agriculture becomes commercialised, men commonly engage in growing high-value cash crops and call on women as unpaid 'family labour'. Women are left increasingly responsible for the labour involved in an increasingly underresourced and devalued food-production sector, resulting in an overall deterioration in their relative position. A number of authors have similarly stressed the deleterious effects of technological change, and increasing markets for land and labour, in agriculture on women's position (Ahmed, 1985; Davison, 1988). Shiva (1989) adds to this body of literature a crucial concern with women's deteriorating position in relation to the use of non-agricultural natural resources.

As subsequent chapters will show, these analyses are of some relevance to gender relations and environmental change in the Gola forest area. For example, the introduction of commercial cocoa and coffee production – as elsewhere in West Africa – has been accompanied by substantial shifts in gender roles. Women's opportunities in this commercial agriculture are restricted by marriage and property relations which sanction certain kinds of control over property and women's labour, and it is possible to identify negative effects on women's economic status and natural resource management activities. However, the usefulness of these analytical frameworks is limited by their conceptual inadequacies.

First, these analyses tend to lapse into sweeping historical generalisations. It is often unclear precisely which period is being talked of, or of the precise dynamics of change involved. However, it is impossible to generalise about processes of 'capitalist transformation' (Moore, 1988: 82); while all scholars agree that both colonialism and capitalism restructured economies and societies and their gender relations, often in profound ways, the accumulated evidence from a large number of historical analyses shows the complex and varied ways in which new socio-economic relations articulated with pre-existing ones.

Second, historical-materialist analyses tend to caricature and simplify the changing nature of gender relations. They reinforce the treatment of women as a homogeneous category, ignoring differences in their experiences of change. They often unquestioningly assume female subordination (Harris and Young, 1981), failing to consider the strategies women may have for dealing with male control. They fail to unpack and analyse the different dimensions of women's work and natural resource use, thus ignoring critical questions about how people are allocated to different tasks, and how the relations between women's different types of work affect their position (Moore, 1988; Whitehead, 1984). Ultimately women's lives remain obscure in these analyses, their reality subsumed to the assumption of male control.

Third, these analyses also fail to address ecological changes (and changes in environmental management) in any but a cursory and presumptive sense. The view that capitalist relations serve to encourage ecologically destructive practices has almost become an orthodoxy from this perspective. But we may need to examine the effects of developmental and socio-economic changes on natural resource-management practices in considerably more detail before venturing such generalisations.

GENDER RELATIONS AND RESOURCE USE

I have argued that these three perspectives – each of which carries its own growing influence, and which are also linked in certain ways – all bring insights to gender–environment relations. But in different ways each is inadequate, and may not only misrepresent women's natural resource-using activities, but also provide misleading guidelines for conservation policy.

In contrast to the comparatively recent gender–environment policy debates, similar questions have been much more extensively discussed in relation to agricultural change. The analytical approach taken in this book draws more heavily on this literature than on the approaches to gender and the environment outlined in this chapter. In particular, a number of gender-concerned studies of African agriculture examine agricultural patterns and possibilities in terms of socially differentiated resource access, use and control.

Agricultural production processes, from this perspective, are seen to involve a number of different resource managers who bring different interests to bear, and have different rights and opportunities to access, use and control the resources and products concerned. The social, including gender, relations which pertain within such resource-using processes have a profound influence on agricultural patterns and on the distribution of their benefits (Berry, 1989; Guyer, 1984a; Linares, 1992). This is also true of forest-resource use, whether or not it is integrated with agriculture. For example, in agroforestry, women and men commonly use and control different trees or tree products, and have different labour obligations to each other (Francis and Atta-Krah, n.d.; Rocheleau, 1987 and 1990). While different resource users may have shared or complementary concerns, these can also conflict (Rocheleau, 1990). The kinds of negotiations which occur, and the different claims which women and men can make in order to press their interests, are therefore central to patterns of natural resource management and use.

Approaching resource use in this way raises important issues concerning the unit of analysis. Focusing narrowly on individual women (or men) is clearly insufficient, as this obscures the relations between them. Equally, extensive research during the 1980s, primarily in the agricultural context, has shown that such relations are often obscured by analysis in terms of social units such as 'the household', 'the farmer' or 'the farm' (Moock, 1986).[9] 'The household' has proved a particularly problematic concept to apply in West Africa, where people commonly belong to numerous nested and/or overlapping economic and social institutions. In as much as households can be locally defined, they are invariably nested within groupings of other kinds. To analyse resource use, it has proved necessary to examine these numerous different groups which acquire importance in different contexts, such as kin, residential, farming, cooking, exchange or consumption groups. As Guyer points out:

> In most rural areas of Africa, access to productive resources is determined by activating a hierarchy of rights: the right to land may be acquired through membership in a descent corporation . . . the right to labour through a complex of interpersonal expectations and negotiations within the family, the kin network and the wider community. Each set of rights is qualified, or contextualised, by the others but is not determined by them. (1986: 94)

As well as taking into account the contextual importance of different groups, understanding resource use involves consideration of the terms of resource allocation and exchange between group members (e.g. in the 'conjugal contract': Whitehead, 1984). Members also maintain links with other groups, and may draw on claims associated with these, influencing intragroup relations. There may also be an interplay between group activities and those which individuals undertake on their own account.

While looking closely at resource-using processes themselves, it is necessary to see how they are embedded in wider sets of ideas and social and political relations concerning gender. Women's and men's relative positions in respect to these structure their interests and opportunities. In subsequent chapters we shall see, for example, how gendered resource use is structured by marriage arrangements and issues concerning descent group politics. Ideas about the characteristics, capabilities and appropriate behaviour of the members of each gender shape (and are shaped) by their practices, being integral to the division of labour and to questions of resource access and control. And structured power relations between women and men are crucial to resource-use negotiations and decision-making processes.

This book applies these approaches, which have been found indispensable in dealing with gender and agriculture in West Africa, to questions of gender and environment in the context of forests. Dealing with resource access and control in this way both necessitates and orientates the detailed understanding of women's and men's interactions with specific environments, and their own perspectives on these interactions, which the following five chapters provide.

Gender relations in resource use also need to be examined over the long term. As Guyer (1986 and 1988) points out, this is necessary to see the ideas and social relations which structure gendered resource use in operation; to recognise which are persistent, and then to see when and why the terms of resource access and control vary and change. An historical perspective also enables us to be attentive to the way that ideas about gender are shaped in the act of using the environment and its socio-cultural significations. It helps us to understand the extent to which, in an iterative way, the ideas and social relations which shape environmental use are also shaped by it. It is this interdependence between the socio-cultural relations of gender and the day-to-day realities of gendered resource use which renders invalid theories that treat either 'gender' or 'environment' as independent variables in their relationship with one another. Finally, analysis of long-term change is important to see how gendered resource use intersects with changes in the wider economy, whether these concern new commercial opportunities or changing local state relations.

PART TWO

Gender and resource use in the Gola forest of Sierra Leone

3

THE GOLA FOREST OF SIERRA LEONE

Chapter 1 suggested that if conservationists are to work effectively with local communities they must understand local resource-management priorities and practices and the ways that these are integrated in social context. Chapter 2 emphasised the importance of social differentiation to conservation-with-development, and suggested an approach to the analysis of the dynamic gender relations associated with forest resource management and use. This section applies such an approach in the Gola forest area of Sierra Leone. We shall see how Mende women and men there manage and use forest resources, how this has changed over the last half century and the perspectives they bring to bear on conservation-and-development issues.

National and international conservation agencies show considerable interest in the Gola forest area. The first part of this chapter discusses some ecological and economic reasons for this, and readdresses the conservation-with-development issues raised in Chapter 1 as they pertain to the Gola forest context. I then introduce the people on whom this study focuses, first in regional context and then at chiefdom and village level. I outline certain key aspects of Mende social, political and gender relations which, as later chapters will show, are crucial in structuring people's forest-resource use interests and opportunities.

THE GOLA FOREST AND CONSERVATIONISTS

The Gola forest reserves lie in the westernmost part of the Upper Guinean forest formation, adjoining Sierra Leone's border with Liberia. The three Gola reserves (Gola East, 228 km², Gola West, 62 km², and Gola North, 458 km²) lie in the Kenema and Kailahun districts of Sierra Leone's Eastern Province (Figure 3.1), and together constitute a substantial proportion of the forest estate currently held by the Sierra Leone government (Figure 3.2). The reserves were designated in 1926 and 1930 primarily for timber production purposes, and they have been subjected to commercial logging since the 1960s. Gola East and Gola West have been substantially logged, but Gola

FIGURE 3.1: Sierra Leone: administrative divisions.
Source: Clarke, 1969.

North, the largest reserve, lies in hilly, isolated terrain where timber is more difficult to access. State timber extraction operations ceased there about twelve years ago with around 85 per cent of the reserve still untouched (Davies and Richards, 1991). The Sierra Leone government has shown some interest in permitting the resumption of commercial logging operations in the reserve by interested private contractors, but it is also considering alternative uses, including conservation.

The Gola reserves have attracted national and international conservation interest largely because they are among the last substantial areas of tropical moist forest remaining in Sierra Leone, and in the Upper Guinean forest

FIGURE 3.2: Sierra Leone: forest reserves.
Source: After Clarke, 1969.

formation more generally. The country has lost most of the high forest cover thought once to exist through conversion to agricultural land uses. Smallholder production of rice and other food crops, which has long been the basis of local subsistence, involves the conversion of forest to farmbush vegetation maintained on rotational bush-fallow systems, and in the twentieth century forest has also been converted to plantations for the production of tree cash-crops such as cocoa and coffee. As Chapter 1 showed, however, deforestation linked to agricultural settlement is by no means a recent phenomenon in this part of the Upper Guinean forest block. The vegetation within the present Gola reserves has not escaped agricultural modification since, historically, much of the area was farmed and fallowed; the high forest vegetation found today regrew only after depopulation linked to warfare in the nineteenth century. The Gola reserves thus contain mature secondary forest rather than primary vegetation. Conservationists who seek primary rainforest must look to other parts of the Upper Guinean forest formation, such as in Liberia and south-west Côte d'Ivoire. Nevertheless, the distinctive history of the Gola reserves gives them special conservation importance as possible sites for the scientific study of forest regeneration processes and of long-term people–forest interactions. Furthermore, Gola North offers particular advantages for the conservation of biodiversity and forest-dependent species. While depauperate in terms of overall species diversity compared with, say, the Korup area of Cameroon (Martin, 1991), the mixed evergreen and semi-deciduous vegetation associations, overlying a landscape of rolling hills, create a diversity of site-specific habitats not widely found elsewhere (Davies, 1987). The Gola forests contain wildlife species of international conservation importance, including the pygmy hippopotamus (*Choeropsis l. libericus*), a small population of forest elephants (*Loxodonta africana cyclotis*), and the red colobus monkey (*Procolobus badia badia*). Their bird populations have been found to be of exceptional international interest as they include eight threatened species, notably the white-necked Picathartes (Allport *et al.*, 1989; Thompson, 1991).

In conjunction with international conservation agencies, researchers and non-governmental organisations, the Sierra Leone government is giving serious thought to the possibility of designating part of Gola North as a biosphere reserve. In keeping with the recent rainforest conservation approaches and programmes of other West African countries, much thought is being given to ways of ensuring that local people benefit from these conservation plans. While conservationists would like part of the forest to be designated as a strict nature reserve, this is envisaged within a broader conservation-with-development strategy involving the surrounding areas both within and outside the present Gola North forest-reserve boundary.

The conservation-with-development agendas likely to prove appropriate in the Gola forest area are strongly shaped by local conditions. In common with many West African rainforest formations, the area around Gola North is currently inhabited by rural communities whose livelihoods are based on agriculture. Village life revolves around a particular kind of forest-derived 'resource': the productive agricultural conditions created through the conversion of the high forest to managed environments on its edges and in clearings. Because agricultural aspects of forest-resource use are so central to local life they occupy the first two of the chapters which follow: Chapter 4 focuses on rice production and Chapter 5 on tree cash-crop plantations. Local livelihoods also involve the use of wild plant and animal products from forest and forest-edge environments, and these aspects are discussed in Chapters 6 and 7. These conditions suggest several particular areas of conservation-with-development concern. First, conservationists are concerned about the impact of existing local agricultural, hunting and gathering activities on forest vegetation and forest-dependent flora and fauna. Second, questions are posed about the relative sustainability of land use around the reserve,

PLATE 3.1: View across Gola North forest reserve from the farmbush surrounding the reserve-edge settlements.

PLATE 3.2: Gola North reserve viewed from the Moro river, Sierra Leone's boundary with Liberia.

especially in the face of increasing population pressure and commercial change. Third, then, there is strong interest in the intensification of local agricultural land use in sustainable ways in order to deter future pressure on reserved forest, and in other rural development activities to supplement and/or substitute for forest-using activities. At the same time, the importance of encouraging local interest in forest protection is recognised, whether through economic measures (e.g. 'extractive reserves') or culturally appropriate dialogue and education (Wood, 1991).

Forest conservation in Sierra Leone is the responsibility of the Forestry Division of the Ministry of Agriculture, Natural Resources and Forestry, whose field staff maintain a wealth of experience and ethno-ecological knowledge of forestry issues despite the difficult economic conditions under which they must operate. There is growing interest in sustainable agriculture and agroforestry within national research centres such as Njala University College, and Sierra Leone's national Conservation Society provides a small but expanding forum for public discussion of conservation issues. Foreign donor support to conservation in Gola North was initiated at the end of the 1980s (Coulthard, 1990). Programmes for the area are still at an early stage of formulation, and were severely disrupted by the war and refugee crises in Sierra Leone and Liberia which deeply affected the Gola forest boundary area from 1990. This book does not discuss specific conservation plans for Gola North in detail, although relevant interventions and approaches considered in Sierra Leone are examined in the conclusion.

THE GOLA FOREST AND LOCAL SOCIETY

The people who live around the Gola reserves in Sierra Leone today all speak Mende, a Mande language[1] dominant throughout the southern and eastern parts of the country. However, this has not always been the case, and the area's complex ethno-linguistic history leaves its legacy even today. There is no clear evidence as to the area's earliest settlement, although oral traditions sometimes talk of an ancient population of dwarves (tɛmuisia). In more recent centuries, the Gola forest was settled by agriculturalists and, at least by the sixteenth century, it came to be occupied mainly by speakers of Gola, one of a number of Mel languages[2] which dominated the region at that time (Davies and Richards, 1991; Person, 1961). Mende has come to dominate the area more recently, as part of its general spread across southern Sierra Leone.[3]

The conditions of forest settlement and subsistence were insecure, and people grouped under leaders who could demonstrate their ability to protect and provide for them, especially as hunters or warriors (cf. Murphy and Bledsoe, 1987). Factional rivalries within and between such groups, often cross-cutting ethno-linguistic boundaries, developed into warfare of increasing scale and specialisation during the eighteenth and nineteenth centuries

(Abraham, 1978; Malcolm, 1939). In this context, patterns of settlement and territorial acquisition involved the building-up of a series of nested ties between 'firstcomers' and 'latecomers' (Murphy and Bledsoe, 1987). Powerful leaders established 'new' villages and founded 'new' territories, either through the settlement of an uninhabited forest area or through the conquest of previous inhabitants. The oral histories of some villages identify a battle as the crucial founding event; other villages trace their origins to a hunter-founder and the growth of a settlement around the site of an elephant kill (cf. Hill, 1984). A leader's descendants would subsequently spread out to establish dependent settlements within the territory, still deferring to the original founder's higher level of territorial control and military protection. Late-comers arrived in each of these levels of territory, often escaping from war in other areas. Those who were deemed politically significant, usually because they arrived with established reputations as hunters or warriors, and followers and descendants of their own, were allocated land and allowed to establish further dependent settlements within the firstcomer's territory. Over time, therefore, territorial relationships built up into a set of nested firstcomer–latecomer ties which constituted a loosely-knit system of political super- and sub-ordination.

Oral history around the Gola reserves relates that in the course of this dynamic settlement process, skilled Mende warriors from the north managed to drive many Gola speakers across the Moro river into what is now Liberia. Many of the conquered Gola speakers who remained in the area adopted the Mende language. Some territories remained under the control of powerful Gola warriors: for example, the northern area constituting much of the modern territory of Malema chiefdom was controlled by the Gola warrior Dafarma and his descendant Kpambu throughout the nineteenth century. Neverthe-less, the Mende language also spread through this area, probably as much through trading relationships as through warfare. The Moro river was desig-nated as the Sierra Leone–Liberia border in the first decade of the twentieth century. This played an important part in the consolidation of ethnic ascrip-tions which took place in the colonial period: ascriptions which have persisted since independence. 'Gola' people were defined as belonging to Liberia, and 'Mende' became associated with Sierra Leonean identity. People around Gola North today consider themselves as Mende, which is how I refer to them in this book. Nevertheless, some still remember how to speak Gola, occasionally uphold their Gola origins, and seem to reflect them in the orienta-tion of certain social values.[4]

In socio-cultural terms, the Gola forest area is best seen in its wider regional context. Mende and Gola both fall within the section of the Upper Guinea Coast which D'Azevedo (1962c) termed the Central West Atlantic Region, because of the common features overlying its ethno-linguistic divers-ity. Societies across the region share a history of migration into a major

TABLE 3.1: Populations in the Gola forest region.

	1963 census	1974 census	1985 census	Increase 1963–85	Increase per yr.
DISTRICT					
Kenema	227,428	266,636	337,055	48.2%	2.2%
Kailahun	150,236	180,365	233,839	55.7%	2.5%
CHIEFDOM					
Malema	6,523	10,056	10,113	55.0%	2.5%
Nomo	1,287	1,738	2,947	129.0%	5.9%
Gaura	9,614	12,243	14,817	54.1%	2.5%
Tunkia	14,262	17,638	22,042	54.6%	2.5%

Source: Davies and Richards (1991: 9).

forest frontier and of warfare; important aspects of kinship and social organisation; and the existence of socially and politically significant male and female 'secret societies' into which all men and women are initiated around the time of puberty. I indicate below how certain of these regionally shared characteristics are manifested in the communities around the Gola forest reserves.

The modern distribution of settlement around Gola North (Figure 3.3) reflects both the influence of pre-colonial settlement processes, and the territorial boundaries created by the British colonial administration after interior Sierra Leone became a Protectorate in 1897. Villages around the perimeter of the reserve lie within four chiefdoms: Malema, Nomo, Gaura and Tunkia. These settlements vary in size from large villages or towns (ta) with populations of four hundred or more, to hamlets containing no more than twenty or thirty people. Many of the larger villages are considered as 'parent' settlements and trace their origins to the 'firstcomer' to the area. Hamlets and smaller villages established by the junior descendants or latecoming subordinates of such firstcomers are considered as dependent settlements, 'under' a parent village. These dependent settlements are referred to as *fula*. A third level of settlement is found in the seasonal farming encampments (*simbɛki*) which were once associated with nearly every village. Today, many of these have been abandoned, but some are still maintained and regularly occupied, especially in the more distant lands linked to larger villages.

Population densities in the four chiefdoms around Gola North, allowing for the uninhabited reserved portions, have been estimated at an average of about 32 persons per km^2 (Davies and Richards, 1991). Notably, this is significantly lower than the surrounding district averages (e.g. 44 persons/km^2 in rural Kenema District). Rates of population increase in Sierra Leone as a whole are around two per cent per annum, and populations in the four chiefdoms around Gola North are growing at a similar rate to those in Kenema and Kailahun Districts as a whole, as Table 3.1 shows.

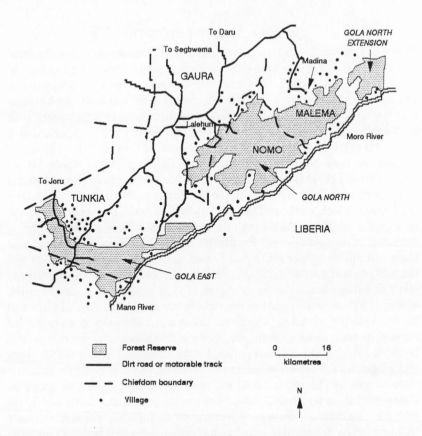

FIGURE 3.3: Gola North: settlement and communications.

Local populations can be temporarily swelled by influxes of short-term diamond diggers, and this probably explains the unusually high 1985 figure for Nomo chiefdom in Table 3.1. But such short-term movements notwith-standing, village-level surveys carried out by Davies and Richards (1991) suggest that rural communities around Gola North are not growing especially fast. Immigration rates into forest edge villages are slightly but not greatly higher than into other areas of the chiefdoms. In short, high and/or rapidly increasing demographic pressure is not an immediate problem in the Gola forest area, although it could clearly become so in the future. This provides an important context for the forest resource use patterns considered in subsequent chapters. It also creates scope for a relatively long-term approach to conservation planning in the Gola forest area (Davies and Richards, 1991).

A GOLA FOREST CHIEFDOM

Figure 3.4 shows the pattern of settlement and communications in Malema chiefdom. Jojoima, the present-day chiefdom headquarters, is the commercial and administrative centre. The main weekly market and the warehouses of government produce-buying agents are located here, and daily public transport (by truck or 'poda') provides links, via dirt roads, to larger towns such as Kenema (c. 70 km) and Daru. Malema chiefdom has experienced a somewhat greater level of commercial development than the other chiefdoms around the Gola North reserve, including Gaura chiefdom where Davies and Richards' (1991) village studies were based. The northern part of Malema chiefdom lies on the outer edge of the zone of intensive trade and cash-crop production which developed in the colonial period. This centred on the railway line which passed through the local towns of Daru and Baima, being extended to its terminus at Pendembu in 1908. A principal pre-colonial trade and military route which had linked Baima with Jojoima, Madina and the villages to the south came, in the early part of the twentieth century, to serve as a major route for the exchange of local produce (e.g. palm kernels and rice) for imported goods in the railway towns. At this time Madina was the headquarters of Malema chiefdom. Cocoa and coffee production expanded rapidly in the chiefdom from the mid-twentieth century. Its export was facilitated during the colonial period by the upgrading of the Baima route and a branch to the town of Salina which served as a mid-point for itinerant traders, and by the extension of the road network in the 1970s under an donor-funded feeder roads development programme. It was in the mid-1970s that the chiefdom administration was moved to Jojoima, which was rapidly building up its present-day status as a commercial centre with an unusually large number of wealthy traders by comparison with many rural Mende towns.

Authority over the chiefdom and its administration is vested in the paramount chief (ndɔlɔ maha), whose residence, chiefdom court and offices are at Jojoima. Mende are noted among societies in the region for accepting female as well as male paramount chiefs (Hoffer, 1972 and 1974). Assisted by a speaker (lavale), he or she provides a link between local society and the state, interpreting laws, regulations and instructions from central government to the chiefdom people and representing their viewpoints to officialdom. The chiefdom is divided into administrative sections, each with its own chief (kpati maha) and speaker (lavale). At village level, the town chief (ta maha) and town speaker are supported by a council comprised of the heads of major descent groups. They represent the village in elections for new paramount chiefs, from among eligible members of the chiefly descent group or 'ruling house'. They arbitrate affairs in the village court, and refer cases left unresolved there to the paramount chief's court.

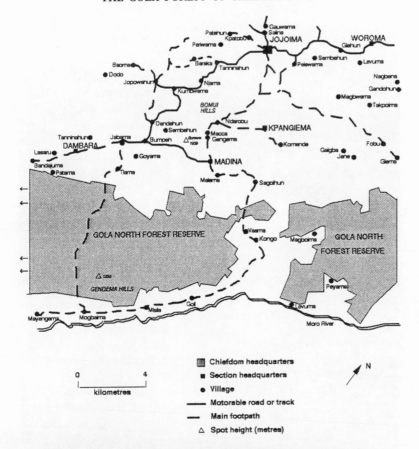

FIGURE 3.4: Malema chiefdom: settlement and communications.

The administrative authority of paramount chiefs has been reduced, since the introduction of internal self-government prior to independence in 1961, in favour of a second politico-administrative hierarchy involving state party officials. The local member of parliament (MP), who also resides at Jojoima, represents his constituency's interests in party affairs. State officials also collect local taxes, a nominal amount paid by those men and women over twenty-one years of age assessed as having an independent income. In rural Mende chiefdoms, MPs and paramount chiefs sometimes compete or combine to attract projects and advantages to the parts of the chiefdom which provide their main electoral support. The relative influence of the 'customary' and party administration on local affairs depends on whether the paramount chief enjoys the support of the MP. In some chiefdoms, local chieftaincies are much more active in local governance than the party administration, especially where forest resource use is concerned; in others, MPs have a strong influence

PLATE 3.3: The interior of the village: the cleared paths and public places contrast with the densely vegetated Bumwe hills behind.

PLATE 3.4: Madina village approached from the southerly path which leads towards the forest reserve, through the surrounding tree cash-crop plantations.

on succession to the office of paramount chief and continue to support those whom they have assisted into power. As is the case in other parts of rural Sierra Leone, central government remains relatively weak and remote from local affairs, and is significantly dependent on the brokerage role of paramount chiefs for the exercise of state power (Richards, 1986).

A VILLAGE ON THE NORTHERN EDGE OF THE GOLA NORTH RESERVE

Madina, which is today one of the section headquarters in Malema chiefdom, lies 18 km from the chiefdom headquarters at the end of a motorable dirt road. Weekly public transport is available from Bumpeh, 4 km away, while produce traders bring trucks to the village every week or so during the dry season. The village's situation relative to local transport and communications is broadly comparable with that of other large villages along the northern perimeter of Gola North reserve, most of which are, today, served by feeder roads. It is very different from the situation of the small villages and hamlets to the south and west, such as Vaama, Kongo, Goli and Misila, which can be reached only by up to a long day's walk on rough, hilly footpaths through the bush and forest. As a result of settlement and descent history, several of these villages are viewed as being 'under' the authority of Madina kin groups. As is common in long-established settlements, there are a number of different descent groups in Madina with different origins, connections with the village's founder and relationships with forest hamlets; by contrast, many of the smaller hamlets centre on a single descent group.

The buildings and public areas in Madina, of red lateritic mud, are kept quite clear of the dense vegetation that surrounds the village. The village itself is laid out in a more or less concentric pattern, as shown in Figure 3.5. Near the centre is the court barri (sɛmɛ), the mosque and church,[5] the government health clinic (one of three in the chiefdom) and the open area where ceremonies take place and where visiting traders operate. Residential buildings form a broad band surrounding these, and behind the houses are the combined kitchens and rice stores.

At the time of study there were about 450 people living in Madina. The census which I carried out during fieldwork in 1988 recorded 451 people, a static figure that obscures real residential fluidity even during the course of a year as people move between villages to visit kin, for marriage, childbirth, initiation, fosterage or apprenticeship, or for economic activity. Nevertheless, supported as it was by demographic information contained in other surveys during the year (e.g. of farming activities), it gives a fairly accurate indication of who was resident in the village for most of this study's main fieldwork period. Notably, this population estimate is very much lower than the figure of 857 given for Madina in Sierra Leone's 1985 national Census. While this discrepancy could, in part, be due to differences in the survey

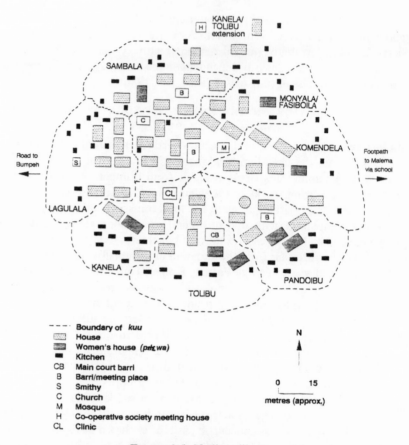

FIGURE 3.5: Madina village.

methods and definitions of 'residence' adopted, it seems too large to be fully accounted for in this way. A more probable explanation is that a proportion of the young men and strangers who were recorded as village residents in 1985 were away in 1988; an idea supported by villagers' own reports of recent, short-term young male outmigration, principally to dig diamonds in Liberia, Kono or temporary local camps, and by data concerning village population structure.

Tables 3.2 and 3.3 show how villagers are grouped by gender and age. Table 3.2 groups villagers' estimates of their ages, according to a calendar of local events, into 15-year cohorts. Adults of 15 years or over comprise 63 per cent of the village population. The table shows a notable surplus of females over males, especially in the 15–29 and 30–44 age categories. Such gender ratios tend to be associated with the poorer, northern districts of Sierra Leone which have high rates of male outmigration in search of work;

TABLE 3.2: Population of Madina divided by gender and age.

Age	Male	Female	Total
0–4	33	46	79
5–14	47	42	89
15–29	42	57	99
30–44	40	56	96
45–60	29	30	59
>60	14	15	29
Total	205	246	451

TABLE 3.3: Population of Madina divided by local categories.

Status	No. of people
Small child (*ndopo wulo*)	90
Child (*ndopo*)	78
Young man (*ndakpa*)	42
Young or unmarried woman (*nyapo*)	22
Adult man (*hindo*)	60
Adult woman or wife (*nyaha*)	112
'Big man' (*numu wa*)	19
'Big woman' (*numu wa*)	13
Old man (*numu wova*)	4
Old woman (*numu wova*)	11

in contrast diamond districts, with high rates of male labour immigration, tend to have an excess of males over females. Davies and Richards (1991: 14) found the Gola forest villages in their sample to have balanced gender ratios, suggesting relatively little disturbance by either diamonds or poverty. The Madina case seems to be best explained by the proximity of diamond-digging opportunities which had tempted a significant proportion of young men away from the village, at least temporarily.

Table 3.3 follows categories commonly used by Mende themselves, and which take into account a range of other status attributes as well as age. The categories are overlapping rather than exclusive since, for example, several elderly women (*numu wova*) are also viewed as big women (*numu wa*). The divisions here are intended only as a rough guide to the numbers of people within each category, since, as later chapters will show, assessments of status vary significantly according to context.

Table 3.3 provides useful reference points for introducing some key aspects of local social organisation and socio-political life. I want to draw introductory attention to these because of their recurring significance for forest-resource use. At this point, I must emphasise that this book is not a comprehensive ethnography of Mende, of Gola forest Mende, or of Mende gender relations; it aims instead to show how ethnographic interpretation illuminates selected aspects of people-forest relations in a policy-relevant way.[6] Further detail

and clarification of issues I can only touch on can be found in the rich
existing ethnographic literature.[7] Nor should the following summary be
taken as a freestanding account of kinship and social organisation. It aims
only to provide essential background for understanding the resource-use
issues discussed later. In turn, subsequent chapters will amplify and add
detail to issues outlined here through the specific discussions of forest-
resource use.

The central importance Mende attach to gender difference from a certain
stage in people's lives is illustrated in Table 3.3. Mende make little distinction
between the sexes for a small child who has not yet reached the 'age of
sense' (around six to eight), and gender becomes only slightly more important
as male and female children (*ndopo*) begin to help older relatives with gender-
specific activities. But at around the time of puberty, initiation into the
men's (Poro, *pɔɔ*) or women's (Sande, *sande*) 'secret society' identifies a
person as fully gendered (MacCormack, 1980), and after this they are almost
always called and described by sex-specific terms. Gender difference, for
Mende, is constantly affirmed by women's and men's different reproductive
capacities. As I have shown elsewhere (Leach, 1990) the performance of
certain activities and tasks in the division of labour also serves to define and
affirm a person's masculinity or femininity, and such 'polarised' tasks are
exclusive to the members of each sex. However, for a post-menopausal woman
(*nyahamagbangoe*), aspects of femininity linked to fertility and reproduction
no longer apply, and gender ceases to be such a pervasive part of her identity.
In old age, gender distinctions are manifested even less often, and an old
person of either sex might be referred to generally as elderly person (*numu
wova*) in appropriate contexts, such as when an old person's advice is needed
on family history or ancestral relations. But gender distinctions do not dis-
appear in old age. Thus while Mende are more inclined to liken men and
women of certain social seniority stages to each other, they do not consider
them able to lose or switch male and female identities. Such persistent male–
female distinctions along with age and status-related differences in how they
are applied are recurring features of gender in West Africa (Oppong, 1983).

The Poro and Sande societies are a central influence on Mende ideas
about gender, and in men's and women's lives.[8] All Mende boys and girls
are initiated, spending a period in a special part of the bush isolated from
members of the opposite sex. Through a series of ordeals and processes
involving 'medicine' (*hale*),[9] they are symbolically transformed into 'pure'
males and females, invested with fertility, and ritually prepared for future
safe mingling with members of the opposite sex (Bledsoe, 1984: 464). Circum-
cision is a prerequisite for boys to enter Poro, but it is not part of initiation
per se and is commonly carried out years beforehand. In contrast, clitoridectomy for girls is carried out in the Sande bush as an integral part of the
initiation process and of the girls' transformation into marriageable women

PLATE 3.5: Girls dance at the final coming-out ceremony of their recent initiation
into the women's society, Sande.

Both male and female initiates are 'schooled' in their understanding of
important socio-cultural issues, for example concerning the proper work
and behaviour expected of women and men, the expectations surrounding
marriage relations, and the control of esoteric 'secret' knowledge (MacCormack, 1975; Bledsoe, 1984). Poro and Sande give men and women access to
gender-specific medicine (*hale*), respective forms of knowledge, and social
and political support which the other gender respects and fears. These
parallel, balanced powers and knowledge support the non-hierarchical values
Mende place on gender; women are subordinate to men in some spheres
(e.g. marriage), but women are not considered inferior as women – they are
'different'.

Secret societies both afford supportive solidarity and create stratification
among the members of each gender. Solidarity arises from the extent to which
the societies transcend socio-political status differences to unite men with
men and women with women, from the enduring bonds created among
initiates of the same cohort (*mbaa*), and from social and political protection
in a person's place of residence (MacCormack, 1975). Each localised branch
of the societies (usually at village level for Sande, across larger areas for
Poro) has its own officials. Mende women and men are usually initiated
near their natal homes, but can claim support from the Sande or Poro
societies which are active wherever they reside. Sande solidarity has been
said by Hoffer (1975) to guard women from unwarranted male exploitation,
abuse or disrespect, act as a political force at village level or beyond, and
provide women with close supportive networks of other women (Hoffer,

1975). But secret society organisation also reproduces social asymmetry. Society leaders are usually members of high-status descent groups who, by controlling important knowledge, gain leverage over initiates, their families and their suitors, and may claim loyalty and material goods from them (Bledsoe, 1984). Initiates and members themselves have varied access to society knowledge and support depending on their prior socio-political status. As Bledsoe (1984) emphasises, Sande leaders are concerned not only with female solidarity, but also with how their Sande positions assist them to create and maintain the socio-political alliances necessary to hold their positions in wider society.

Secret society leadership is one means of becoming a 'big man' or 'big woman', a crucial aspect of status illustrated in Table 3.3. A big person (*numu wa*) is a powerful patron on whom others depend for political or economic assistance. Aspects of social and political life in which 'wealth and security rest on the control of others' (Bledsoe, 1980b: 48) are common to societies in the Central West Atlantic Region, and have been variously termed by ethnographers as 'wealth in people' (Bledsoe, 1980b; D'Azevedo, 1962b: 509) or 'patron–clientage' (Richards, 1986). Mende often express the notion of being under someone's patronage as being 'for' them (*ngi X lɔ va*; 'I am for X'), or 'in their hand' (*ngi lɔ X yeya*). One offers allegiance and services to one's contextual *numu wa*, and can expect social, political or material support in return. Patrons seek to expand the clientele they 'hold' *vis-à-vis* rival patrons in various ways. Amidst the insecurities of pre-colonial forest settlement, people depended heavily on the support of hunter or warrior-patrons, and it was through prowess in these activities that big men expanded their followings. Patrons (*numu wa*) in Madina now acquire and maintain their power in various ways, whether through high status in descent groups, holding local political offices, playing brokerage roles, or dispensing economic resources, and clients need protection against modern insecurities. Patron–client relations do not just structure local socio-political dynamics, they are also integral to wider political and economic processes in Sierra Leone (Richards, 1986). These relations link villagers with the wider political economy, whether through the brokerage roles played by village *numu wa* or through the support of external patrons (e.g. in trade or urban areas) which they seek for themselves.

Patron–clientage is important to gender relations. Mende fully accept that women as well as men can become successful patrons. Doing so depends not only on people's ascribed positions, but also on their different opportunities to create relationships of obligation and dependency with other people. But men's and women's relative opportunities are uneven, because of their respective positions in the social relations considered below and in later chapters. Thus, while women do become 'big women', they do so with more difficulty – and in different ways – than men become 'big men'. These

PLATE 3.6: A senior Sande society official and an acknowledged 'big woman'.

'wealth in people' relations pertain not only when a publicly recognised village *numu wa* is involved. As Bledsoe points out, 'Any individual, whether adult or child, needs protection and mediation with superiors; in return the subordinate must accede to demands from those who perform these services' (1990: 75). Parents, senior relatives, or co-wives can all play such support roles. The notion of 'wealth in people' thus pervades many aspects of relations between women and men, and among the members of each sex, in day-to-day life.

Kinship organisation around Gola North can be seen to reflect a tension between 'wealth in people' objectives and patrilineality. While patrilineal ideals are upheld in many contexts, matrilateral relationships are frequently invoked during social and political processes. This is underlined in recent Mende ethnography (e.g. Cunningham, 1991), whereas early ethnographers such as Little (1967) determinedly allocated the Mende a 'patrilineal kinship system' and had difficulty in accounting for apparent divergences from this. The importance of relationships with maternal uncles and other matrilateral kin is even more strongly recognised in the ethnography of Gola (D'Azevedo, 1962b) and related West Atlantic language groups such as the Kissi (Paulme, 1954). In the Gola-Mende areas of Gola North, patrilineal descent is considered the most reputable means to trace rights to land, titles, family property and secrets. Descent groups which uphold direct patrilineal descent from an important settlement-founding ancestor can usually claim the highest local status in matters pertaining to land and local political office-holding, as discussed further in Chapter 4. Those who cannot trace direct patrilineal descent to a founding ancestor might trace it through women or a maternal uncle (*kenya*). High-status descent groups and their members also use such matrilateral ties to create useful alliances with other groups, to expand their numerical strength and to ensure that they retain secure control over titles or property. Extending kin relationships 'horizontally' through such matrilateral ties therefore assists kin group viability and the acquisition of 'wealth in people' (D'Azevedo, 1962b). Whereas patrilineal ideals operate to restrict women's control over resources and people, as we shall see in later chapters the 'wealth in people'-oriented aspects of Gola forest kinship open up significant opportunities for women.

As Murphy and Bledsoe (1987) have emphasised, matrilateral ties are central to binding and legitimating the relationships between 'firstcoming' and 'latecoming' descent groups established during settlement processes. An important latecomer to a settlement is often given a wife from the landowning descent group whose protection he seeks. His group of descendants, constituting a politically subordinate lineage, is subsequently in a position of classificatory 'sister's son' to the firstcomer's as 'mother's brother'. Linked to this relationship of subordination between such 'senior' and 'junior' lineages, the term maternal uncle (*kenya*) around Gola North is used as a

TABLE 3.4: Citizens and strangers in Madina.

	Male	Female
Citizens (*tali*)	74	75
Strangers (*hota*)		
born in Malema chiefdom	12	40
born outside Malema chiefdom	39	43
Total population	125	158

metaphor for political seniority more generally. Matrilateral cross-cousin marriage between a mother's brother's daughter and father's sister's son is an important strategy for the further binding of senior and junior lineages, and as such is a preferred marriage form around Gola North, often repeated generation after generation. Such marriages often use the arrangement known as *kenya huaŋ wui* in which a man gives one of his daughters to his maternal nephew without receiving bridewealth, although expecting continued socio-political allegiance from him and his descendants.

In the large, long-established villages around Gola North, such as Madina, such marriages between descent groups within the village are often encouraged because they help to retain existing citizens, both male and female, within the village. Smaller, more recently established settlements (including the forest hamlets around Gola North) tend to be relatively more concerned to attract marriageable strangers from other communities. This distinction shows up clearly in Davies and Richards's (1991) comparison of the marriage patterns in the different villages in their sample. The incorporation of strangers (*hota*, pl. *hotɛisia*) is, nevertheless, an important way for all Mende settlements, kin groups and patron–client groups to increase their numerical strength. Strictly, a stranger is anyone born outside the settlement in question, or, in the case of small dependent forest villages, outside the parent settlement. Some strangers are short-term visitors, such as for diamond-digging or other economic purposes; others prove to be longer-stay immigrants.

Table 3.4 divides people resident in Madina according to their origins as strangers or as citizens (*tali*), born in the village. Strangers constitute 47 per cent of the total adult population. Forty-one per cent of village men are strangers, and 52 per cent of village women. Davies and Richards's (1991) surveys found villages located on the forest-edge to have a significantly higher proportion of strangers than settlements further from the reserve boundary; strangers constituted 58.5 per cent of the adult population in their forest-edge sample, compared with 36.1 per cent in the non-forest-edge villages. This difference seems to reflect both the marriage-related issues discussed above, and the attraction of strangers to the particular economic opportunities available in forest-edge villages. The proportion of strangers in Madina, as a long-established village close to the reserve boundary

with strong opportunities to engage in cash-cropping activities, is understandably intermediate between the two extremes.

Strangerhood is part of a process of incorporation rather than a fixed
social category. A newly arrived male stranger is expected to place himself
under the patronage, protection and representation of an established member
of the community (*hota kɛɛ*, literally 'stranger-father'), who is either a citizen
(*tali*) or sometimes a longer-established stranger (*hota wovɛi*, 'old stranger').
Mende consider that new strangers cannot be relied upon to stay and to
respect local authority and customs, and such strangers' status in matters
related to forest-resource use reflects this. Indeed, the behaviour of large numbers of short-term visitors, such as around diamond-digging sites, is evidently
and locally recognised as hard to control. But a stranger who proves his commitment to remaining in the community and his allegiance to his stranger-
father's family gradually acquires status more equivalent to a citizen's. He may
be incorporated into his stranger-father's family by marriage to a woman from
it, or by fictionalising his genealogy. Of the fifty-one male strangers in Madina
in 1988, twenty-one were unmarried, twenty had married a citizen woman
and ten had arrived with their wives. Of the latter ten, six were from non-
Mende-speaking districts: three were Fula traders of Guinean origin and
three were from Liberia.

For a woman, the experience of strangerhood is generally associated with
arriving in a community already as a wife. Often a Mende wife moves to her
husband's village on marriage. This pattern conforms with patrilineal ideals
and is most common when men are from high-status descent groups. But
remaining with natal kin offers advantages to spouses and their families,
and is generally preferred. Women from high-status descent groups often
do remain in their natal homes, marrying an incoming stranger. Yet as we
have seen, marriages also occur within the village, between descent groups
or to consolidate relations between descent group segments. Of the fifty-
four wives in Madina resident in their natal home, twenty were married to a
stranger, thirty-four to a citizen. Negotiation over residence can continue
after marriage, if either husband, wife or their respective families can convince
the other of a pressing reason to move. Thus of the married women in Madina
in 1988, fifty-four (45 per cent) were living in their natal homes, and sixty-
eight (55 per cent) had married into the village from outside. On widowhood
or divorce, women often return to their natal kin; twelve out of seventeen
widows and ten out of thirteen divorcees in Madina were living in their
natal homes.

Because marriage is so important to alliance-making and patronage politics,
the control of women's marital and childbearing potential implies control of
an important political resource. This underlies many ideas and practices
which construct women as irresponsible jural minors who need to be controlled by men and older people while they are of childbearing age. As we

TABLE 3.5: Marital status, men.

	Age				
	15–29	30–44	45–60	>60	Total
Not yet married	25	7	1	1	34
Married, 1 wife	10	18	12	4	44
Married, 2 wives	4	8	8	1	19
Married, 3 wives	1	3	4	4	12
Married, 4 wives	—	1	2	—	3
Married, 5 wives	—	—	1	1	2
Divorced	1	3	—	1	5
Widower	1	—	1	2	4
Polygyny rate*	33.3%	37.9%	55.5%	60%	45%

NB: Total number of wives does not tally with Table 3.6 as some wives were resident elsewhere at the time of the survey.
* Polygynous men as percentage of currently married men.

TABLE 3.6: Marital status, women.

	Age				
	15–29	30–44	45–60	>60	Total
Not yet married	5	—	—	—	5
Married	46	51	19	4	120
Divorced	6	4	4	—	14
Widow	—	1	7	11	19
Total					158

shall see, these ideas and practices significantly restrict women's opportunities to acquire control over resources and over other people. However, various factors assist women to overcome this image, and to benefit from control in their own marital affairs and over other women's marriages. Older women can exert control over their children; Sande officials acquire leverage over initiates and their suitors, and senior co-wives may control the acquisition of junior wives for their husbands (cf. Bledsoe, 1980b).

Polygyny is common in Mende marriage, and Table 3.5 shows current polygyny rates among Madina men. Having several wives has always indicated power and wealth and polygyny rates tend to be higher among older men, although polygyny is not such a prerogative of old age as it once was. Mende co-wives are ranked according to their order of arrival into the marriage. The senior or 'big' wife (nyaha wa) has authority over the junior wives (nyaha wulo, small wife), each of whom is ranked above successively acquired wives. A young junior wife often refers to her senior as mother (nje), and the senior calls her child (ndopo), but co-wives also refer to themselves simply as 'mates' (mbaa). Several factors interact with the 'order of arrivals' to affect co-wives' relative status, including their respective ages and whether or not they are living in their natal homes. Mende emphasise

TABLE 3.7: Residential house types in Madina.

House type	Occupants	No.
Multiple	Male kin and clients of house inheritor; wives of monogamous men; wives' children	21
Big (pɛlɛ wa)	Female kin and wives of house inheritor; wives of polygynous men; wives' children	8
Small	House builder or inheritor, with own wives, dependents and children	26

TABLE 3.8: Women's house occupancy.

	Marital status		
Usual sleeping place	Single wife	Co-wife	Unmarried, widow or divorcee
Room of multiple house with husband	25	—	—
Room of small house with husband	5	—	—
Own room in small house	3	—	13
Shared women's room in small house	4	23	—
Pɛlɛ wa	22	38	25

that there should be no jealousy among co-wives: a principle taught to girls during Sande initiation. They also emphasise that husbands should treat all their wives equally. In practice, however, husbands do often single out one of their wives as a favourite 'love wife' or 'companion wife' (*ndoma nyaha*).

Residential arrangements within the village are linked to the organisation of kinship and descent, marriage and polygyny. The village is divided into sections or *kuu*, which were shown in Figure 3.5. These are quarters held by particular families, housing all the members of a particular descent group together with those people attached to it through marriage or clientship. Within each *kuu* are one or more residential compounds (*mawɛɛ*, from *mu wɛlɛ*, 'our house'), accommodating those relatives and clients who share the accommodation and patronage of a single *mawɛɛ* head, and in the past, as Chapter 4 will show, united for many other purposes. There are several kinds of house within each *mawɛɛ* compound, and these are shown in Table 3.7. Multiple houses and big houses were built in the past by *mawɛɛ* heads to house their dependents. Multiple houses are sub-divided into rooms which today house men or monogamous couples. Big houses (*pɛlɛ wa*) are undivided 'dormitories' shared – and preferred – by women. Co-wives commonly sleep in these, taking three-nightly turns to sleep in their husband's room. Today, men prefer to construct separate houses for their own wives and dependents, including a room for co-wives to share, and these 'small houses' are increasingly common in the Gola forest area. Table 3.8 shows the house types occupied by women according to their marital status.

In the chapters to follow, we shall see how the aspects of social and political life introduced here are related to forest-resource use. People's different positions in patron–clientage, secret societies, kinship and descent, marriage and residence influence and are influenced by their resource-using activities, interests and opportunities. As people interact with their environment, they also interact with a wide range of social groupings and sets of relations. It is to forest-resource use that we now turn, beginning, appropriately, with the agricultural system which has long provided the basis for local subsistence in the Gola forest area.

4

FARMING, FOOD AND FALLOWS

The cultivation of annual crops on a rotational bush-fallow system has long been the mainstay of local livelihoods and social life in the Gola forest area. Fertile land for food production is an essential forest-derived resource in villagers' eyes. Mende create sites for farming out of bush or forest, growing the culturally valued staple, rice, with a range of other food and cash-oriented crops. This chapter examines how Mende classify and deal with different parts of their forest environment in the context of annual farming, and looks at aspects of the conceptual framework within which they consider the relationship between farmers, farm-sites and the bush. It examines women's and men's involvement in the farming and fallowing process, and their differential use of resources in this context.

Conservationists are concerned about the effects of local farming practices on forest vegetation, and about their long-term sustainability under changing demographic and socio-economic conditions. Given that population densities around the Gola North reserve are relatively low, there is no immediate pressure to shorten fallow periods or expand cultivation into forested land. Nevertheless, farming patterns have changed over the last thirty years. Food production has intersected with new socio-economic conditions and opportunities, especially those linked to the expansion of tree crop cultivation for cash, which Chapter 5 discusses in detail. Here I show how the relative use of different bush and farm-site types is changing, with implications for both food security and forest ecology. The causes are best illuminated by looking at the organisational dynamics of food production, and at gender relations in the use of land resources, labour and products (Leach, 1991e and 1992c).

BUSH TYPES, FARM TYPES

The hilly, forest-dominated Gola landscape offers a range of types of bush with farm-site potential. Mende categorise these according to position on a catena with different slope, soil and moisture conditions (cf. Richards, 1986,

Figure 4.1). Uplands (often steep) are entirely rainfed and have free-draining gravelly soils (*kɔti*). Low-lying areas near the base of the catena (*bului*) are partially fed by runoff from upper slopes. Inland valley swamps below them (*kpɛtɛ*) are permanently moist and some are seasonally flooded.

In vegetational terms, Mende often refer generally to all the land outside the village itself as bush (*ndɔgbɔ*). In many contexts they also distinguish fallow bush (*ndɔgbɔ*) from high forest (*ngola*), containing trees older than about 30–40 years. Several categories of fallow bush are also distinguished, including strong (*ndɔgbɔhinti*, *c.* 15–30 years), fairly strong (*gbɔɛɛ*, *c.* 11–14 years), and young farmbush fallow (*njɔpɔ*, <10 years). The criteria used are age of secondary succession, vegetation form and indicator species.

Different sites have different food production value. Upland farming has long been the mainstay of local subsistence. There, local rice varieties, selected and placed to suit micro-environments within the site, are inter-planted with a wide range of other crops. These include vegetables and leaves important as sauce ingredients (e.g. chilli pepper, egg plant, tomato), and root crops and grains which act as seasonal hunger foods (e.g. cassava, sorghum, sweet potato). *Bului* plots support short-duration (three month) rice varieties which mature in the hungry season, acting as important hunger breakers, and a more limited range of intercrops. Upland and *bului* land is sometimes farmed for a second or third year with non-rice food crops before being left fallow. Inland valley swamps (*kpɛtɛ*) are planted with flood-tolerant long-duration (five month) varieties (locally termed *yaka*). Swamp soils are too wet for intercrops to be grown in the rainy season.

Sites cleared from secondary fallow can be successfully cultivated with rice only for a single year. In comparison, land cleared from high forest offers certain advantages and disadvantages. Forest farms (*ngolagbaa*) give higher yields of rice and certain intercrops (e.g. pepper) and can be success-fully cultivated with rice a second time within five years. However, clearing high forest is difficult and labour demanding. More commonly, farmers prefer to use the more readily cleared bush already 'captured' within the bush-fallow cycle, of 8–15 years (i.e. *gbɔɛɛ* or mature *njɔpɔ*). Young fallow (<7 years) is normally avoided as it has insufficient fertility and too many weeds for rice production, but sites cleared from swamp fallow of this age are often successfully cultivated. When farmers do take new forest land into the fallow cycle, they often extend a *bului* plot up the surrounding slopes. Much of the earlier Mende settlement of the forest probably took place according to this pattern (Richards, 1991).

SOCIO-ECOLOGICAL CONCEPTS
Farm-sites, farmers and the bush

Settlement and farming have converted much of the forested landscape to a shifting mosaic of forest, farm-site and bush in various stages of regrowth

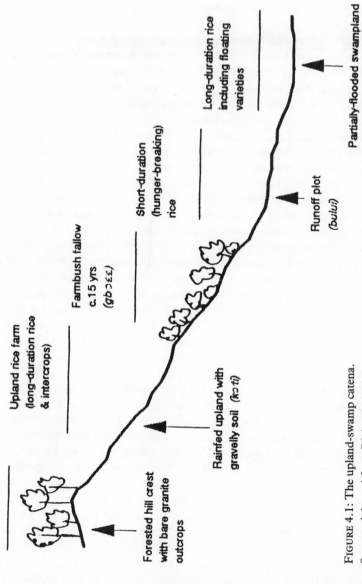

FIGURE 4.1: The upland-swamp catena.
Source: Adapted from Richards (1986).

PLATE 4.1: A mosaic of (1) farm (*kpaa*); (2) farm bush (*ndɔgbɔ*); (3) last year's farm (*njɔpɔ*); and (4) high forest (*ngola*).

(Plate 4.1). For Mende, it is this conversion, harnessing the fertility to grow rice, which has enabled settled social life.[1] But Mende acknowledge the fragility of the relationship between their food-production operations and the forces of the bush. Productive farm-sites are only a precarious moment in a place's annual and longer-term agro-ecological and social history, in an area cultivated and left fallow by different farmers at different times.

As Davies and Richards (1991) emphasise, Mende conceive of farming as an annual process within which 'farms', as such, exist only briefly. Farmers enter bush (*ndɔgbɔ*) to choose a new upland farm-site in December each year. Between January and March (Figure 4.2) they prepare the land by 'brushing' (*ndoe*) undergrowth, converting the area to *ndoeke* (*ndoli yeke*; literally 'new born part'). The large trees are subsequently felled (*po*) with an axe, transforming the place into *pokpaa*. The cut vegetation is left to dry and then burned, as late as possible in the dry season. Unburned branches are, if necessary, gathered into heaps and re-burned. After burning the place is known as *mɔtiihun*. As the rains set in in May–June, rice and intercrops are broadcast and the soil is turned lightly with a hoe to cover them. Strictly only a fully planted site is referred to as *kpaa*, 'farm'. Having achieved this a farm hut is built to cook and rest in and farmers await the harvest, between late October and December, with anxious expectation. Once the rice is harvested and packed safely into store for later threshing and de-husking the farm-site is referred to as *mbawoma* ('behind rice'); it subsequently becomes *njɔpɔ* (young bush) and eventually bush (*ndɔgbɔ*) again.

The parallel sequence of stages in swamp farming usually begins between April and July, and ends with harvest the following December–January (Figure 4.2). Vegetation is cleared by hand rather than burned, and rice may be transplanted rather than broadcast.

Cleared farm-sites are light, hot and dry, like the village, but they remain surrounded by the cold, dark bush which – although it provides the fertility for food production – also presents innumerable dangers to farmers and their operations. Along with climatic events such as storms and early rainfall, and accidents such as tree fall, farmers must contend with aspects of the bush which constantly threaten to reassert themselves, jeopardising the rice and its cultivators. People engage in a constant struggle to restrain these. Animal pests can devastate ripening crops, especially large cane rats (*Thyronomis swinderianus*), monkeys and birds. Farmers carefully fence the farm in an attempt to deter the former, and must keep constant guard against the latter while the rice is ripening. 'Weeds' which compete with the rice must be removed. Farmers refer to all weeds as *ngulu*, tree, regardless of whether the plant is in fact a germinated sapling or an herbaceous plant (and contrasting with *kpiti*, 'grass', the name for an herbaceous plant growing outside a farm boundary), thinking of them as aspects of the bush (which will eventually comprise trees) reinvading (Davies and Richards, 1991).

PLATE 4.2: A man fells a forest tree to open up a new upland farm-site.

PLATE 4.3: A catenary upland rice farm fully planted with rice and intercrops.

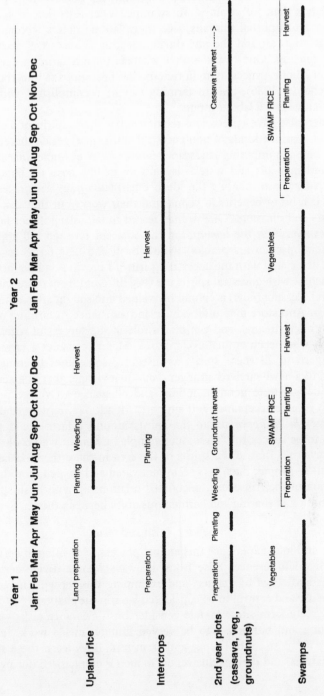

FIGURE 4.2: Calendar of main annual farming activities.

While such hazards affect all farming, they are notably more pronounced for uplands than for swamps. In swamps, water-retention in soils reduces the effects of unusual rainfalls, rice transplanting deters weeds, and piling cut vegetation around the site during clearing reduces the need for pest-control fencing. One result is that whereas upland farming needs peaked inputs of labour, especially to fit time-bound operations to uncertain rainfalls (cf. Richards, 1986), swamp farming can be accomplished with steadier, more evenly spread labour inputs.

Farmers also have a precarious relationship with the spirits of the surrounding bush. Various kinds of non-ancestral spirit (jina) reside there, especially where there are imposing landscape features.[2] For example, tingɔi and njalɔi are found in pools and waterfalls, and dwarf-like tɛmu on large hills and rocks. Ndɔgbɔjusu inhabits the 'deep bush' (susu/jusu: deep/recess). These jinanga can bring benefits to people and their work, but they can also cause accidents and disasters. One woman feared to fall asleep in her farm hut on hot afternoons lest the tɛmuisia on the adjacent forested hill approach her with their mischievous pranks. Fallow bush and new farms made therein are also associated with the ancestral spirits[3] of previous cultivators. People's relationships with ancestral spirits are very different from those with jinanga. Ancestral blessing (bayi) is commonly valued and sought after, often through sacrifices. Ancestors may offer advice and assistance to farming operations, often through dreams, and can play a role in the successful regeneration of the bush when each annual cycle ceases. Mende consider a farmer's status with regard to all these spirits as insecure, sometimes likening it to the position of a newly arrived stranger (hota) to a village. Just as a new stranger should demonstrate good intentions and allegiance to village residents in order to receive acceptance and support, Mende say, farmers should 'show goodness' (fe kpɛkpɛya ve) to the spirits around a farm-site if their farm work is to be successful. Thus, for example, a woman who cooks in a farm hut always calls first to the spirits of the area to share the food before dishing it out to people. Such acts seem motivated and shaped more by people's perception of their insecure, negotiated relationship with bush spirits, than by any notion of sharing and harmonious unity between them.

Gender, bush and farm

Women and men experience this annual process of farming in very different ways. Broad differences arise from the ways Mende divide certain tasks, activities and crops by gender, and examining this set will enable issues of resource use and control to be considered later in the chapter.

Men create farm-sites. Mende consider bush clearance tasks – brushing, tree felling and burning – to be very definitely 'men's work', along with building the pest control fence and farm hut. Boys learn these skills from male relatives, and their exclusiveness to men is emphasised during initiation into the men's society, Poro. Mende draw explicit links between bush clearance and warriorhood: the annual carving of a farm out of the bush recalls warrior-founders' carving of territories out of the forest during settlement history, and men describe clearing as 'fighting the bush', often bringing their cutlasses and axes to bear with warlike aggression and cries. The intense bursts of energy and high levels of risk involved are consistent with other work thought appropriate only to men. In short, to clear bush is to emphasise one's status as a man. Clearing high forest emphasises male capability most of all, as the large trees are so difficult and dangerous to fell. Expert tree fellers tackle huge trees with special climbing techniques and the help of leaf medicines (*hale*), drawing on specialised knowledge which 'ordinary' members of society do not possess. It is inappropriate for a woman to clear any kind of bush for rice production. Those who do so might be labelled *hindogbahama* (a man-like woman). Generally only post-menopausal women, who are accepted as 'like men' in certain respects, ever brush their own farms without risk of deleterious comment and accusation.[4]

Other food-production tasks are emphatically 'women's work', including processing and cooking the rice. Sande emphasises the female-exclusiveness of these activities. A man performing them consistently, especially in the public eye of the village, would be called *nyahagbahama* (a woman-like man) and risks disapproving threats from Sande-supported women and uneasy laughter from other men. Between these strongly polarised and relatively inflexibly divided tasks lie a range of others. Weeding is normally women's work but it is not inconceivable for men to help out. Planting, bird-scaring and harvesting can be divided more flexibly between the members of each sex according to changing social and economic circumstances, as we shall see.

Men initiate the annual farming cycle while, as rice processors and cooks, women complete it. And it is the rice that women cook and bring to men while they work at bush clearance which supports them in the opening of the new cycle. Mende sometimes say that 'the bush is men's, but the farm is women's'. Such statements seem to refer both to gendered agricultural work, beginning for men in uncleared bush but for women, with planting, in a cleared farm-site, and to the notion that men make the bush productive by converting it to a place where rice can be grown, while women 'make the farm productive' by converting the rice to a form in which it can be eaten and used in social life.

Women are involved with each upland farm-site for longer than men. While rice is a joint concern, intercrops are primarily a concern of women. These mature at different rates and women continue to collect them long after the rice has been harvested, often right through the following farming year as Figure 4.2 showed. Thus for men the rice harvest signals a conceptual boundary between 'food production place' and regenerating bush (*njɔpɔ*),

PLATE 4.4: A woman digs for the sweet potatoes she intercropped with her
household's rice during the dry season following the rice harvest, amidst
regrowing bush fallow vegetation.

but women experience a more gradual transition. Young *njɔpɔ* remains a source of crops which they collect amidst progressively reinvading bush plants and animals, ceasing regular visits to the place when it becomes 'too bushy' and inaccessible even if the crops have not yet finished.

Mende emphasise that these gender-divided roles are complementary and interdependent; neither gender's work is possible and useful without the other's. The idea that gender roles are different but balanced and complementary permeates many other spheres of Mende life, from ideas about human reproduction to the balanced powers of male and female secret societies (cf. Bledsoe, 1984; MacCormack, 1980). In some senses the food production cycle provides an annually repeating locus for the affirmation of these broader ideas.

Such a division of labour, based on sex-specific tasks and tools combined in sequence, is characteristic of many of the 'old world' staple crops found in the West African forest zone, and such sequences often provide means through which wider ideas about gender relations are created and expressed (Guyer, 1984b). However, over the last thirty years there have been considerable changes in the organisation of rice production and therefore in exactly what farming roles 'say' about social relations. As we shall see, the production process is also a means by which people continually legitimate rights in each other and in resources and products (Guyer, *op. cit.*), in ways which are also changing. Mende ideas about land tenure provide both a third dimension of the conceptual framework for food production, and a way into examining these resource-use relationships and changes.

Land tenure

The ideas of farming as a process, and of short production cycles embedded in longer-term land histories, are linked to Mende concepts of land tenure. There is no notion of land as property in the sense of something that can be owned or possessed. Two distinct concepts are important. First, there is the holding of land (*ndɔlɔ*) by or on behalf of groups of people, legitimated by the group's claimed place in the territory's history. Second, people may make use of land resources (such as cultivation space, soil (*pɔlɔ*), minerals, vegetation, water, etc.) for a temporary period, according to nested sets of use rights.

Although *ndɔlɔ* is the basic term for land, it is better translated as 'territory' (also country, ground or world). All the territory of the chiefdom is held by the paramount chief (*ndɔlɔ mahei*); nested within this, landholding families (*mbonda ndɔlɔ*) hold areas linked to particular settlements. Elders, usually members of the core patrilineage (*ndehu*), administer landholding on behalf of family members. While patrilineal principles favour men as descent-group heads, Mende would nevertheless give control to a woman rather than allow it to pass to an unsuitable (personally irresponsible, too young) man who might manage it badly or risk losing it.[5] Landholding implies both power over and obligation towards the people and resources within the territory. These are 'for' the landholders, who have the right to use and allocate land resources and to expect allegiance from occupants, but also duties to protect both land and people.

Nested landholding groups are integral to local politics. Key leadership roles are generally occupied by members of the most powerful landholding descent groups. Paramount chiefs and speakers are elected from the chiefdom's ruling house; within villages, secret society leaderships and the 'native authorities' who vote in chieftaincy elections are occupied by members of important landholding families. The relative status of landholding descent groups is legitimated according to a 'code of arrivals' (Murphy and Bledsoe, 1987)[6] ultimately traceable to a settlement's 'firstcomer' warrior or hunter-founder. Groups whose landholding rights are nested within those of a more powerful descent group may trace descent only from a politically subordinate latecoming group, or only more weakly through women or alternate male and female ancestors. These relations are highly dynamic, depending heavily on achieved successes in the acquisition of clients and wealth, and subordinate immigrant groups occasionally gain in wealth and status to outstrip earlier arrivals. In such circumstances public versions of family and territorial histories are commonly reworked to accommodate current political relations (Hill, 1984; Richards, 1986). One of the reasons why family and land histories are often closely guarded secrets is to avoid bringing unwanted discrepancies to light. It is these political relations as much as 'land' *per se* which are at stake in interfamily land disputes, which are arbitrated in the paramount chief's court.

People who want to farm must acquire rights to use land resources from descent-group elders, who also arbitrate competing claims over land use. Male and female family members have unquestionable rights to be granted the use of family-held land resources. Notably for Mende *mbonda* (family) is an incorporative concept, with none of the exclusive sense surrounding the concept of a lineage or line of descent (*ndehu*). *Mbonda* can encompass a very wide circle of kin and clients, including the husbands, wives, in-laws, matrilateral relatives and clients of descent-group members. All these may request the use of family land, although an in-marrying wife would normally be expected to liaise through her husband, and a male stranger-client through his patron. Members of other families and newly arrived immigrant strangers may also be allocated land-use rights, but only in exchange for a gift (*famalo*, greeting present) acknowledging the landholder's position. The *famalo* is waived for a longer-established stranger, a signal of his or her incorporation as an established 'family' member. These use rights diminish after harvest, and land control reverts to the landholding family. Landholding and land-resource use are linked, in that bush clearance by people to whom a landholding group has allocated land-resource use constitutes a reaffirmation of their territorial control. Indeed, control over land can become more ambiguous if it is left out of use under high forest for a long period. The desire to reinstate old family-land claims can be an important reason for making forest farms.

Within this broad range of possibilities, the numbers and types of 'social unit' requesting land use for farming each year have shifted over the last few decades, as has the sort of land requested. Nested within rights to use land resources for a rice farm are other rights to land resources which depend on the existence of a cleared farm-site. These include rights to use space and soils to plant intercrops and to cultivate an additional separate crop, either alongside the rice or after its harvest. These rights are especially important to women and to 'junior' men, but again, as we shall see, their roles have been subject to change.

Territory currently lying within the Gola Forest reserves is formally subject to different tenure arrangements, under the custody of the government rather than local communities. Local people are not permitted to farm there. But villagers interpret the arrangements from their own conceptual framework, again emphasising the distinction between landholding and land-resource use. The original Forest Ordinances as arranged with local paramount chiefs apparently acknowledged the reserved areas to 'belong' to local communities, but that the (then colonial) state would take them into trust on indefinite lease. Many Mende family heads interpret the state to have obtained only land-resource use rights, and emphatically assert that local families are still the landholders of the reserved areas. Encroachments on the reserve are relatively rare, but in recent cases they have been motivated by the desire to reassert these old claims to family land rather than by any shortage of adequately fallowed land outside the boundary. Other villagers accept the reserve arrangements without opposition, emphasising the state's (legitimate) long-term land-resource use rights. But they are surprised that the state has made no productive use of the resources at their disposal (cf. Davies and Richards, 1991).

These ideas and experiences of the relationship between farm-sites, farmers and bush, gender and land tenure provide an enduring framework for Mende food-production operations. But within this, actual patterns of activity, resource use and control are varied and dynamic. If we turn to look at farming organisation and relations of land-resource use, labour and product rights, we find these to have changed significantly over the last few decades. This has had differentiated effects on women and men, and has influenced food-production security and forest ecology. The resource-use patterns that prevailed during the mid-twentieth century provide the context for examining these recent changes.

FARMING BEFORE THE 1960s

During the early- to mid-twentieth century, groups of forty or fifty people commonly produced rice together, uniting as a *mawɛɛ* (Little, 1948a). Between seven and ten of these *mawɛɛ* groups regularly farmed in Madina. The *mawɛɛ* revolved around a group of brothers and sisters, their spouses, some children and grandchildren, and various more distant kin and clients, under the headship of a *mawɛɛ-mɔ* (*mawɛɛ* person). Most *mawɛɛ* heads were male, but influential senior women could acquire the title by inheriting it from a dead husband or male relative in the absence of suitable male heirs (Little, 1948a). As a food-production group, *mawɛɛ* members were obliged to contribute labour each year to make a 'big farm' (*kpaa wa*) from which the *mawɛɛ* head ensured their subsistence. The *mawɛɛ* was also a residential and patronage grouping, offering members many other kinds of social and economic support.[7] At this time all male members shared large divided houses and women slept in large undivided 'big houses' (*pɛlɛ wa*) in village-based *mawɛɛ* compounds, while 'domestic slaves' were sometimes housed in more distant farming camps. *Mawɛɛ* heads were important local patrons (*numu wa*) who, as well as ensuring members' food security, offered other material assistance such as with taxes, fines and court fees, and clothing. Cloth was given to male and female members after their respective main farming tasks (Little, 1948a and 1951). Members' dependence on the *mawɛɛ-mɔ*'s economic support assisted the *mawɛɛ-mɔ*'s control over their labour. Importantly, *mawɛɛ* heads often paid brideprice for male members, giving them leverage over the labour of both the man and his new wife. Other men (including immigrant strangers) were given wives from the *mawɛɛ* without paying brideprice, but were then obliged to work for the *mawɛɛ* to fulfil brideservice obligations (Crosby, 1937). The production, patronage and residential dimensions of *mawɛɛ* organisation were mutually reinforcing, and the annual farming cycle was a means to reaffirm them, year after year.

Farming activities and responsibilities were divided among *mawɛɛ* members. The *mawɛɛ* head generally secured land-resource use rights for the group; a straightforward process as *mawɛɛ* heads and landholding descent group elders were often one and the same. While the *mawɛɛ-mɔ* took responsibility for decisions such as farm-site location and size, a male head's senior wife (*nyaha wa*) shared (and occasionally took over) decisions about *mawɛɛ* labour and product use (Crosby, 1937).

The division of labour for production of the *mawɛɛ* rice yield did not depend solely on gender. Among men, there were important cross-cutting distinctions based on age and descent-group status. High status men participated in the socially significant male tasks involved with bush clearance but would then turn to hunting and local political activity, leaving subsequent 'men's work', such as fencing the farm-site against cane rats, to young men,

PLATE 4.5: A young woman harvests upland rice.

strangers and clients. These 'junior' men worked with women to plant and harvest the rice. Notably, rice-planting by women and junior men is a standard pattern among Liberian and southern Guinean peoples in the Upper Guinea coast region, but among the Temne and Kpa Mende, further north-west in Sierra Leone, it is the men who plant. The Gola-Mende area around the Gola North reserve seems to have followed the Liberian pattern. There were also divisions between women. The *mawɛɛ* head's senior wife usually organised, but took little physical part in, women's work. Female *mawɛɛ* members sometimes divided into groups associated with each of their sleeping houses (*pɛlɛ wa*) to accomplish their tasks, each group working with an allotted complement of 'junior' men. *Pɛlɛ wa* groups oversaw the cooking of rice, in huge pots, to feed the entire group of workers (Little, 1948b).

The large size of *mawɛɛ*-based production groups gave them flexibility to take advantage of different bush and farm-site types. *Mawɛɛ* 'big farms' (*kpaa wa*) were nearly always intercropped uplands with *bului* plots for hunger-breaking rice. Groups to meet the peaked labour needs of upland farming (especially at clearing, planting and weeding stages) and, if necessary, to clear high forest could be assembled within the *mawɛɛ* (Little, 1948b). If peak labour needs exceeded *mawɛɛ* capacities, their heads could draw on kinship or patron-client ties to obtain help from members of other *mawɛisia*, or employ a labour group. A common form of men's labour group around Gola North drew on old forms of warrior organisation (*kugbe*). Village chiefs sometimes directed these groups, which mainly comprised young men and strangers, to work on each farm in the village in turn. Patrons had socio-political as well as economic interests in assembling group labour at peak periods, since this was a way publicly to demonstrate their status and to create and consolidate patron-client relations. As others emphasise, such political motivations often contribute to farm-labour organisation in West Africa (Berry, 1989; Guyer, 1984b; Johnny *et al.*, 1981; Linares, 1981).

Interlocking with *mawɛɛ* rice production were two sorts of nested land-resource use, directed towards producing crops which were subject to different forms of control. The picture probably varied across Mendeland, but around this part of Gola North it appears to have been as follows. First, the *mawɛɛ-mɔ* would allot small portions of the cleared upland farm-site to important male, and occasionally female, dependents (Crosby, 1937). This 'small farm' (*kpaa mumu*) was considered a separate undertaking, whose labour responsib-ilities and proceeds belonged entirely to the farmer concerned. A married man was expected to feed his wife/wives and children from his *kpaa mumu*, relying on rice from the *kpaa wa* primarily for security. Nevertheless, work on the *kpaa wa* took priority, and 'small farm' cultivation was not allowed to interfere with it. Second, female *mawɛɛ* members had rights to use cleared farm-site space to plant intercrops. This usefully obviated the need for separately cleared sites for such crops, which, given the prevailing task divisions, women would find difficult to clear for themselves. Although some hunger foods belonged to the whole *mawɛɛ*, women planted and owned root crops, vegetables and cotton which they used for consumption and gift exchange among their kin.

Since the 1960s this organisation and resource use pattern has shifted as farming has intersected with changing social and economic conditions. In particular, the small-scale cultivation of commercial tree crops (cocoa, coffee and oil palm) and diamond digging have expanded, affecting food production both directly and indirectly. Current farming organisation, product control and labour divisions and relations reflect these influences, and underlie recent changes in the distribution of farming across different bush, farm-site and crop types.

FARMING SINCE THE 1960S

Organisation

Rice-producing groups on the scale described above are rarely found today. Madina had ninety-two farm-households in 1988 and eighty-four in 1991, with a mean (in 1988) of 2.8 adult members (Figure 4.3). Normally farm-households are now 'sub units' of the *mawɛɛ*, which is now principally a residential/patronage group. Modern 'small' farm-households may also be called *mawɛɛ*: as functional levels have separated, so the meanings of the term *mawɛɛ*, which was always polysemic, have multiplied.

Changes in farming organisation are linked to increasing opportunities for social and economic independence. As people acquire resources through trade or cash crops they rely less heavily on patrons and senior relatives, and can more easily extricate their labour from their control. As one man explained, 'Once we made farms for a big man. But now we farm for ourselves.' While Little (1948b) noticed a progressive decrease in farming-group size in the 1940s in Sierra Leone's Southern Province, Gola forest elders highlight the role of expanding cocoa and coffee production in the 1950s and 1960s. Cocoa and coffee incomes helped many men to pay for taxes, fines, clothing and support for wives and dependents for themselves. By paying their own brideprice, such men could avoid indebting their labour so heavily to a *mawɛɛ* head in order to marry. It became expected that a man would establish his own farm-household at, or soon after, marriage.

Today, farm-households commonly consist of a husband and wife/wives, unmarried children, and sometimes an additional member such as an elderly mother. Unmarried strangers often farm alone, while widows and separated women, once 'embedded' in large *mawɛɛ* farming groups just as married women were, may now head their own farm households. Farm-household headship has become important to notions of adult male identity: to 'being a man' in the sense of a supporter of wives and dependents. A man who still farms with a patron or senior relative is often referred to as 'only a small

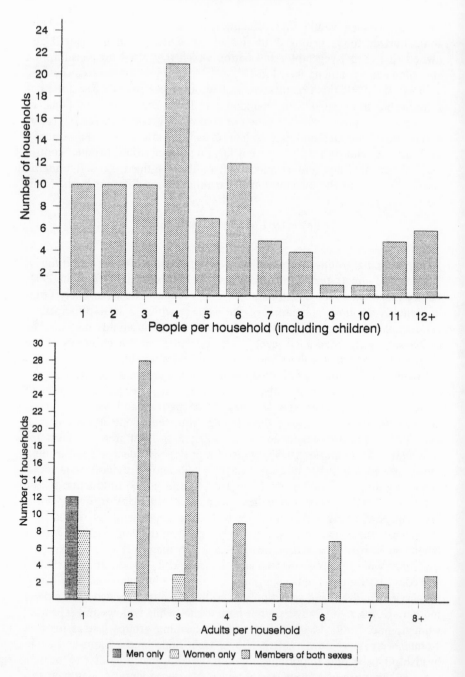

FIGURE 4.3: Size and composition of rice farm households in Madina, 1988.

boy'. The annual farming cycle has also acquired associations with marriage, affirming the complementary unity of a husband and wife's roles. Men's clearance of bush now connotes the fulfilment of married male responsibility; failure to clear it constitutes grounds for divorce in local customary law. For women, the phrase 'he does not make farms for me' encapsulates the deterioration of marital relations.

One result of these changes is that a larger number of farm-household heads, each year, make use of their rights to use land resources. To gain land, most farm-household heads have a range of possibilities. Men and women living in their natal villages can use land of their own descent group, or of their maternal uncles'. Male and female strangers – including widows living in their deceased husband's home – derive land from a spouse's or a patron's descent group, and farm-household heads may also 'beg' the use of another descent group's land for the year. No farmers complain of general difficulty in gaining access to land resources, and the range of options gives most people potential access to the full range of bush and farm-site types (cf. Richards, 1986). However, family heads are sometimes called upon to arbitrate competing usage claims: for instance, where two farmers wish to use the same piece of bush. Such cases are judged partly in terms of the relative strength of each party's claims (those of a landholding descent-group member normally supersede those of a more distantly related family member, perhaps through marriage, or of a stranger), but also, like Mende dispute settlement more generally, according to each claimant's relative political strength and social influence.

It would be wrong to see these organisational changes as a smooth transition from *mawɛɛ* to conjugal farm-household. First, there can be tensions between farm-households and larger, patronage-based or *mawɛɛ* groups. Currently powerful village patrons and *mawɛɛ* heads often try to recruit junior kin, clients and their wives into their farm-households for the season, thus enhancing their status and authority, even if 'juniors' would prefer to farm only with their own wives. One 'big woman', an elder of an important landholding family, so incorporated her son and his three wives to create a group with ten adult members, explaining that 'this year we want to make a very large farm'. In 1989, in the aftermath of a severe hungry season and foreseeing heavy rice needs to feed community labour during a forthcoming building project, Madina's town chief and family heads decided that each residential *mawɛɛ* should make a group farm additional to sub-unit household farms. In short, the trend towards small farm-households has not stabilised; they remain nested within the organisational possibilities of '*mawɛɛ* as production group' and 'patrons as production group heads'.

Second, farm-household arrangements vary from year to year as different circumstances and dilemmas arise. For example, in 1988 a recently divorced woman joined her married daughter's farm-household to avoid male labour difficulties, and in 1990 refugees from Liberia used a common stranger–citizen arrangement when they joined Madina farm-households for the season, 'departing' with a prearranged proportion of rice after harvest (Leach, 1992a; cf. Richards, 1986).

Coincidental with changes in farm-household organisation are shifts in the levels and roles of members' additional 'small farms'. Present household big farms (*kpaa wa*) are often of similar size and labour force to the small farms (*kpaa mumu*) of the past. The *kpaa wa* is now considered the main source of food security for farm-household members. Small additional plots, made by individual farm-household members such as unmarried sons and clients, daughters and wives, are now even smaller.

Independent food provisioning raises new ambiguities: how much is tolerable before the gender-interdependence of household farming, and the integrity of marital relations with which it is entwined, is threatened? Notably, some women now feed themselves and their children from their small farms for a large part of every year, claiming that a husband is not fulfilling his rice-providing responsibilities, and this can presage marital breakdown. And co-wives who predict the eruption of interpersonal tensions during communal operations sometimes prefer to farm independently, despite the cultural ideal that they should work in unity with their husband. In 1990 three co-wives each worked separate farm-sites with their adult sons, their husband taking little part except to eat from each farm's proceeds.

Product control

These tensions, whether between wider kin and patron–client networks, or between conjugal-based farm-households and individuals' interests, importantly affect control over the products of farming. The harvest and storage of the farm-household rice is supervised by the farm-household head and his senior wife. A senior wife or another mature woman is considered the ideal rice-store keeper. Such women carefully emphasise their responsible diligence in knowing and budgeting-out the household's rice economy, which can include covertly appropriating small quantities for their own use or sale. Household rice is intended to meet members' food needs as far as possible into the hungry season before the next harvest. But there are also pressures to give rice to others, such as to offer political hospitality, to contribute to family ceremonies, or to help hungry kin and clients during or after harvest. Helping with harvest in return for a share ('finding rice'), or requesting it directly, is a common and accepted way for people to augment scarce rice supplies. This becomes an essential coping strategy for those who are sick or whose own farms have yielded poorly.[8] Giving rice to others creates security by allowing farmers to cope by 'calling in their debts' should their future fortunes fail. Both socio-cultural ideals and material concerns favour such networks of interdependence over food 'self-sufficiency'.

Farmers are nevertheless anxious to control unwanted drains on their rice supplies. They may therefore be secretive about starting to harvest rice, and reluctant to announce good yields. Furthermore, while all household members experience this general tension between the need to give out rice and giving too much, they may disagree over particular instances of giving. A wife may feel that her husband's relatives are making too many claims, but male household heads are also concerned that wives do not give household rice too freely to their own kin and friends. Women attempt to protect their fragile control by perpetuating myths about the fate of men who enter rice stores, saying that such men start to smell bad (*a maguelɔ*) and become weak and sickly. Disagreements occasionally erupt into 'palavers' which usually result in the husband taking over the rice-store key.

Individual wives and junior men consider the rice from their separate plots to give them useful security against the failure or inadequacy of the household farm, and, importantly, to provide inputs into the networks of interdependence which they maintain for themselves. Junior wives find independence from their senior co-wives as important as from their husband. As one woman said: 'It is good to have your own rice if you want to cook for your own children and your friends. If you try to use the household rice your husband or co-wife might cause problems.' Personal rights to rice are legitimated by its production in a well-defined place with individually organised (rather than farm-household) labour. But these rights, relatively clear when rice is in the farm, can become more ambiguous post-harvest. A farm-household head may try to bring individuals' rice into joint use, as food for all, either to supplement or to replace diminishing *kpaa wa* supplies. While a wife or son may agree with this priority, individuals seem more often to consider their own and farm-household rice as separate, even opposed, interests. They insist on retaining private control through careful, separate storage.

Some upland farm intercrops belong to the whole farm household, while others are shared by female members to use as sauce ingredients for common meals. Female household members, however, can also use intercrops on an individual basis in separate cooking, as gifts to their own kin or friends, and increasingly for cash sale. Women have developed means to identify separate ownership of such crops planted in a shared farm-site. For example, they use branches to bound small sections (*kaka*) within which broadcast intercrops (but not the rice) are individual property. They plant maize and root crops in recognisable points and lines, between designated branches or around particular tree stumps or termite mounds. They create 'in-farm gardens' (*kpaa hu gadi*) by planting sweet potatoes, pepper and egg plants in distinct clusters. Women consider individual intercrop ownership especially important when crops are to be sold, and when their relations with their co-wives are disagreeable. In this sense the mixture of joint and privately owned crops built up during the upland planting season can provide a record of short-term economic, social and interpersonal relationships between female household members. Figure 4.4 illustrates this for one farm-household.

Labour relations and production security

As farm-household organisation has changed, so production security has become more variable and more dependent on non-household labour. Smaller farm households, especially, often suffer from labour shortages and this is a prime reason for unsuccessful farming (cf. Richards, 1986). Group labour for demanding operations must usually be assembled from outside the farm-household.

Mende recognise a range of means to obtain labour, including drawing on kinship or patron–client ties, joining a reciprocal labour group, or paying individuals or groups by the day, but people's opportunities are highly differentiated. Influential male or female village patrons and senior family members can most easily call on junior kin or clients. Patrons can also manage the social negotiations to assemble large labour groups (kɔmbi), 'paying' them with a combination of money, a midday meal (kɔndi) and promised future support.

Most women, young men and strangers, however, have more limited access to others' labour (cf. Guyer, 1984b; Roberts, 1988). Women often need male labour for bush clearance, whether because they are husbandless farm-household heads or on their individual plots which are no longer necessarily portions of a cleared main farm-site. Women find kɔmbi recruitment difficult and can draw on only a more limited range of kin ties. Middle-aged women often receive help from adult children and sons-in-law, although they complain that changing marriage and economic arrangements are weakening their claims. Women have developed arrangements to help cope with female activities. Sisters, sleeping house and kitchen mates often help each other with weeding and planting. For harvest, women link reciprocal labour arrangements with rice gift and security networks. A woman invites her female kin and friends to cut the rice she has helped plant, 'paying' each helper three to four 'ties' of rice per day, expecting to be invited back to the helper's farm when rice is harvested there. But access to male labour for bush clearance and pest control remains a more serious problem. Women must often resort to paying male labourers for daily or task-based 'contracts', but willing workers are hard to find and contracts often break down. Others request help covertly from their lovers.[9] Wives are sometimes unable to embark on individual cultivation because they lack male labour to clear bush. And commonly left unfenced, female-managed farms are especially vulnerable to attack by cane rats.

Overall rice production sufficiency among farmers in eastern Sierra Leone is generally thought to be declining (ILO, 1990). Madina villagers, for

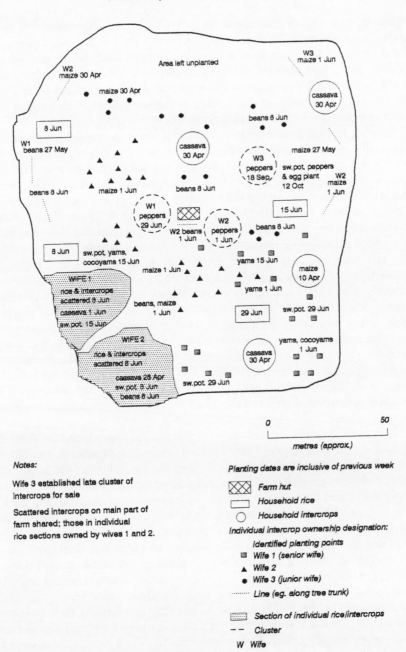

FIGURE 4.4: Intercrop planting patterns.

example, now expect only about ten per cent of farm-households to have own-grown rice until the next harvest. Others must buy imported rice from local traders, 'find' rice from kin, or eat hunger foods to fill the hungry season 'gap'. Many Mende link these changes directly to tree-crop cultivation. First, much of the expansion of cocoa and coffee cultivation has taken place on low-lying *bului* land, at the expense of the short-duration rice which was once an important hunger-breaking crop but is now hardly grown.

Second, tree-crop cultivation has introduced competing labour demands, especially for men whose tree crop maintenance tasks fall at the peak of the rice production season.[10] As one put it, 'Once we worked only on rice, but our work is all scattered now.' Only a few patrons, with the help of claims on other's labour, can invest fully in both tree crops and rice. Other farm-household heads resolve the rice–tree crops dilemma in different ways. Some consistently clear undersized rice farms on the grounds that they can fulfil their food-provisioning responsibilities to wives and dependents by purchasing rice with tree-crop revenue. In reality, as we shall see in Chapter 8, numerous other financial pressures tend to dissipate men's dry season tree crop revenues before the hungry season. Wives, realistic about this, privately express their wish that their husbands would concentrate on food production. Other men take a 'rest' year from rice farming every five to six years to concentrate on tree-farm development (cf. Engel *et al.*, 1984). For many farmers, each year becomes different as they struggle to balance dynamic organisational arrangements, labour access and social obligations with fluctuating and unpredictable cocoa and coffee prices. In 1988 many men in Madina concentrated on tree crops; in 1990 and 1991 rice seemed to return to the forefront.

Men's involvement in tree-crop cultivation has contributed to shifts in gender divisions of responsibility for food production in general, and labour inputs in particular. Wives partially compensate for declining farm-household rice production through their individual production, and women seem increasingly concerned with this. Although bush clearance remains 'men's work', the division of labour in the subsequent tasks of planting and harvest – once performed jointly by women and junior men in this area – has altered. A husband may now be the only male member of a farm household, yet claim to face time-conflicting tree-crop tasks at planting and harvest time. Furthermore, the conceptual basis for his participation in these activities is ambiguous. Is his the role of a past *mawɛɛ* head (usually nil) or a 'junior' man (full participant)? In these circumstances, planting and harvest have devolved mainly on to women, with a husband's contribution understood as voluntary help (*gbɔ*), not obligation. Young men, strangers and poor farmers seem to 'help' their wives more than senior men. Among female farm-household members, junior wives and daughters often seem to bear the brunt of the extra work burden, leaving them less time for their individual farming activities. In some farm-households, the annual production process is no longer a sequence of interdependent male and female tasks, but a process initiated by men and carried through by women.

These labour issues – and their social and cultural meanings – are important to recent patterns and changes in the use of different types of bush, farm-site and crop.

BUSH, FARM-SITE AND CROP TYPES

First, high forest farms (*ngolagbaa*), always relatively rare, may be especially so today as farmers cannot easily find sufficient labour. Only two farm-household heads in Madina tackled high forest in 1988. But associations between clearing this most difficult and dangerous kind of bush and male power remain as strong as ever. It demonstrates a now rare capacity to assemble sufficient labour. And now that rice production and marriage are so directly entwined, some men see high forest clearance – like bush clearance generally, but more so – to express husbandly authority and capabilities. Such social and political issues can motivate high forest farming regardless of economic or demographic considerations. For example, one of Madina's 1988 high forest farmers felled a large area but subsequently showed more interest in hunting and village politics than rice. The intent behind his dramatic performance appeared to be more to demonstrate his power to the family members whose support he sought in forthcoming chieftaincy elections, and to reassert his authority over three wives who – following recent marital and co-wife conflict – intended each to farm individually. The need to plant such a large area eventually brought about a concerted group effort and recreated – at least temporarily – the ideal of a group of co-wives working in complement to their husband.

Second, swamp (as opposed to upland) farming is becoming more common as it better suits the circumstances of certain farmers. Because swamps can be cultivated with spread-out (rather than peaked) labour inputs, they suit small farm households and those with limited access to extra-household labour (Engel *et al.*, 1984; Johnny *et al.*, 1981). Swamps also carry a slightly different set of task divisions; (men's) bush clearance is less lengthy and arduous, involving less tree-felling and burning, while rice-transplanting into swamps (even more than upland-planting) is thought of as women's or young men's work. Male tree-crop farmers sometimes prefer swamps as their labour inputs can be reduced. Eleven of the thirteen Madina farm-households headed by widows and divorcees also farmed swamps rather than uplands in 1988. Although a female swamp farmer must still find male labour for the initial brushing, she need not retain it through a long sequence of clearing operations, and because she can spread out her labour inputs she can easily intersperse her swamp work with other work demands. Table 4.1 shows the relative frequency of farm-household swamp and upland farming

PLATE 4.6: A woman, helped by her daughter, transplants rice seedlings into
her personal inland valley swamp farm.

TABLE 4.1: Farm-household site types in Madina, 1987–90.[11]

| Farm-site type | No. of farm-households | | |
	1987	1988	1990
Upland	58	49	40
Swamp	29	43	35

in Madina in recent years. For similar reasons women and junior men find swamps an easier option for their additional small rice farms, and these are now hardly ever uplands.

Third, swamp cultivation for rice affects women's production of vegetables. When a farm-household head chooses to clear a swamp rather than an upland site, female members lose their access to places to plant intercrops as these cannot be grown in wet swamp soils. Women have similarly lost such land-use rights when farm-household heads have decided to concentrate on developing a water-controlled swamp, and this is now recognised as one of several serious drawbacks to swamp development as an agricultural development strategy for Sierra Leone (Johnny et al., 1981). Women have therefore had to find other ways to meet their continued need for sauce ingredients and hunger foods and, increasingly, for vegetables to sell for cash. One way is through resource-use arrangements with other women. Women in swamp-farming households sometimes arrange to plant and harvest their intercrops in other women's upland farm space, in effect negotiating inter-household use rights to land resources. Elderly women commonly plant cotton in younger relatives' farms. Women also allow each other to take intercrops from the farms of their kin and Sande cohort members, provided they take them only for consumption and are restrained in the amounts they harvest. A woman will sometimes invite a close friend to join her in a major vegetable-finding expedition before a market visit, when each gathers and sells for herself.

Women's other means of obtaining vegetables is to cultivate them in vegetable gardens (hakpa yadi), making more use of a well-established cropping pattern. Women have long used the spaces behind their kitchens to establish a close and convenient vegetable supply. But the available space is limited, and largely occupied by senior women, so new vegetable gardens must now be established in the bush. Women consider bului plots ideal, but as we have seen cocoa and coffee cultivators have occupied most of these. Thus constrained, women create gardens on two types of rice-production site, introducing vegetables as a separate stage in the land-use fallow sequence. These were shown in Figure 4.2. They make the first type of garden in swamp land, only during the dry season, abandoning the site to fallow or swamp rice production in the rains. Women create the second type during the rainy season by recultivating a recently rice-farmed upland site (i.e.

njɔpɔ of 1–2 years old). Occasionally women cultivate both complementary types in the same year, transferring their crops and their attention from the upland to the swamp in the dry season. Women experiment with varieties that thrive in these different agro-ecological conditions, exchanging successful ones with each other in gift networks (Leach, 1991a). Women find separate vegetable gardens well-suited to market production; they provide for greater and more predictable production, and clearer personal rights over produce than when vegetables are planted as intercrops (cf. Klomberg and van Riessen, 1983).

Upland vegetable gardens are but one form of a fourth increasingly common land-use pattern: the cultivation of uplands for a second or third year before they are left fallow. This is a useful practice for various types of farmer and crop. Women and young men increasingly produce groundnuts to sell in local markets as a source of independent cash income. Some farm-household heads now use second-year plots to plant cassava (perhaps with other root crops such as sweet potatoes) as hunger food to help compensate for shortfalls in farm-household rice production generally, and the lack of hunger-breaking rice on *bului* plots in particular. Swamp-farming households, lacking places to plant household hunger foods as intercrops, sometimes cultivate second-year plot cassava instead. Other men and women grow root crops on second- and third-year plots primarily for cash sale in local markets, responding to the increasing market demand – especially for cassava – which the Gola forest area shares with other parts of southern and eastern Sierra Leone.

The technical characteristics of these root crops intersect favourably with current social, economic and organisational pressures in farming. Because they have low and flexible labour requirements, an individual can, if necessary, manage them alone. And because indigenous varieties can thrive on relatively infertile second and third year soils, they obviate the need to carve an entirely new site from bush or forest. This is an advantage for women and for farmers with limited access to male labour. Furthermore, unlike bush clearance for rice farming, second and third year site preparation is not a socially loaded key male task. Women acceptably brush the low vegetation regrowth in the *njɔpɔ* away for themselves with a cutlass. Pest control remains a problem, and some women do not embark if they cannot find a man to fence their cassava or groundnut plot against cane rats. But others manage to make mutually beneficial arrangements with male kin and friends. For example, two women and three young men grouped to perform their respective tasks in preparing, protecting and planting a large cassava and groundnut site, subsequently designating, tending and harvesting their own plots within it.

As in this example, Mende farmers often combine together for second and third year cropping and vegetable cultivation in ways which cross-cut and transcend groupings such as farm-household and *mawɛɛ*. This is matched by new configurations and nested interrelationships of land resource-use rights. Farmers do not necessarily obtain second year and vegetable gardening sites from areas just farmed by their own farm-household. They can sometimes make use of sites previously farmed by other households in order to obtain access to suitable land resources (e.g. upland or swamp soils), or to combine with particular people.

Changing site type and cropping patterns give scope for new kinds of conflicting interest over land-resource use: conflicts which may well intensify in the future as growing populations place increasing overall pressure on land resources. Throughout eastern Sierra Leone there is growing competition among swampland uses and users, for rice production, vegetable gardening sites and tree-crop development. Similar pressures may soon affect upland use for different types of extended cropping, such as for varied annual crops on second- and third-year land, and tree-crop development. There is as yet no evidence of overall strain on the processual framework within which Mende consider land tenure (cf. Davies and Richards, 1991). But people with weaker claims and/or lesser political influence may well lose out in the competition for access to increasingly scarce and valuable sites, and in ensuing disputes over resource use. Recent cases in which strangers' swamp use has been revoked in favour of patrilineage members testify to this possibility. Situations in which land-use decisions undermine other users' nested resource-use rights are also proliferating. The negative effects of a farm-household head's decision to cultivate swamp sites on women's and juniors' use of upland farm space have already been discussed. As uplands and swamps are put to more permanent uses, such as for tree crops, women's and young men's access to second-year sites may also be reduced.

These patterns of site use and cropping also have ecological implications. They imply shifting pressures on soils and vegetation within different parts of the upland-swamp catena, over and above the general changes in soil and vegetation composition that are thought to occur with successive cultivation cycles (Davies, 1990). Ecological changes resulting from farming are felt more strongly where population densities are higher and fallow periods generally shortening, as is visible further north around Bo. But even in the Gola forest area the growing pressure on certain types of bush and farm-site is leading to non-cyclical ecological change. This is true of inland valley swampland, while second- and third-year plot cultivation may damage the potential for bush fallows to recover through coppicing (Nyerges, 1989). The ecology of bush-fallow systems is not well-known, especially with reference to their edaphic characteristics, and major questions remain about the precise dynamics and agro-ecological consequences of soil and vegetation changes. To a certain extent, pressures and changes in the Gola forest area are 'buffered' by the continued overall availability of high forest and plentiful fallow bush. But, as we have seen, questions of tenure, organisation and labour mean these buffers are not necessarily available to everyone at all times.

CONCLUSION

Changes in farming patterns have implications for forest resource use and ecology of direct relevance to forest conservation. This chapter has not sought to document these changes quantitatively or to investigate their precise vegetational dynamics, either in outside scientists' terms or those in which Mende might see them. Rather, I have looked at how and why different forest, bush and farm-site types are used. I have tried to show that natural resource management and changes need to be understood in terms of different people's interests and opportunities, and the dynamic relations between them. This has involved examining how resources of various kinds are managed, distributed and used, seeing beyond, within and across categories such as men and women, or particular social units (households), to the changing configurations in which people combine themselves and resources in different circumstances.

The activities, exchanges, combinations and recombinations, and dilemmas people engage in when managing forest resources for farming go far beyond the production of food. They also reflect and reproduce wider socio-cultural ideas and relations, whether these concern the relationship between farmers and the bush, or the proper organisation of marriage. As Guyer (1984b) emphasises, agricultural production cycles do not only describe the material means of subsistence, they are also a symbolic means of validating social arrangements. From day to day, resource use shapes and is shaped by the ways people get on with and think about each other. As new economic and ecological dilemmas are thrown up by processes of change, provoking creative responses, so new dilemmas emerge. I have highlighted, for instance, the ambiguous relationship between more independent forms of food production and relations of authority at *mawɛɛ* and conjugal levels. Similarly, women's and men's current range of separate production involvements are associated with new strains in the conjugal contract (Whitehead, 1984) and over marital obligations, issues explored further in relation to food provisioning in Chapter 8. Changes in resource management and use have had differential socio-economic consequences for women and men. But these changes seem to be accommodated within a broad and flexible set of concepts of people–bush relations, gender interdependence and complementarity, and land-tenure relations which shows no signs of fundamental change. The dominant sense is of shifts within an enduring repertoire (cf. Guyer, 1988).

The illustrations in this paper preclude the notion of unilinearity in either economic or ecological trends. For instance, studies of West African food production commonly talk of the progressive 'break-up of family farms' into more individualised production units. But the Gola forest material suggests the contextual reversibility of such processes; it may be important to recognise the persistence of larger-scale organisational forms which certain people can reinvoke in certain circumstances. The relationship between cash-oriented and subsistence production is not a question of one progressively overriding the other in response, for example, to price changes, but a structural tension which farmers with different social obligations and resource endowments deal with in different ways from year to year. Most clearly, forest use change cannot be seen as a steady process consequent, for example, on increasing population pressure or poverty. Such pressures are mediated through a complex of relations and factors influencing site choice and cultivation patterns which ensure that they will be unevenly manifested in space, time and across different social groups. This theme – the ecological significance of local resource-management strategies, and the social influences on them – recurs in the next chapter, where we look more closely at tree cash-cropping.

5

TREE CROPS, CASH CROPS

Tree cash-crops such as cocoa, coffee, and oil palm have come to play important roles in the rural economy of the Gola forest area in the last thirty to forty years. The small mixed 'plantations' are now a common feature of the forest-edge landscape. This chapter addresses the use of resources associated with Mende tree cash-cropping from both social and environmental perspectives, and in relation to the dual attributes of cocoa, coffee and oil palm as 'trees' and as 'cash crops'.

The introduction and expansion of cocoa and coffee production has associated Mende villagers with an export-oriented cash economy. This has involved major shifts in gendered access to and control over resources. In eastern Sierra Leone, as elsewhere in the West African forest zone (Berry, 1975; Bukh, 1979; Okali, 1983), women have 'underinvested' in tree cash-crops. For the most part, they participate in tree-crop cultivation by working on farms owned or managed by men rather than by planting and acquiring farms of their own (Berry, 1988). Tree cash-crop production has also become associated with different divisions of labour and produce from annual food production, and these reduce women's control over certain resources. Although in some respects the Mende situation supports Boserup's (1970) well-known thesis of women's deteriorating economic position under commercial crop production, this chapter emphasises the need to go beyond such generalisations to see which women are so affected and why. This entails examination of how tree cash-crop production opportunities intersect with historically particular socio-economic relations; specifically at how different people are positioned in relation to land and tree tenure, labour arrangements and inheritance negotiations. Each of these issues is dealt with in turn.

In rainforest conservation terms, crops such as cocoa and coffee receive a conflicting press. On the one hand, smallholder cash-crop production is viewed as a major displacer of forest (Martin, 1991; Serageldin, 1990). On the other, as 'trees', cocoa and coffee may be considered to contribute to 'indigenous agroforestry systems' with a useful role to play in conservation activity. This chapter introduces Mende perspectives to this debate by considering ecological aspects of local plantation management strategies, and the ways that social organisation, labour and tenure arrangements affect plantation conditions. Chapter 6 will build on this discussion, showing the importance of plantations as places where Mende also manage a range of timber and non-timber forest products.

Comparisons with selected agroforestry activities in other parts of the West African forest zone make this analysis relevant to more general concerns with tree planting. This chapter considers ways in which gender relations shape local people's practices, interests and opportunities when it is 'trees' that are in question, rather than 'cash crops'. The multiplicity of claims over tree crops that arise because of their long lifecycles show the significance of gendered experiences to forest-resource use.

PLANTATIONS AROUND THE GOLA FOREST RESERVES

Some people in Madina view the introduction of cocoa and coffee as having instigated a new and profitable era of forest-resource use, saying that 'The bush really benefits us now.' However, this view is not shared by everyone, as we shall see. The Gola forest lies within the belt of Sierra Leone where cocoa (*Theobroma cacao*), coffee (*Coffea robusta*)[1] and oil palm (*Elaeis guineensis*) can all be successfully grown. Cocoa and coffee were first introduced into the country in the early twentieth century. Their cultivation spread under the influence of colonial agricultural policies. In the relatively isolated Gola forest area, production became established after the Second World War and expanded under the influence of high prices during the 1960s and 1970s. Oil palm plantations are a more recent introduction originally linked to government attempts to promote 'improved' palm varieties as a cash crop in the 1960s. These were distributed by the Eastern Integrated Agricultural Development Programme (EIADP) in the 1970s and early 1980s along with development loans to assist in their establishment. While plantation palms (*mosanke*) are locally considered as part of a realm of cash crops, and share many social and resource-management characteristics with cocoa and coffee, people continue to manage and use native wild palms which they consider quite differently. Wild palms are considered in detail in the next chapter.

Tree cash-crop production and marketing linked Gola forest farmers to a national export economy. During the colonial period the British administration purchased the produce from traders in marketing centres established along the railway. Since independence in 1961 the export of cocoa, coffee and palm kernels has been managed by the parastatal Sierra Leone Produce Marketing Board (SLPMB) and several private produce-exporting agencies which, following recent economic reforms, now operate more or less fully competitively with SLPMB, setting their own prices to farmers. Farmers in Malema chiefdom sell to buying agents in Jojoima or to village produce-traders who act as middlemen. Local produce traders commonly provide loans to tree-crop farmers, and these creditor-debtor relations often endure as patron-client relations which bind the local-level marketing structure.[2]

Mende refer to areas planted with tree crops as gardens (*gadi*) or plantations (*tuhani*). While cash-crop production is a major goal of indigenous plantation management, it is not the only one, and farmers create and maintain their tree-crop gardens to be multiple-use environments which also help to fulfil subsistence and forest-product needs. Kola and fruit trees, such as citrus, mango and bananas, are intercropped with the cocoa and coffee. Farmers carefully preserve and manage a range of wild trees to maintain a suitable micro-climate for the tree crops, and for their other uses as timber or non-timber forest products (Davies and Leach, 1991). Chapter 6 will examine these wild plant products' uses in more detail and assess the relative significance of plantations as gathering grounds. Here, we consider indigenous plantation-management strategies in ecological terms. Far from being simple displacers of forest vegetation as monocrop plantations would be, locally managed, multiple-use plantations offer advantages in terms of forest conservation.

Farmers establish their plantations through one of two alternative land-use sequences, using tree-crop seedlings which they have nursed from seed, transplanted from another plantation, or (in the case of oil palms) purchased from a supply agency. In the first and most common method, farmers plant the seedlings in forest (*ngola*) or long-fallowed bush (*gbɔɛɛ*). Initially, the entire tree cover is left to provide shade for the young seedlings over the first two or three years. Subsequently, the shade trees are thinned to regulate light and shade conditions and humidity as the tree crops mature. The second method involves transplanting the tree seedlings to land cleared for annual crop cultivation, from which all but the largest trees have been removed. For the first one or two years the seedlings are intercrops, and provided with necessary shade by rice and other food crops. After the food harvest the area is devoted to the tree crops, and suitable trees are permitted to regrow from coppice or re-colonise from seed to provide shade. Farmers commonly establish coffee and oil palm on upland farms or *bului* plots, and cacao (with its higher moisture requirements) in *bului* or inland valley swamps (*kpɛtɛ*). They plant bananas simultaneously to harden the swamp soil by absorbing water, and to provide additional shade. In Madina, the second method has become increasingly common as the supply of well-developed farmbush for thinning near the village has diminished, and as farmers seek to minimise the labour demands of plantation establishment.

Whichever establishment method is used, farmers carefully select which wild trees to preserve or encourage according to clear ideas concerning species characteristics and relative use priorities. They give high priority to the regulation of shade, and consider that the shallow, broad crowns of the *Albizia* species, combined with light foliage in the case of *Albizia ferruginea* and *Albizia adianthifolia*, are ideal. Other preferred shade trees include *Spondias mombin*, *Pseudospondias microcarpa*, *Funtumia africana* and the broad-canopied *Macaranga barterii*. Certain trees are selectively removed because of their potentially damaging effect on the cocoa and coffee crop. Those with exceptionally dense canopies are normally felled. While *Albizia ferruginea* is a useful shade tree, it has brittle branches which snap off in high winds, damaging the cash crops beneath, so tall individuals are killed off leaving only small trees. Many farmers claim to remove fruit-bearing trees known to attract monkeys, as this encourages pest damage to the cocoa crop. Most important in this respect are those trees such as *Parinari excelsa* which bear fruit during the cocoa ripening period (July–October). Trees selectively preserved for their economic uses include wild oil palms, timber trees and those bearing useful non-timber forest products. In deciding which individual trees and species to leave, plantation managers carefully balance the requirements of the cash crops with the economic values of these wild trees in ways considered further in Chapter 6.

As a result of these shade tree-management strategies, the plantations around the Gola reserves have many superficial similarities with the rainforest itself: cool, shady conditions in the understorey, and an overstorey of forest trees. They replicate the multilayered structure of the forest, with the exception of the understorey layer which in plantations is kept clear. This provides a range of ecological and conservation-related advantages over industrial monocrop plantations. As in forest, nutrients are recycled from the fallen leaf litter of canopy trees, and this helps mitigate the long-term decline in site fertility often attributed to cocoa and coffee monocropping. Ecological surveys carried out in three plantations in Madina show that a large diversity of tree and animal species which would be eliminated from monocrop plantations survive in locally managed plantations (Davies and Leach, 1991). When these findings are compared with the results of similar surveys undertaken in high forest and fallow environments, however, it is evident that relatively few forest-dependent trees and animals are among the surviving species, although plantations support more elements of the climax closed-canopy forest vegetation than does farmbush. The lack of forest-dependent trees preserved partly reflects the priorities of local resource managers who, as we shall see in Chapter 6, do not accord the same value to high forest species as do conservationists.

The extent to which plantations mimic forest does not suggest that Mende think of plantations as an entirely harmoniously integrated 'part of' the bush. As in food production, they recognise the fragile balance between their carefully maintained agricultural operations and the forces of the bush, both natural and spiritual. While soil and vegetation resources from the bush provide the necessary fertility for tree crop production, farmers must also check the tendency of 'unwanted' elements of the bush – such as undergrowth which smothers young seedlings and invites crop pests – to reinvade. However, unlike annual crops, for which farmers struggle to maintain an entirely cleared place over short periods, tree crops with long life-cycles involve a less intense struggle drawn out over long periods. In this sense the ring of plantations surrounding the village provides a little-changing buffer between the life of the village and the ever-changing mosaic of bush and farm-sites beyond.

PLANTATION CONTROL

Patterns of plantation control show strong gender disparities. In 1988 there were eighty-five more or less distinct plantations in Madina. Three were planted only to oil palm, five only to coffee, one only to cocoa, and the rest were mixed cocoa and coffee. Figure 5.1a and b shows the rate of plantation establishment in Madina and the ages of the farms presently worked by villagers.[3]

Only four of these plantations (one oil palm, and three mixed cocoa and coffee) were more than about two hectares in size; the others were all less than one hectare. Fifty-one of the men resident in Madina in 1988 had planted tree crops. A further seven had acquired control over the plantation of a relative or deceased planter. Fifteen had both. Thus in 1988 fifty-eight men (46 per cent of male residents) controlled a plantation, although eleven of these controlled only immature trees. In comparison, only four resident women had established a plantation and a further four acquired control over one through other means. These eight female tree-crop owners constituted only 5 per cent of the resident female population. However, more than half the women in the village had planted a few coffee, oil palm or fruit trees, either behind their kitchens or as clumps within the plantation of a husband or male relative.

What are the reasons for this pattern and what implications does it have for women's and men's respective control over tree-crop products? In exploring this, several levels of explanation are required. First I consider the social context of the introduction and use of tree cash-crops: issues concerning the 'cash crop' aspects of tree crops. I then consider tenure arrangements, labour arrangements and product control associated with tree crop establishment in turn: issues concerning the 'tree' aspects. Comparison with agroforestry activities in other parts of West Africa shows the relevance of tenure and labour arrangements to women's and men's respective involvement in tree-planting activities more generally.

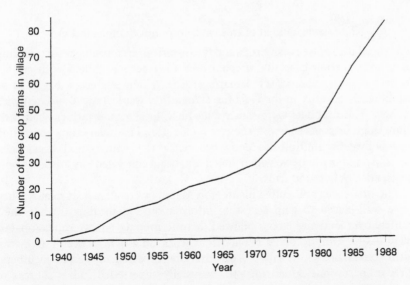

FIGURE 5.1A: Cocoa and coffee farm establishment in Madina, 1940–88.

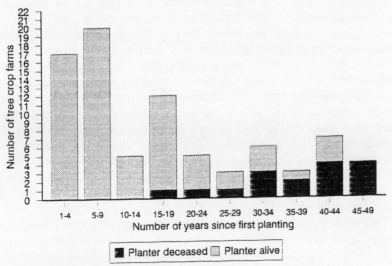

Trees under 5 years of age not yet bearing.

FIGURE 5.1B: Ages of tree-crop farms in Madina, 1988.

The social context of tree cash-crop introduction and use

The social uses of tree cash-crops and the historical circumstances surrounding their introduction crucially affected how they become linked with certain forms of gender control (cf. Linares, 1985). When tree crops began to be established seriously in the Gola forest area they were firmly associated with money. The products were rarely consumed locally, and farmers had little knowledge or concern about their post-sale use. Tree cash-crops contrasted with polivalent, multiple use food crops such as rice, which could occasionally be sold, and with trees which had long been cultivated on an occasional basis, such as kola and fruit.

The first cocoa and coffee planters in Madina were all *mawɛɛ* heads. They were well-placed to gain access to information and seedlings, while their control over land and labour allowed them to produce a new crop comparatively easily. Oral accounts explain that work on a *mawɛɛ* head's tree-crop farm joined the set of labour contributions expected of *mawɛɛ* members. Tree-crop revenue added to, and eventually superseded, other sources of money that *mawɛɛ* heads used to meet their dependents' cash needs, such as sales of bushmeat or wild palm kernels.

Junior men became increasingly interested in planting for themselves, especially during the cocoa and coffee price rises of the 1960s and early 1970s. At first juniors' plantations were established on a similar basis to 'small farms' for annual crops. They were treated as a subsidiary enterprise to *mawɛɛ* farm work which planters could use to help meet their own and their dependents' cash needs. However, tree-cash crops provided an unprecedented means for men to accumulate relatively large amounts of money independently of their patrons and senior relatives. This helped them to marry and support their own wives and children without indebting their services so heavily to a 'big person' (*numu wa*). This in turn contributed to the changes in food-production organisation discussed in Chapter 4, and in the organisation of economic provisioning more generally. As one man put it: 'Once we were for a big man, but once we realised the benefit of tree crops, we scattered, and now we are for ourselves in everything.'

This statement presents only one side of the coin, however. The increased availability of money through tree crops seems to have facilitated less a breakdown of 'wealth in people' relations, than a growing ability of 'junior' men to compete on more even terms with elders and family heads in acquiring clients of their own. Control over and use of money currently reflects tensions between patrons' interests in maintaining dependent clients, and clients' interests in acquiring economic independence from patrons but acting as patrons to further dependent clients of their own. Why did *mawɛɛ* heads and senior relatives apparently make little attempt to restrict their dependents' cocoa and coffee cultivation in order to retain their leverage over them? One reason may be that the land and labour organisation of tree-crop cultivation, which I discuss below, militated against patrons' potential control, as dependents could easily develop small tree farms on secluded forest plots during their spare time. However, a few *mawεε* heads are reported deliberately to have encouraged members' cocoa and coffee planting. Equally today fathers and patrons sometimes help sons and strangers establish plantations as investments towards their marriages. One explanation may lie in the polivalent meanings of such help. In that tree crops represent economic independence, it is disadvantageous for junior kin and clients to have them; but in as much as the help itself is construed as patronage it binds the receiver's allegiance and is a basis for calls on other services from them.

Mawεε heads did not similarly encourage female members to plant tree cash-crops. Instead, wives and female kin were expected to assist with the tree crops of their husbands and male kin, a pattern common throughout the West African forest zone (Berry, 1975; Guyer, 1984a). Associations between tree-cash crops and men were also encouraged by colonial agricultural policies, and later by the EIADP, which targeted men in all its extension support and credit to help with cocoa, coffee and oil-palm establishment and maintenance.

Over time, control of tree cash-crops has become important to male status and identity in Malema chiefdom. Most men now consider tree-crop revenue important to the adequate support of wives and children. Men expect and are expected to provide rice in the hungry season with tree-crop revenue, either through direct purchase or through loan arrangements using tree crops. The provision of clothes for wives and children is no longer linked to rice-farm work as it was in the 1940s (Little, 1948b) but is now assumed to mean purchases made in the dry season with tree-crop proceeds. Men without tree cash-crops are thought especially likely to fail in meeting these obligations. Parents regard a potential suitor's possession of tree crops as an indicator of his ability to support their daughter and provide an inheritance for their grandchildren. Young men and their parents, therefore, now consider the planting of tree crops as an investment in future married status.

These associations help to account for the low frequency of plantation establishment by women. As tree cash-crop cultivation is now part of the role of responsible supporter of dependents, it is considered inappropriate for women while they are supported. I never came across a woman who had embarked on tree-crop cultivation on her own account while part of a marriage that she considered viable and in which the husband was nominally 'in charge'. Current wives do not consider it a possibility, explaining instead that, 'My husband's tree crops are for all of us.' A wife can acceptably plant small groups of economic trees behind her kitchen or within the plantation of a husband or male relative. Equally, women acceptably plant fruit trees, whose products are mainly for use and sold only on a small scale. But a wife

who established a separate plantation of cash-oriented trees would be seen
to challenge her husband's authority – and even to disown his support.
Wives in Madina have occasionally embarked on tree-crop cultivation when
they have been intent on separation. The town chief's senior wife started a
coffee plantation in her parents' village three miles away ten years ago,
when relations with her husband were bad and she had intended to divorce
him and return to her family.

Plantation control does not contain such challenges to male authority for
some types of woman. Women who have been 'married up to' by a younger
or stranger man and who therefore already have authority over a husband
can sometimes manage a plantation on both their behalfs. Equally, when a
woman has been deprived of male support by death or divorce, she may be
helped to acquire tree crops by men, such as through a gift or specified
endowment on a planter's death. Thus while plantations are conceptually
linked with certain male roles, they are not linked with masculinity *per se*.

The social meanings of these tree cash-crops, which are specific to the
historical and social context of their introduction and establishment and to
their cash orientation, would clearly not apply to all planted trees. Trees
planted as part of a conservation-oriented social forestry programme, for
instance, might take on quite different meanings associated with their previous
history (in the case of indigenous species), their intended use, and whom was
approached by any outside agencies involved. But this particular social context would nevertheless be relevant to emerging forms of gender control (cf.
Bradley, 1990; Cashman, 1991).

Land and tree tenure

Tenure arrangements over land and trees also shape people's relative opportunities to establish tree-crop plantations. As for annual crop production,
prospective planters must seek rights to use land-resources from the heads
of landholding families, either requesting rights to thin fallow bush or
permission to extend use rights to a rice farm-site by planting trees on it. The
long life-cycles and inheritance possibilities of tree crops might be expected
to complicate tenure arrangements. How have Mende understandings of
land and resource tenure accommodated tree crops?

It is often assumed that where land is held on a 'communal' basis, such as
by landholding descent groups, people have little incentive to invest in 'permanent improvements' to the land such as planting trees. They cannot be sure
that they will reap the benefit of their investment themselves. But an important
counter to this argument is that tenure over trees can be considered separately
from that over land. Regardless of tenure arrangements over land, tree
tenure can provide sufficient security to encourage planters (Bruce and
Fortmann, 1989; Fortmann, 1985). This has been the case throughout much
of the West African forest zone, where the expansion of commercial cocoa

and coffee cultivation has been based on private tenure over trees on communal holdings (Berry, 1975; Hill, 1963).

Mende, similarly, do not consider planted trees as part of the land they stand on. Trees can be the property of their planter while the land remains under the control of the landholding descent group. In theory if a land user was dispossessed in favour of patrilineage members he or she could expect to be compensated for the value of the trees. This sometimes happens when a planter leaves an area and is not expected to return. Equally, transactions concerning trees, such as transfer to others through sale, inheritance, gift or pledging, do not affect land status. Pledging of cocoa and coffee trees is a particularly common way in which Mende raise cash loans, the creditor harvesting the trees as interest on the loan until it is repaid. As in parts of Nigeria, trees are frequently used as security for loans even though farmers cannot legally mortgage land (Berry, 1975).

For similar reasons, tree-planting has not contributed to the privatisation of land rights. This is suggested as a possibility where tree-planting is considered to establish ownership claims over the land, or because long-term usufruct of the land in tree-planting eventually confers *de facto* control over it (Bruce and Fortmann, 1989).[4] In the Gola forest area, the conceptual separation of tree and land tenure, the concept of land resources as able to be used but not owned, and social and political relations based on land-controlling groups, would all have to alter fundamentally to accommodate a shift towards land commercialisation. Instead, a market in trees and their products has developed independently of land. Money is sometimes exchanged for rights to use land but such 'leasing' and 'renting' arrangements affirm rather than undermine the land-allocator's control, and give the lessee nothing equivalent to freehold rights (Davies and Richards, 1991).

Similar land relations emerged in the context of cocoa and coffee cultivation elsewhere in West Africa. For instance, although in parts of Ghana and Nigeria landholding groups often began to demand payments from tree-crop cultivators who were profiting from the use of family lands, and new terminological distinctions arose between 'landowners' and 'tenants', these were usually considered as tribute in recognition of the landholders' authority, not rents in a standard economic sense (Okali and Berry, n.d.). In Yoruba areas the same amount of tribute was collected from each 'tenant' regardless of differences in the size or yield of their farms (Berry, 1975).

In some parts of West Africa, tenure issues are reported as a major barrier to tree-planting by women and male strangers. Landholding descent groups are sometimes reluctant to grant land-use rights to non-kin group members, making tree-crop establishment difficult for male strangers and for women who marry in to their husband's community and acquire land-use rights only through their husbands. Women can also be restricted from planting trees on their own patrilineage land, since this would pass to her husband's lineage when the trees are inherited by her children (Berry, 1988; Bukh, 1979). In Mende areas, these difficulties are reduced both by the inclusive understanding of family (*mbonda*) as the relevant landholding group – a grouping that can include in-married wives and long-established stranger-clients as members – and by the separation of tree and land tenure. In Madina, women consider access to land to be an insignificant barrier to planting tree crops, considering that they could plant either on their own or their husband's family land. Equally, male strangers are rarely prevented from planting tree crops for directly land-related reasons. The land remains under the control of the landholding family; if the stranger leaves he is either compensated or the trees become the property of his patron.

Mende strongly link tree-planting with residence and allegiance, however, and this influences both wives' and strangers' opportunities. Only eight of the fifty-one male strangers resident in Madina in 1988 had planted cocoa or coffee. A newly-arrived stranger is rarely granted land for tree crops by his host, but he may be allowed to plant tree crops after several years (cf. Engel *et al.*, 1984: 61). Local concern about letting strangers establish tree crops centres on its implications for a stranger's entrenchment in the community and stranger-father's family, rather than on the possible loss of land. Newly arrived strangers are regarded simultaneously as potential allies and potential subverters of their host's family and of the community as a whole. People are reluctant to let a male stranger establish tree crops before he has proved his loyalty and allegiance, and is found 'responsible in town business', by which time he may be integrated with his host's family through marriage. This serves to emphasise that 'strangerhood' is not a determinant category but a process of gradual incorporation. Plantation establishment is, in turn, an accepted indicator of a stranger's long-term identity with a place or kin group.

Certain women and men can be constrained from long-term investments in tree-planting by marriage arrangements which render them as only temporary residents. Compensation for lost benefits should they leave is far from assured, especially if this goes against the interests of more influential people. Both young unmarried women and men can be unsure of their future place of residence. Although a woman commonly moves to a husband's home, families are often anxious to keep their daughters as well as their sons with them to enhance their size and political strength, so the daughters of high status families are often 'married up to' by incoming men from lower status families. Given these uncertainties, it is not surprising that unmarried women rarely plant trees, and that the young men who do so as an investment for marriage are usually those from high status families who can be most sure of remaining in their natal home once married.

Women might be expected to be more interested in planting trees once settled in a married home. However, a Mende woman may move around a great deal in the course of her married life. She may stay with her mother from late pregnancy through the post-partum period of sexual abstinence. She may move through a series of marriages in the serial polyandry which is the common counterpart to polygyny for men[5] (Bledsoe, 1987). Marital instability may lead to prolonged recuperative stays with natal kin or to complete separation. A married woman who makes a major investment in tree-planting, therefore, may prefer to do so in a nearby natal home, perhaps where a brother will help to maintain the trees. As one woman put it, 'Here in Madina I am not a permanent resident.' Women tend to become more interested in long-term investments such as tree-planting in middle age and especially post-menopause when they acquire more control over their own marriage arrangements. It is common for a middle-aged widow to return to her natal home, and either to live with relatives or to marry a younger, 'stranger' husband. Such women are especially likely to invest in tree-crop cultivation, and three of the eight female plantation owners in Madina in 1988 were in this position.

Local attitudes towards the allocation of land-use rights for tree-crop cultivation also reflect the current relatively easy availability of acceptable sites. In parts of eastern Sierra Leone the scarcity of suitable sites leads to competition for tree-crop land in which those with weaker claims lose out (Klomberg and van Riessen, 1983). But in Madina, while there was probably competition for the best *bului* sites close to the town during the early phases of tree-farm establishment, this competition ceased about ten years ago when these sites were fully occupied and new planting was transferred to 'open' bush. Farmers prepared to use upland forest and fallow sites face no shortage of tree-crop land. However as Chapter 4 showed, incipient competitive pressures are emerging over swamp-site use, for tree crops as well as other land uses.

Labour issues

Of the women in Madina who do not control plantations, the majority claim this to be for labour-related reasons. Labour issues severely constrain many women's tree-crop farming opportunities. Before examining the task divisions and labour-access arrangements that make this so, some general consideration of tree-crop labour patterns will be necessary.

Figure 5.2 summarises the annual cycle of possible tasks involved with the establishment and maintenance of cocoa, coffee and oil-palm plantations. Many farmers continually replace old trees with new young seedlings, so in any particular year 'maintenance' tasks are interspersed with 'establishment' tasks.

New seedlings are planted at the start of the rainy season. Farmers use an axe to regulate the shade cover by the selective removal of shade trees. They clear unwanted bush regrowth from plantations between May and November.

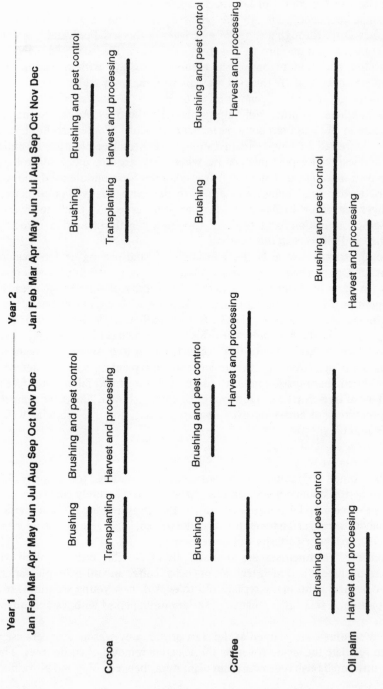

FIGURE 5.2: Calendar of main tree-crop farming operations.

This assists tree-crop growth, facilitates the harvest, protects young seedlings and deters pests. Certain monkey species and squirrels are serious pests of cocoa, and additional measures to deter them include building traps at tree level, patrolling plantation areas with a gun, especially during the early mornings and evenings, and felling fruit trees which attract them. Young oil-palm seedlings must be watched almost constantly to protect them from cane rats.

Oil-palm harvesting is concentrated in the dry season, when palms are climbed to cut their fruit. It is subsequently processed into oil either in the village or in a special pit in the bush. Cocoa is harvested between August and December. Farmers pick or cut the cocoa pods, collect the fallen pods from the ground into heaps, and extract the cocoa beans in the farm by cracking each pod in turn on a large stone, and scraping out the contents into a basket. In town, the cocoa is covered and left to ferment for several days. Coffee is harvested between December and February. The berries are either picked or are scraped from each branch and collected from the ground. Both crops are spread on mats to dry, watched and turned, and coffee is then de-husked by pounding with a pestle and mortar.

Local cocoa and coffee management strategies avoid peak labour inputs and thus enable a single person to work the crop alone. A farmer can develop a plantation gradually, adding more tree seedlings and felling shade trees as time allows. Undergrowth and pest-control activities can be conducted at a minimum level with only occasional visits to the plantation, and a farmer need harvest only as much cocoa or coffee as is deemed worthwhile. This flexibility is especially useful given that the main period for tree-crop seedling transplanting and undergrowth clearance (May–November) coincides with the peak season for rice production work.

Plantations managed in this way are low-yielding. This is not to say that well-timed peak labour inputs do not benefit their productivity; farmers who can summon the resources to brush, prune, protect and harvest their trees fully do achieve higher yields (Alpha, 1988; Goba, 1984; Konneh, 1988; Minah, 1981). However, low input, low output management, often proves a more suitable use of resources for resource-poor farmers on a year-to-year basis. It is compatible with the multiple-use of plantations as sources of timber and non-timber forest products. Farmers can also reduce their management inputs when cocoa and coffee prices are low, turning their attention to rice, retaining their plantations as forest-product gathering grounds and as security against a time when prices might be higher or when labour is available to rehabilitate them. They also treat their trees as long-term assets that can be sold, pledged or mortgaged to meet sudden needs for cash (Chambers, Conroy and Leach, 1992; Chambers and Leach, 1989).

By comparison farmers find it more difficult to cope successfully with tree cultivation activities that require heavy and sustained labour inputs,

PLATE 5.1: A woman works on the harvest of her husband's coffee crop in a mixed coffee/cocoa/kola plantation established in thinned-out forest.

PLATE 5.2: A husband and wife work together to collect and break harvested cocoa pods in his plantation; she will supervise their fermentation and drying.

especially if these fall at times of year that cause conflict with food production activities. Local experience with oil-palm plantations is telling in this respect. The labour demands of oil palm are less flexible than those of cocoa and coffee, and young seedlings, especially, can be devastated if they are not carefully protected and kept clear of undergrowth. Labour shortages have discouraged most farmers in Madina from embarking on their cultivation, while the three plantation palm owners in the village are all family heads with secure access to labour from their junior kin and clients.

The overall and seasonally heightened labour shortages that affect West African farmers have been noted in relation to agroforestry development activities (Okali and Berry, n.d.). Indeed, agroforestry systems such as alley farming, in which leguminous trees are intercropped with food crops, have been thought appropriate in the West African forest zone in large part because they do not increase overall labour demands. In the systems introduced by the International Livestock Centre for Africa (ILCA) in Nigeria, for instance, *Leucaena leucocephala* is intercropped with food crops to improve soil fertility and to provide fodder, fencing and firewood. Some extra labour is required to plant and prune the trees but not for the crucial task of weeding the young *Leucaena* seedlings as the interspersed food crops would need weeding anyway. Economic analysis showed the system to be profitable to 'the farmer' (MacIntire *et al.*, 1985).

However, debates conducted at the level of 'the farmer' have proved very limiting, since there is rarely a single farmer who makes all the relevant decisions and to whom all the 'costs' and 'benefits' accrue. Experience with alley farming in Nigeria shows that divisions of labour and the arrangements through which different people's labour comes together, and the multiple loci of control to which tree cropping is subject, are crucial to its relative success (Francis and Atta-Krah, n.d.; see also Leach, 1991c; Okali and Berry, n.d.). In the Gola forest area, such issues crucially affect who is able to embark on cocoa, coffee and oil-palm cultivation and the kinds of yield they are likely to expect.

Certain of the tasks involved in tree-crop cultivation are firmly associated with each gender. It is considered appropriate only for men to clear unwanted trees and undergrowth from plantations. Both sexes state categorically that, 'Women cannot brush tree crops.' Such a division would apparently gain precedent from annual crop farming, where 'brushing' and tree-felling are so closely associated with male status. Indeed, the work carries the same name (ndoe, to brush a rice farm; huloe, to 'brush inside' a plantation) in each activity. However, unlike rice-farm clearance, tree-farm brushing does not accomplish a dramatic conversion from bush to 'social' place. Rather, it is a gradual, carefully calculated process carried out over a number of years. Symbolic resonances with fighting and warriorhood are thus absent. Tree-crop brushers must be careful not to let the axe or cutlass damage the tree crops and work more in the spirit of careful protectors of planted things than as attackers of the bush. Correspondingly, tree-crop brushing is not a source of male prestige and men are rarely admired for their strength and skill in the work. However, the fact that only men brush tree crops supports assumptions that men are the most appropriate controllers of tree-crop farms, justifying men's advantage over women in tree-crop inheritance, as I show below. The tasks involved in pest control are also considered as 'men's work', as they are explicitly associated with the activities of exclusively male hunters (Chapter 7).

Women carry out much of the work involved in harvesting and processing tree crops. Tasks that involve 'cooking' and pounding, such as the various stages involved in processing palm oil and the pounding of coffee, are firmly considered to be 'women's work'. None of the other tasks involved in tree-crop harvest and processing are considered gender-specific. The stages can be flexibly allocated to men or women, performed jointly, or by a single individual of either sex, as labour availability dictates. However, women are usually expected to help, and the long-drawn-out character of tree-crop harvesting work – resembling other aspects of women's activities – seems to support the assumption that they should do so. When men and women harvest cocoa together they often divide labour within the task. For example, men cut cocoa pods from tall branches with the long-handled knife, while women and children cut the pods from low branches, and they all work together to gather, break and carry the produce to the village.

These task divisions make it much more difficult for a woman to establish and maintain a plantation on her own account than for a man. Whereas a man needs female labour only for coffee-processing, and could otherwise develop a plantation slowly without any additional help, a woman cannot cultivate tree crops without male labour for brushing and pest control.

Labour access

Tree-crop farmers may need access to other people's labour both for additional assistance or to perform tasks inappropriate to their gender. But opportunities to recruit others' labour are also gender differentiated. Most men are better placed than women to gain access to labour through kinship and patron–client relations. Husbands can call on their wives for help at harvest and for coffee-processing, as a loosely defined part of the conjugal contract. Many male farmers can call on male junior kin (sons, sons-in-law, nephews) and clients to assist with brushing and pest control, and male and female kin (daughters, nieces) to assist with harvest. Long-term arrangements are also made in which a planter who has grown too old or sick to manage his own tree crops appoints a client or young male relative to take over year-to-year responsibility for brushing and harvesting. This role is referred to as *hugbatε* (arrange, take care, prepare). These labour arrangements usually carry indirect, rather than direct, rights to tree-crop produce, as I discuss below. As in rice farming, people with authority and political influence in their family or at town level tend to be better able to recruit labour through kinship or patron–clientage, and to manage larger, higher yielding plantations as a result.

In some parts of the West African forest zone the spread of tree-crop cultivation has led to widespread increases in labour-hiring, as farmers have used the revenue from tree-crop farms as a source of working capital for paying labourers (Berry, 1988). Farmers in the Gola forest area tend to hire labour for tree crop maintenance work only irregularly, even though a number of labour-hiring arrangements have developed. Farmers pay male labourers by the day (at a rate of 20 leones per day in 1988) for brushing. They employ work teams less often for tree-crop work than for rice farming. Two male farmers known for their diligence and regularly high yields used tree-crop revenues to hire labour for brushing and pest control every year. One grew no rice and concentrated only on tree crops. Harvest labour 'contracts', superficially similar to those used in rice-farming, have also developed. Women and some young men work both individually and as part of groups to pick the coffee or cut and break the cocoa pods of a plantation manager. At the end of the day, each worker keeps two or three thruppence pans of cocoa, or, currently, one-third of the coffee which they have picked. Women now sell their labour for coffee-pounding, at a rate, in 1988, of 100 leones per completed bag of de-husked produce.

While women, like male plantation managers, can make use of these harvest labour arrangements, most women find it difficult to secure the male assistance they would need for plantation establishment and maintenance. Husbands are not obliged to give this. As one woman put it: 'Women can't plant cocoa and coffee, because women can't brush, and husbands are concerned only with their own business and won't help us.' Most women lack secure access to male labour through kinship and patron–client ties. Hiring labour can also be problematic, both because women have difficulty in negotiating secure employment contracts with 'unreliable' young men and because they find them hard to pay for. Women's pressing day-to-day financial responsibilities, and hand-to-mouth income and expenditure patterns (Chapter 8) make it more difficult for them to forego current income streams to invest in tree crops which take four to five years to yield a return (cf. Guyer, 1980). Even if a woman could find male labour for brushing, however, a married woman would find it difficult to harvest a whole tree-crop farm of her own, since her obligations to her husband's trees would severely limit her available time and energy for her own cocoa and coffee. As men's tree-crop cultivation has left women to assume more of the labour burdens of food production (Chapter 4), women's labour availability to move into tree-crop production on their own account has further declined.

It is not surprising, then, that only four of the cocoa and coffee plantations in Madina were established by women, and that all these women had unusually secure control over the labour of others when they began to plant. One of these was an elderly female member of a high-status descent group who married a younger man after she was widowed, and controlled his labour. In 1985 she requested that he brush a tree-crop farm for her, and he now maintains her plantation as well as his own. She copes with the burden of doubled harvest and processing operations with the help of her two adult daughters. Another female planter is a widow whose age, kinship position and personality assist her leverage over her resident son-in-law, whom she persuades to clear and maintain a coffee farm for her. However, loss of control over labour can prove disastrous for women's plantation management. The town chief's wife's plantation in her natal village, initially maintained by her brothers, has gone to ruin since they left the village three years ago. In the absence of sufficient leverage over her son, who claims to be fully involved with his own tree crops and has refused to work for her, the farm has been left to devastation by undergrowth and animal pests.

The two kinds of place in which women most often plant trees for themselves are notable for their avoidance of these male labour difficulties. First, women who plant small groups of cocoa, coffee, kola or fruit trees in their husbands' and male relatives' farms avoid male labour difficulties, since the trees are brushed and pests controlled along with the male farmer's own.

Second, women plant trees behind their kitchens. These areas are often already fenced to protect vegetables which may be planted there from goats, and this serves adequately to protect the young tree seedlings. Here the 'brushing' to protect young tree seedlings becomes indistinguishable from the 'weeding' of the vegetables which may already be planted there. Defined as weeding (normally women's work) rather than brushing (normally men's work), it is unproblematic for women to perform this task. This serves to emphasise that tasks may carry different cultural definitions according to where they are performed, and what they imply about control over produce. Whereas men's brushing is important to legitimate their claims over the trees in plantations, the trees which women plant behind their kitchens are clearly their own, and no such issues are at stake.

In a similar way, gender divisions emerging in any 'new' tree-planting activity would depend partly on how the tasks involved were defined and interpreted. If trees in an agroforestry activity were considered as valuable cash generators to be controlled by men, and activities to maintain them as 'brushing' to be performed by men, it might be difficult for women to plant trees on their own account or to benefit from joint enterprises. Alternatively tree- and food-crop maintenance might be considered as 'weeding'; this would increase women's opportunities for independent agroforestry but might also invite new demands on their labour on men's and joint household agroforestry plots, risking an increase in their workloads and a reduction in their time for private enterprises. And women might not weed effectively if they were unsure of gaining any benefit from the trees. In Igbo areas of southern Nigeria, alley farming by conjugal households has sometimes failed because women perceived the trees to be men's, and either did not bother to weed them effectively or planted the food crops for which they were responsible at times and in ways which jeopardised tree-seedling survival (Francis and Atta-Krah, n.d.).

Clearly questions of product control would be crucial to any such arrangements. In the case of cocoa and coffee, it is relevant that the trees are used for cash. Trees planted for intended use as firewood, mulch or food might be subjected to quite different gendered product rights, taking more precedent from divisions of rights and control over annual crops (Chapter 1) and over 'wild' trees used for such purposes (Chapter 4). However, the long life-cycles of trees also raise product control issues that could be expected to apply regardless of their intended use. It is to questions of product control that we now turn.

PRODUCT CONTROL

Until now, I have implied that tree crops are 'owned' by their planters. But claims over trees in cocoa, coffee and oil palm plantations should be properly re-stated as 'degrees of individual control' (Hill, 1963: 112). Because tree crops are invested in over a long period of time, they tend to accumulate multiple, overlapping rights to their produce (Berry, 1988). These mechanisms include labour arrangements, inheritance practices, and the selective reporting and interpretation of significant events in the plantation's history. I shall consider these in turn.

Not only do rights in particular tree-crop farms tend to proliferate; the same mechanisms also allow individuals to accumulate rights to the produce of a number of plantations. These rights can enable people who have not planted them nevertheless to gain access to tree crops and their produce. However, as these rights vary strongly by gender and social position, they provide for greater produce access for some people than for others. Furthermore, there is often conflict, overlap and ambiguity over the relative status of different people's claims. In these circumstances, as elsewhere in West Africa, 'individuals' access to tree-crop farms has depended more on their ability to exercise their claims *vis-à-vis* those of other rightholders, than on the way in which they acquired their rights in the first place' (Berry, 1988: 4).

Labour arrangements

As in other parts of the West African forest zone, it is possible for people in the Gola forest area to build up a proprietary interest in tree crops by working on them. People who have worked in a particular plantation over a period of years may acquire direct or indirect claims over the tree-crop proceeds, especially if they were not fully compensated for their labour when it was performed (cf. Berry, 1975; Okali, 1983). Mende advance this argument especially for wives, junior kin and clients, and it is an important context for understanding the minimal rewards they receive for their tree-crop labour in the immediate term.

Mende wives acquire few direct rights to tree-crop produce from their annual labour on their husbands' tree-crop farms. They are entitled only to glean inferior and fallen produce, such as early fallen, rotten coffee berries (*kɔfi womi*), disease-blackened cocoa (*kakalo yenduli* or *yemɔngɔi*), produce scattered during picking, and oil pressed from the palm-fruit fibres left after the main oil extraction. Gleaning is so painstaking and slow that many women cannot afford the time to exercise their claims.

This gender division of proceeds in cocoa, coffee and plantation palm-oil production contrasts with the division in rice production (Chapter 4) and in wild palm-oil production (Chapter 6), in which husbands and wives who work together both receive rewards for their labour. Whereas husbands and wives consider food-production cycles to be joint processes, wives describe their tree cash-crop work as 'for my husband', not 'for us'. Women resent this and, as we shall see, have various strategies of resistance.

Several arguments are advanced to justify this arrangement. First, a woman's work on her husband's plantation is said to be part of her obligations as a wife. It is thus embedded in a bundle of obligations in the conjugal contract (Whitehead, 1984). Although tree-crop farming husbands are expected to buy food and cloth for their wives with tree-crop revenue, a wife has no grounds for specific additional claims in return for her tree-crop labour. Wives who consider themselves inadequately supported are expected to direct their public claims towards their husbands themselves rather than towards their plantations or their produce. A woman may receive a 'gift' of produce from a husband if his yield is large; about five per cent of married women in Madina received such gifts after the 1987–8 harvest. Such gifts are not considered to be direct rewards for labour, but gestures of appreciation of a wife's fulfilment of a bundle of conjugal obligations of which tree-crop labour is only a small part.

Second, men argue that it is inappropriate to 'pay' a wife for her work, suggesting that payment (*pawa*) is inappropriate – even denigrating – to the morally loaded ties which bind a married couple (Todd, 1971). Whereas regular shares of cash-oriented produce suggest payment, occasional voluntary gifts can be deemed entirely fitting to husband-wife relations.[6] Third, it can be argued that a wife who works faithfully on her husband's tree-crop farm can expect a share of the farm or its proceeds after his death. Several such endowments have occurred. One of the first planters in Madina, for example, is said to have specified that his favourite senior wife should receive a portion of his plantation when he died in recognition of her loyalty, fidelity and the work she had contributed to the trees in his lifetime.

A widow is not formally entitled to a regular share of the proceeds of her deceased husband's tree crops, but a widow who maintains cordial relations with the plantation manager might receive a voluntary gift. For example, one man explained that: 'If there is plenty of coffee I give them [the planter's two surviving widows] a bushel each, because they worked hard on it when their husband was alive.' More often a wife's work on a husband's plantation is said to be 'for her children'; that is, she may benefit through her children's future claims on tree-crop produce and the economic assistance they might give her. Childless widows are sometimes given direct 'gifts' of trees or their produce to compensate for the lack of this indirect benefit, especially if they have other dependents to support.

Like wives, close kin who work for a tree-crop owner gain little or no formal access to the produce in the short term. Male junior kin are expected to assist with brushing for no immediate reward. Women who help with the harvest receive clear-cut shares of produce only when they work a formal 'paid contract' for non-relatives, but are often unrewarded by their fathers, elder brothers and uncles. As one woman, returning empty-handed from a cocoa-harvesting day, explained: 'He gives to me if he pleases, but he is my

TABLE 5.1: Tree-crop caretaking labour
arrangements in Madina, 1988.

Relationship of planter to caretaker	No. of arrangements
Father	4
Father's brother	2
Brother	1
Stranger-father	4
Unrelated patron	2

uncle so if he gives me nothing I just drink the water (sweet cocoa juice)
and come to town.'

Tree-crop owners justify their failure to remunerate close kin immediately
in several ways. First, it is said to be inappropriate to 'pay' close relatives,
just as it is inappropriate to pay wives. Second, farmers suggest that their
labourers can expect economic assistance from them in future as a result of
their positions as junior kin, and will therefore benefit indirectly from the
tree-crop revenue. Third, farmers claim that as junior family members,
labourers will eventually inherit access to the proceeds of the farm.

Where long-term labour contracts between junior men and patrons and
senior relatives, are concerned, two sorts of arrangement operate. Mende
refer to both of these as *hugbate*: an 'arrangement' or 'caretaking' (Table 5.1).

Sometimes an unrelated man – usually a recently arrived stranger – takes
over the management of part of a patron's tree-crop farm and is rewarded
with half the annual produce. This appears similar to the *'abusa'* sharecrop-
ping contracts reported in Ghana and Côte d'Ivoire (Dupire, 1960; Hill,
1956; Robertson, 1983). In the second, more common arrangement, the
planter recruits a junior kinsman (e.g. his son, younger brother or an established client) to manage the plantation. The labourer is expected to hand
over all the produce after harvest, and is not formally entitled to a share
although a gift of produce may be given. In this latter case, junior kin and
clients often hope that the patrons whose farms they work will assist them
with the eventual establishment of tree crops of their own. Senior men also
suggest that when they die, their junior caretakers will inherit the role of
manager of the tree crops on behalf of other family members. Thus caretaking
arrangements – as Robertson observes for the Akan – 'may provide a gradual
and unostentatious strategy for patrilateral deposition inter-vivos' (1983:
468). Because junior kinsmen who work for them will acquire long-term
rights in tree farms, patrons explain, it would not be appropriate to reward
them now.

In practice, neither wives nor junior kin can be sure of these future long-
term benefits. In the case of wives, they rest on 'discretionary' bases; in the
case of junior kin and clients, they are uncertain because of the tensions

which, as we shall see, surround inheritance negotiations. In both cases, the ambiguities and long time-scales of such arrangements leave them open to reinterpretation as economic circumstances change or as social, political and personal relations between farm managers and past labourers alter (cf. Berry, 1988: 11).

Labourers often compensate by taking or 'stealing' (*huma*) immediate rewards for their labour for themselves. As one wife said bitterly, 'We get no benefit unless we steal it.' Women and young men can consider this a form of resistance to a situation of unequal resource access which some evidently resent. This emphasises that husbands' and patrons' control over their labour is neither complete nor uncontested. Nonetheless, as Chapter 8 will show, crop appropriation responds to wider social and economic dilemmas than simply the question of rewards for labour, and plantation owners are frequently well aware of – but choose to ignore – what is going on.

Tree-crop appropriation is a common practice. Forty per cent of women and young men interviewed admitted that they had appropriated cocoa and/or coffee during the 1987–8 harvest, while others had refrained only because the plantation yielded so poorly that the farmer would immediately have noticed the loss. As one woman explained, 'If it is plenty I steal, but it is not plenty.' Cases suggest that some tree-crop farmers have as much as twenty or thirty per cent of their harvest 'redistributed' in this way. Women, often in cooperation, appropriate small quantities of produce at a time, while they are harvesting and processing it.[7] Young men engaged in *hugbatɛ* arrangements can appropriate relatively large quantities at a time, since the owner expects to be handed the produce only at the end of the season, not after each day's labour. As one young man explained: 'It is easy, and he doesn't find out. I finish drying the coffee, and carry it to him, and he is pleased, and gives me small money for cigarettes. He doesn't know how much I have kept.'

Inheritance

After the death of a planter, Mende consider planted trees crops to become 'family property' (*mbonda haŋka*). Whereas Mende inheritance of moveable property is normally from brother to brother, where planted trees in this Gola–Mende area are concerned this principle coexists with the idea that trees are 'for the children' (*ndenga va*). This leads to considerable ambiguity, and sometimes conflict, over respective inheritance claims. The planter's brothers and all his male and female children are considered to have rights to the tree produce. Plantations can therefore accumulate multiplying claims on their produce generation after generation, limited only by the point at which the trees cease to be productive. People may accumulate inherited rights in a range of plantations over time. Although people with a direct patrilineal relationship with the planter have the strongest claims over produce, connections with a

TABLE 5.2: Inherited tree-crop caretaking
roles in Madina.

Relationship of planter to caretaker	No. of arrangements
Father	9
Maternal uncle	2
Father's brother	1
Brother	4

planter through matrilateral ties (e.g. by a maternal nephew) or traced through a woman are a weaker, though acceptable, basis for claims. Each plantation continues to be referred to by the name of the planter who becomes, in effect, the focal ancestor of a 'conical clan' of claimants, to borrow an apt phrase from D'Azevedo's (1962b) account of Gola kinship and inheritance.

Whereas a male planter's trees are inherited by all his children by all wives, the tree crops of a woman in a polygynous marriage are inherited only by her own children. Women who plant small groups of cocoa and coffee trees in their husbands' plantations sometimes say they do so in order to have 'something to leave for my children'. Local notions of 'family property' which allow for rights to be traced through a woman rather than along strictly patrilineal lines are important in legitimating such rights. This is a major reason for women's interest in planting trees themselves, since a polygynous wife's children's access to their deceased father's tree crops is far from assured.

One member of the inheriting group is appointed to take main responsibility for managing the plantation. People refer to this role, like the labour arrangements described earlier, as *hugbate*. It is described merely as an 'arranging' role: the *hugbatɛmɔ* (caretaker) organises labour for maintenance and harvest, arranges produce sale, and distributes the proceeds to other claimants at family meetings held in the dry season. The caretaker is usually chosen amidst the arrangements for the distribution of a planter's other property at the family meetings that take place after his or her funeral. Ideally, the role is inherited within the planter's patriline. If a son can be said to be too young to cope with the demands of *hugbate*, brothers or matrilateral relatives may inherit. If there are no suitable male caretakers living in the village, a female patrilineage member is sometimes put in charge. Mende consider a woman a better steward of family property than an unsuitable male. However, the argument that 'women cannot brush' tree crops, and thus would need to find male labour to take care of them, means women are less likely to be put in charge of tree crops than other forms of family property.

Table 5.2 shows the relationships between planters and caretakers for family plantations in Madina. Only three of the caretakers are female. One of these inherited from a brother who left no children, and another as an only daughter.

For good reasons, arrangements in practice do not simply follow these stated ideals. First, there is often competition between corporate claimants to 'family' tree-crop produce, and those with weaker claims and/or less influence tend to lose out. Individuals may be interested in obtaining greater shares for themselves, and are reluctant to let others benefit at their expense. They may try to bargain with the caretaker to favour their claims and attempt to deter other right-holders from claiming, sometimes through face-to-face negotiation, but more often through *hale* (medicine). They threaten competing claimants with *hale nyamu* (bad medicine) which can make them ill or damage their property. If a planter left many children by different wives, the widows often push their own children to stake greater claims. As one tree-crop owner put it: 'They will force them and show them their rights, saying "If you sit back, you will get nothing tomorrow, so I will find ways and means (i.e. *hale*) to put you ahead of these others".' Thus people, especially young men and women, commonly find it difficult to obtain real access to annual produce unless they are influential within the family, well-protected with *hale*, or have a politically or medicinally powerful relative behind them.

Second, there are tensions between the rights of corporate claimants and those of the caretaker, rendering the latter a difficult and ambiguous role, sought after by some and avoided by others. Although Mende often say that the caretaker has no greater product rights than other claimants, in practice caretakers sometimes acquire a relatively high degree of individual control. This can happen if the planter left few children, or they all move away and cease to claim their produce shares. It can also arise when politically successful and medicinally well-protected caretakers deter other rightholders from claiming their shares, and hold on to the entire yield. While claiming that they will use the revenue to meet 'family expenses' such as funerals and school fees, such caretakers nevertheless gain from superior opportunities to distribute the revenue as they choose, and to enhance their leverage over junior kin and clients by dispensing it as patronage.

These possibilities of individual control create competition for the role of caretaker. In these circumstances even well-entitled women and young men usually find it difficult to press their claims to the role. But not all women are so placed. Notably the third of the female caretakers is a 'big woman' whose age and authority enabled her to acquire custodianship of her brother's plantation over and above her male kin. Although she was intended to control the farm only until her brother's son was old enough to manage it, she had retained control because he feared her superior protection with *hale* and dared not challenge her.

People also consider plantation caretaking a socially difficult and dangerous role. Several deaths and chronic illnesses in Madina over the last decade have been attributed to 'bad' medicinal actions associated with 'this family tree crop business', and one man spoke for many when he said that, 'When taking care of family property you must be very careful, otherwise you won't stay long.' For example, one man took care of his father's coffee plantation, but constantly received threats of harm from his father's brothers in Jojoima. They resented his control over the plantation, and he knew them to have strong *hale*. Tree-crop inheritance and produce distribution have become sensitive issues which people fear to raise in public. Most caretakers now invest heavily in protective medicines; one reputedly spent over 2,000 leones on *hale* from a specialist in 1987, for example. Whereas medicinally protected and powerful 'big' men and women may treat family tree-crop conflicts as opportunities to demonstrate their powers and enhance their status, other people are reluctant to get involved, and most women consider *hugbatɛ* an unsuitable and undesirable role.

Plantation histories

Claims over particular tree-crop farms and their produce can also proliferate and change through the interpretation of past events, transactions and arrangements concerning them (cf. Berry, 1988: 5), including those connected with inheritance. It is relatively common for plantations to be claimed on the basis that they were pledged to the person concerned in exchange for a loan. As up to 30–40 per cent of plantations in Madina are under pledge at any one time, often for long periods when debtors are unable to raise the money to redeem them, such claims may be publicly difficult to challenge. Events concerning planting and subsequent inheritance rights may also be so reinterpreted. For example, a plantation whose control had passed to the planter's eldest son was claimed several years later by this caretaker's father's brother, on the grounds that it was actually a generation older and had been established by his own father, giving him, as eldest son, prior inheritance rights.

Like Mende oral histories concerning settlement, land and descent, then, tree-crop 'histories' do not represent exact chronologies of past events, but have often been reworked to accommodate the present distribution of power and wealth. When disputes arise over such claims, settlements are based more on the relative political influence of competing parties than on the 'truth' or otherwise of the history at stake. Furthermore, conflicts over tree-crop inheritance can address much wider issues than the distribution of annual tree-crop revenues. Rights in family farms have become a pivotal focus for the expression of broader intra- and inter-familial tensions. In the case cited above, for example, the son and father's brother were from two competing lines for the paramount chieftaincy. Each faction considered control of family tree crops to contribute to its political resources; competing for them became a specific channel for the wider political competition between them.

Multiple claims and conflicts over tree crops can directly affect plantation management. Mende consider family tree crops differently from individually planted and controlled ones. They have been incorporated into family conflicts and local politics, and are not considered to be 'for money' as individually planted trees are. The insecurity surrounding family plantations can deter caretakers from making strenuous efforts to brush and maintain them. Plantations over which there is serious, ongoing conflict are sometimes neglected entirely, and several disputed plantations in Madina have been abandoned to return to bush. Mende seem to consider this an appropriate process. Managing the fragile balance between people and bush ecology for human benefit also necessitates the maintenance of balanced and productive social relations. When these break down into irresoluble dispute, so it is right that the no-longer manageable site should return to bush once again.

CONCLUSION

Having considered the range of ways in which Mende villagers gain access to and control over tree crops and their produce, it is evident that as a group women have received disproportionately few of the benefits of cocoa and coffee production. Few have acquired a high degree of individual control over tree crops and their produce, either by establishing their own plantations or inheriting a farm portion or a management role. Most have only limited, insecure access to produce through shares of family tree-crop proceeds, gleaning and covert appropriation. At the same time women have taken on work as, in effect, unpaid labourers for their husbands and male relatives, although this is not entirely uncontested.

The reasons for this pattern of resource access lie in the ways cocoa and coffee production intersected with the kinship and socio-political relations that structure women's and men's respective opportunities. Among the constraints on women's plantation establishment are marriage relations that limit their secure length of residence in any one place, a gender division of tasks which deters women from embarking alone, limited authority over kin and clients who might provide labour, and competing labour obligations on the tree farms of male relatives. Patrilineal ideals work against women in inheritance negotiations. Ideas about roles in providing for dependents give men greater scope, as husbands or patrons, to claim control over tree-crop income, and the use of these incomes to support wives and clients has in turn become central to the identity of such supporters.

Differences in tree-crop access do not run neatly along male:female lines, however. Young men and recent strangers (with no, or only immature, tree crops) are often in a temporarily similar position to the majority of women, while some women are positioned so as to overcome these constraints and thus to achieve relatively high degrees of individual control over tree farms.

Widows no longer face constraints associated with marriage; middle-aged, elderly and 'big' women often have considerable control over young male labour; and senior women who support junior kin and clients are considered quite appropriately to have tree crops.

Furthermore, as this account of tree crops emphasises, resource access depends not on an immutable set of rules but on processes influenced by power relations. There is no fixed framework against which all court cases or family inheritance arrangements, for instance, are judged. Rather decisions are reached in ways that reflect the relative strength and influence of the people concerned; influence they might have gained through processes un-related to tree crops themselves. In this sense, both male and female patrons (*numu wa*) have greater opportunities to stake and uphold claims over tree crops, and may see participation in disputes concerning them as an opportunity to enhance their reputations and authority. Where women's or young people's access to resources is constrained, it is often less because they have limited claims within systems of kinship and property rights than because they find it difficult to assert these claims *vis-à-vis* competing claimants.

Many of these issues are just as relevant to trees that are not cash crops. Their long life-cycles mean questions of investment as related to residence are relevant, and that they are likely to accumulate multiple, overlapping claims on their produce and become subject to inheritance negotiations. And associated insecurities can lead to reduced management. The ecological and distributional issues raised by the proliferation of claims over tree crops are therefore highly relevant to conservation-oriented tree-planting activities.

The environmental impact of cash crops such as cocoa and coffee clearly depends less on what is grown and more on how they are managed. The indigenous techniques used to establish and maintain cocoa and coffee planta-tions in south-east Sierra Leone, replicate the forest structure and provide habitats for vegetation and fauna. This is partly because local management regimes, geared to the use of timber and non-timber forest products as well as cash-crop production, involve the selective preservation of useful wild species. While plantations as currently managed do not offer an alternative habitat for the conservation of forest-dependent flora and fauna, they consti-tute an integral and sustainable part of the forest-edge mosaic, and could play important roles in conservation-with-development strategies to enhance the sustainability of land use around protected reserves. Furthermore, villa-gers might well respond to shifts in the relative prices of cash crops and 'wild' forest products, due to further declines in cocoa and coffee prices and/or improved forest product-marketing conditions, by shifting their plantation management emphasis further towards forest products, preserving more forest trees and simultaneously enhancing plantation value for conserva-tion. Thus while plantation management does not currently fully marry conservationists' and local resource-management goals, there are grounds for seeing in it a focus for productive dialogue between villagers and conservationists.

Finally, a key feature of local low-intensity, multipurpose plantation management strategies is that they make effective use of scarce labour. By contrast, a few wealthy farmers in Malema chiefdom have heavily capitalised enterprises and the capacity to hire large labour forces. It is they who can afford to – and do – engage in more destructive monocrop enterprises, such as large oil palm plantations.

6

TIMBER AND NON-TIMBER FOREST PRODUCTS

Chapters 4 and 5 have shown the centrality of agriculture to local social and economic life around Gola North forest reserve. It is clear that for Mende villagers, key 'forest resources' include the useful farm and plantation environments which derive from the conversion of forested land. Nevertheless, villagers also make extensive use of 'wild' plants: of timber and non-timber forest products. This chapter examines local interests in these resources and the ways in which their collection and use are integrated with agricultural activities. Whereas common stereotypes often portray forest communities as dependent directly on high forest for useful wild plants, whose collection is a distinct, separate activity from agriculture, this chapter shows the crucial importance of environments shaped by agricultural interaction and human management as gathering grounds.

Across the main categories of wild plant which Mende collect and use, many product interests and roles in their collection and use are differentiated by gender. After outlining who uses which products and why, this chapter looks at where women and men collect them and at the social arrangements controlling their access. The significance of different gathering places needs to be understood in terms of tenure arrangements controlling access to forest products, people's different work routines, and management opportunities related to agricultural land uses. Women's and men's relative interests in these products has altered with changes in their commercial and socio-economic value. As land-use changes and commercialisation alter people's relative access to forest products, disjunctions can emerge between gendered interests in particular forest products, and gendered opportunities to manage and preserve them. Such changes are highly significant for conservation-related activities concerning non-timber forest products.

FOREST PRODUCTS AND THEIR USES

Mende villagers broadly categorise forest products[1] as foods, materials for construction and equipment manufacture, fuelwood and medicine. Responsibilities and interests in the collection, processing and use of all of these are often divided by gender.

Food

Many wild plant products are used as food, including the leaves and roots of herbaceous plants, the fruit and seeds of trees and creepers, a large range of edible fungi, and oil from palms and other trees with oil-bearing seeds. Gathered foods play two main roles in the local diet: first as sauce ingredients and second as hunger foods. Women are responsible for providing the sauce component of the diet and, as well as using gathered sauce ingredients in their cooking, they value them to give to other women as part of networks of gift exchange.[2] Men share responsibility for staple food provision and as such often have strong interests in gathered hunger foods. In addition, women, men and children often collect wild food products as snacks.

In Madina, participant observation of daily activities throughout the year gave many opportunities for qualitative assessment of the roles of different gathered foods. These observations can usefully be compared with the results of surveys carried out by Davies and Richards (1991) of a sample of households in Lalehun, Gbahama and Sembehun, which used seven-day recalls to record the frequency with which items appeared in women's cooking in three different seasons. Forty-eight per cent of all items recorded during these surveys were vegetable products, confirming qualitative observations in Madina of the importance of women's sauce ingredient collection to Mende wild food use. Women rely on wild vegetables when planted ones are scarce or inaccessible, and for variation. For example the leaves of the small plants *poponda* (*Piper umbellatum*) and *gbɔhui* (*Triumfetta cordifolia*) are consumed in sauces throughout the year, while *kikpɔ* (*Crassocephalum crepidioides*) is eaten in the early dry season. The fruit of *kposi* or *ndɔgbɔmaggi* (*Solanum verbascifolium*) are used as a flavouring, a useful substitute for the locally popular 'Maggi' brand stock cubes from which they get their name.

Edible fungi (*fali*) such as *kpɔwɔ* and *koma-vale* (*Schizophyllum commune*) accounted for thirty per cent of the recorded survey items. As Davies and Richards (1991) point out, these clearly play a greater role in Mende subsistence than has previously been recognised. Men and women in Madina often say they are equivalent to meat, and value them as a useful meat or fish substitute during the rainy season. Roots, nuts and seeds accounted for a respective fourteen per cent, six per cent and two per cent of recorded gathered foods. Of particular note are the seeds of the forest trees *bɔbɔ* (*Irvingia gabonensis*), *hela* (*Bussea occidentalis*) and *fawa* (*Pentaclethra macrophylla*), which women gather in the dry season and use to thicken sauces. However, while Davies and Richards (1991) reported only this use of *Pentaclethra* in their late dry season recall surveys, discussions and observations in Madina suggest that an equally, if not more, significant use is as a source of oil for cooking and soap-making. For this, women usually store seeds collected in the dry season to process and use in the rainy season when other oils (e.g. palm oil) are scarce and expensive.

Oil from the wild palm *tɔkpɔ* (*Elaeis guineensis*) is ideally a sauce ingredient in every meal. Thirty-five per cent of women in Madina processed the highly valued red palm fruit oil in 1988; many of those who were unable to, largely for labour-related reasons discussed below, took care to gain access to some through local purchase or as a gift. It is those women whose economic situation most limits their access to palm oil who seem to make most use of 'wild' oil sources such as *Pentaclethra*. Red palm oil is also employed in sacrifices to ancestors, and is said to have medicinal properties, whether eaten (Mende say it 'makes one's blood good'), rubbed on the skin,[3] or incorporated into local soap.[4] The importance of the oil palm to villagers around Gola North extends far beyond red oil itself, however. The tree is central to a complex web of economic, social and ritual uses;[5] as one villager put it: '*tɔkpɔ: mu yɛngɛlɔ kaka* (the palm tree: we work it a lot).' Many uses in construction and equipment manufacture are discussed below. Palm wine is tapped from oil palms as well as from the raffia palm, *nduvu* (*Raphia hookeri*). Although muslim prohibitions limit the consumption of alcohol in the Gola forest area, palm wine is frequently consumed in private, especially by young married men who attribute to it virility-enhancing powers. Hofstra (1937) describes a ceremony, *tɔkpɔgɔlei*, which Mende performed in the past to acknowledge just how dependent community life was upon the oil palm.

Wild plants are also used as hunger foods to tide people over seasonal shortages and periodic severe hunger periods. Most regularly important in this respect are 'bush yams' (*Dioscorea spp.*, especially *ngawu*) which are commonly dug up and eaten as a staple between May and October when rice is scarce. This seasonal importance is shown in Davies and Richards' (1991) surveys which report bush yam consumption by 67.8 per cent of respondents in the rainy season, 57.8 per cent in the late dry season but only 7.5 per cent in the early dry season. In Madina, observations focusing on the social differentiation of food gathering suggested that members of small and female-headed farm households consume more bush yams than others, since they more often suffer shortfalls in their staple food production. Bush yam use can also vary considerably from year to year. While in 1988 a similar survey to Davies and Richards', if carried out in Madina, might well have had similar results, in 1990 hunger linked to the hosting of Liberian refugees forced virtually everyone to turn to bush yams (Leach, 1992a). It is in severe hunger periods such as this that villagers around Gola North also resort to a range of other wild hunger foods. These include bush yam varieties normally avoided for their bitter taste, and palm hearts which are usually rejected because their extraction irrevocably damages the tree. Oral history frequently

PLATE 6.1: Co-wives extract red oil from palm fruit in the special pit (*bundei*) in farmbush near the village. They will keep the leftover nuts to process later into kernel oil.

links past hunger periods with the name of the product most important for survival. For example, during *Kpatoi*, in the 1940s, people relied on seeds from the tree *kpatoi* (*Pterocarpus santalinoides*) – which are borne during August, the height of the hungry season – as a staple. Today, wild hunger foods remain as important as ever in the context of declining rice sufficiency, shortages of cash to purchase it and the frequent insufficiency of farm-grown hunger foods.

Most wild plant foods are collected by those who use them, rather than according to a task-specific division of labour. Thus it is women who collect sauce ingredients, snacks and staple foods on a day-to-day basis. Men occasionally help, collect snacks for themselves, and might participate in collecting staple and hunger foods. Mende do, however, link certain wild plant collection and processing activities with gender-specific skills. The pounding and boiling necessary to extract oil from palm fruit and tree seeds is women's work, and the cooking-like skills involved in ensuring that the oil 'comes out well' are part of the realm of kitchen-based knowledge largely controlled by women. Some women claim to have a 'touch' (*doahungbɛ*) for this which they attribute to powers derived from Sande. Tasks involving tree-climbing – the cutting of palm fruit, palm wine tapping and honey collection, from hives in high branches – are exclusively men's work. Such tasks are associated with masculinity. In the colonial period palm-climbing was a central part of boys' 'training' during their initiation into Poro, and it was said that, 'A man who

does not know how to climb a palm tree is regarded as only half a man'
(Hofstra, 1937: 108). There is acknowledged danger of serious accidents in
scaling slippery palm trunks up to ten metres high with only the aid of a
hoop (*mbale*), very likely encountering a poisonous snake at the top. Men
who were fearful or physically incapable of climbing – there were always a
few in every village – were considered unmanly. A few men accumulated
admirers and followers through their reputations as 'expert' palm-climbers.
They claimed that a woman's touch would spoil the medicines (*hale*) they
used to assist their work. Honey collection by climbing trees, smoking out,
and cutting open the bee hives closely resembles palm-climbing in the
actions, skills and symbolism involved.

Sometimes men's and women's gender-specific tasks are combined in
sequence. This is the case for palm-oil production, an important dry season
activity. Men cut palm fruit and women then process the deep red oil
(*ngulɔgbɔu*) from their pericarp. Women process palm fruit either in their
kitchens or, if large quantities are involved, in a special pit (*bundei*) in the
farmbush near the village. The kernels are kept to be processed later into
kernel oil (*ndawulɔ*), a useful pericarp oil substitute in the hungry season. As
in upland rice farming, men initiate the cycle and women complete it. And
like rice production, palm-oil production has long provided a means to affirm
the complementarity and interdependence of gender roles. This broad conception seems to have persisted despite significant shifts in women's and men's
palm-product control which, as we shall see, have occurred in the last few
decades.

Construction and equipment manufacture

In contrast with women's predominance in collecting and using food products,
most of the tree and plant materials which Gola forest villagers use to
construct and repair buildings, furniture and items of household and agricultural equipment are collected and processed by men. The knowledge and
skills involved in the manufacture of many equipment items are learned as
part of Poro initiation, and women usually avoid the activities for fear of trans-
gressing forbidden men's society boundaries.

Where construction is concerned, boards sawn from timber trees are
used for the roof beams, doors and shutters of mud block or cement-
built houses and for furniture. Like industrial foresters, Mende consider
certain hard, dense rainforest trees such as *yawi* (*Heriteria utilis*) to provide
good, long-lasting timber. But the preferred species for regular use are
semei (*Chlorophora regia*) and the yellow *baji* (*Terminalia ivorensis*), which
are more easily cut with an axe and sawn with local technology, the two-
man pit saw. Most timber for local use and sale within the village is
obtained by village men in this way.

Timber boards are only one of a large number of locally important building

TABLE 6.1: Building materials used in villages around Gola North.

Category of use	Species	Times collected in one year
BUILDING POLES (10 most important species)	*Harungana madagascariensis*	58
	Musanga cecropioides	29
	Margaritaria discoidea	27
	Anisophyllea laurina	26
	Diospyros sp.	24
	Erythrophleum ivorense	23
	Microdesmis puberula	19
	Chlorophora regia	17
	Terminalia ivorensis	15
	Afzelia africana	14
THATCH (4 most important species)	*Raphia palma-pinus*	82
	Elaeis guineensis	22
	Raphia hookeri	22
	njasei	4

Source: Taken from Davies and Richards, 1991: 32.

materials. Every upland farming household builds a farm hut in the field each year. Men build kitchens-cum-storage barns in the village for their wife/wives,[6] renewing these every 10–15 years. Unlike sleeping houses, which today are roofed with zinc pan, these buildings are thatched. Such regular construction activities account for a relatively high proportion of raw material use by villagers around Gola North. Annual recall surveys of all instances of raw material collection by 116 people in Lalehun, Gbahama and Sembehun (Davies and Richards, 1991) found that building poles and woods accounted for 27.3 per cent of occasions, and thatch for a further 10.6 per cent. Table 6.1, which draws on these surveys, shows the main species collected for these uses. Madina men confirm that whereas thick poles or mature trunks of strong, termite-resistant trees such as *kpɛdɛi* (*Afzelia africana*) serve best as uprights, lighter species such as *yoŋgoei* (*Harungana madagascariensis*) make the best cross-poles. Of the species of palm used for thatch, *tɔkpɔ* (*Elaeis guineensis*), *nduvu* (*Raphia hookeri*) and *keli* (*Raphia palma-pinus*), men in Madina (as in the other villages) prefer to use *keli* as it is the most durable.

Many of the items of equipment used in everyday life, whether in village or bush-based activities, are manufactured by villagers from wild plant products. Even today there are few accessible substitutes for these; Sierra Leone's economic situation renders non-local materials scarce and expensive, and imported tools and equipment, even if available, would be well beyond the means of the materially poor communities around Gola North.

Inventories carried out by Davies and Richards (1991) of items made from wild plant products in 89 households in Gbahama, Lalehun and Sembehun found that nearly all households had mortars, pestles, rice 'fanners' or winnowing trays, wooden spoons, scoop fishing nets (*mbembe*), large crop-carrying/storage baskets (*samba*), mats, brooms, hoe handles, benches or stools, and notched ladders for reaching the kitchen rice store. Half to three-quarters also had a smoking basket for fish or meat, palm-tree climbing harnesses, fish traps, fishing baskets (*piyɛ*), hammocks and bird-driving slingshots. Observations suggest that villagers in Madina possess a similar range of items, although not all are obtained and owned on a 'household' basis. A farm-household head is expected to supply those items needed for the household farm enterprise, replacing them as necessary (e.g. tool handles, pestles and mortars used in the farm hut, baskets and mats for carrying and drying household rice). Other items, such as mortars and fanners, are owned by women, and co-wives usually possess their own. Sons and male clients commonly have their own equipment for their independent activities, such as palm-climbing harnesses, fish traps and cutlass handles. A husband or male household head is not obliged to provide such items for his wife/wives and male dependents. Some 'help' by making them, and women sometimes receive them as gifts from male relatives, but others have to buy them for themselves from other men. Scoop nets for fishing are a notable exception, since women weave these for themselves.[7]

Palm products play central roles in agricultural and household-equipment manufacture; palm leaves and leaf ribs are used, while soaked, rolled leaf fibres make effective string. In Davies and Richards' household inventories mentioned above, *Raphia hookeri* accounted for 22 per cent of all citations, being used to make stools, bags, hammocks, slingshots and baskets. *Elaeis guineensis* accounted for a further 13.4 per cent, largely because of its importance in the manufacture of scoop nets and brooms, and *Raphia palma-pinus*, used to make chicken baskets and mats, for 9.1 per cent. Baskets and rice-winnowing trays are principally made from 'rattans' (climbing palms). Three rattan species accounted for 17.1 per cent of citations in the Lalehun, Gbahama and Sembehun inventories. Madina villagers seem to make heaviest use of *mbalu, Eremospatha macrocarpa*.

Other items are made from wood. In Madina, as in the other villages around Gola North, notched rice-store ladders are generally made from *Musanga cecropioides*. Several species are used as pestles: *Anisophyllea laurina* and *Diospyros heudelotii* were found to be predominant during the Lalehun, Gbahama and Sembehun inventories, and villagers in Madina use these as well as *Vitex micrantha* and *Smeathmannia sp*. Mortars, which are commonly purchased from specialist craftsmen in the village, are usually made from *baji* (*Terminalia ivorensis*) or *semei* (*Chlorophora regia*). Soft woods, notably *Funtumia africana*, are used for carving items such as spoons and clothes paddles. For hoe handles, by far the most commonly used species in Madina is *Newbouldia laevis*, and for axe handles, *kafo* (*Rubiaceae*).

PLATE 6.2: A man makes a pot trap for fish from *Raphia hookeri*. The hammock he sits in is woven from string derived from the same species of palm, one of the raw materials most frequently used by Mende.

An important category of product that women, as well as men, collect and use for themselves is material for wrapping and tying. As Davies and Richards (1991) emphasise, in a society without paper, synthetic string or plastic, 'ropes' for joining building poles to rafters, suspending hammocks, constructing traps and tying firewood bundles, and large leaves for wrapping items such as fish, meat and vegetables, are extremely important. During their annual recall surveys of raw material use, these were the two most important categories of end use, accounting for 15.9 per cent (tying) and 15.8 per cent (wrapping) of all citations (Davies and Richards, 1991). Observations in Madina suggest that even these figures are underestimates, since many of these uses are by women, who wrap food and tie firewood bundles on a near-daily basis: a frequency difficult to recall over an annual period. The most widely used tying materials are *koko* (a species not yet identified), rattans and palm leaves. By far the most popular leaf for wrapping around the Gola reserves is *mbonda* from *mbɔwɔ* (*Mitragyna stipulosa*), which is invariably used to parcel and store kola nuts; banana leaves are also used.

Gathered materials are also used to make the drums and masks so significant to Mende secret society business, funerals, religious festivals and celebrations. Slit drums (*keli*) are normally carved from *Chlorophora regia* or *Musanga cecropioides*, conical drums (*sangba*) from *Pycnanthus angolensis*, and masks from light woods such as *Musanga*. Certain society masks are bedecked with raffia, obtained from one of the commonly used *Raphia* species.

Fuelwood

Women need fuelwood every day, whether for cooking, for smoking fish or meat suspended above the cooking fire, or for processing palm oil. During the rainy season a fire may be kept burning in the kitchen or farm hut all day to drive away cold and damp. Water is also heated at this time of year for evening bathing. Fuelwood is easily available at all times of year and only dead wood is used.

It is mainly women who collect fuelwood for domestic use, although it is not unusual for husbands and male children to help. Women emphatically distinguish good fuelwood from poor. Table 6.2 shows the species they prefer to use. 'Good' wood ignites easily, burns with a strong hot flame and is slow to burn down: features that matter most in the rainy season when fires are long-burning and damp wood may be hard to light, but which are useful whenever a woman must cook or process food in between other pressing tasks. Women substitute other species for those they most prefer when necessary, but select 'good' wood when they can. In each of three surveys conducted at different times of year I found at least 80 per cent of women to be burning one or more of their three favoured species on their kitchen fires.

TABLE 6.2: Preferred fuelwood species, 60 Madina women.

Species	Percentage of women naming species as one of her three most favoured fuelwoods
Macaranga sp.	83
Phyllanthus discoideus	60
Funtumia sp.	17
Xylopia aethiopica	13
Coffea robusta	13
Uapaca guineensis	10
Vitex micrantha	10
Terminalia ivorensis	6
Others	2

Medicines

One man told me that, 'We Mende feel that all plants can be medicines (*hale*),' commenting on the enormous range of leaves, roots, barks and seeds that are locally used to prevent and treat conditions of both body and mind. Plant products remain central to Mende medical practice despite the increasing availability of Western medicines from local government clinics and itinerant drugs pedlars. Even leaving aside the difficulty of affording them, they are used alongside traditional medicines which retain their social and cultural importance (Bledsoe and Goubaud, 1985). A detailed discussion of Mende medicine is outside the scope of this book, and various aspects have been covered effectively elsewhere (e.g. Gittins, 1987; Jedrej, 1976; MacFoy, 1983; MacFoy and Sama, 1983). However, several points are relevant to the concerns of this chapter.

Mende distinguish between the 'ordinary' medicinal use of plant products, and the activities of specialist medicine-users (*halemɔ*). The former encompasses much of the everyday use of medicinal plants in Mende life, such as in the treatment of common ailments such as wounds, diarrhoea, scabies, headaches and fever, and to promote good health and fertility. A small survey carried out by Davies and Richards (1991: 49) in Lalehun suggests that ideas about many of these cures are consistent across the community, leading to repeated reliance on the same broad range of plant products. Fifteen informants gave 214 instances of plant-product use in the treatment of eleven common ailments. All, for example, cited only the leaf of *Tetracera potatoria* as the treatment for diarrhoea, and the bark of *Enantia polycarpa* as the remedy for jaundice. In total 29 different species, cited three or more times, accounted for 63 per cent of the citations.

Such treatments rely principally on the 'natural' properties of the substance concerned, and in principal anyone can prepare and use them. The nine female informants cited most of the treatments for worms (81 per cent), malaria (68 per cent) and coughs (64 per cent); data that support the comments of Madina villagers that women know more than men about treating those illnesses which most afflict children. It is also women, of course, who specialise in ailments associated with pregnancy and newborn babies. However, such knowledge and product use is not strictly gender-differentiated. Nor is it confined to recognised healers, although a handful of elderly women and men in Madina are admired and often approached for their accumulated skill in these everyday treatments, which they give either for free or in return for a token gift (dofa va).

In contrast with these day-to-day uses of plant medicines, specialists often claim their knowledge to have been acquired in a dream and the efficacy of the plant to derive ultimately from God (ŋgɛwɔ). Specialists can be male or female, and include herbalists, male Islamic teachers (karamoko), male or female secret society leaders, 'professional' male hunters (kamajɔ) and members of descent groups which exclusively control the knowledge of certain cures (e.g. fracture treatment). According to Davies and Richards (1991: 52) specialist healers are said to rely particularly heavily on four forest trees when formulating treatments, of which the most important is ndolei (Distemonanthus benthamius) and another is sowolikpɔi (Canthium subcordatum), a tree sacred to the Sande society. A person seeking treatment must make a series of specific payments to request the healer to collect the medicine and have it administered effectively, and other heavier payments to acquire the knowledge to prepare and administer the medicine him or herself.

Medicine applied by specialists is associated not only with specific conditions and ailments (usually of a rare or intractable kind), but also with a wider notion of hale as power, able to bring about transformations such as those which boys and girls undergo at initiation (Gittins, 1987). The exclusive control of 'secret' medicinal knowledge by these people can allow them to claim more general support and other material resources from others (Murphy, 1980 and 1981). However the distinction between 'specialist' and 'ordinary' medicine depends more on the context of use than on the person, product or ailment concerned. For instance, a man might use a leaf to treat a cutlass wound, and apply the same leaf to a hunting medicine while working as a kamajɔ under very different auspices (Chapter 7). The same woman who treats a child's everyday illness might also, as a Sande official, administer medicines to assist childbirth in a very different context from which men are strictly excluded. And someone whose condition fails to respond to a widely known local treatment (and perhaps to the application of Western medicines) might subsequently seek the help of a local specialist. Furthermore, someone who 'buys' medicine from a specialist is subsequently allowed to know and practise with it on their own account, and 'ordinary' people can therefore begin to build up specialist reputations for themselves.

FOREST PRODUCTS AND THE MARKET

In addition to their wide range of direct uses in village life, wild plant products are also sold for cash. Sales of timber and non-timber forest products both provide economic benefits to the communities around the Gola forest reserves, although of different kinds and to different groups of people.

Commercial timber exploitation involves several levels of organisation. The first concerns the forest estate administered by the government Forest Division,[8] including the Gola reserves, which is partially managed and exploited on behalf of the state to meet national demand for industrial timber supplies. Government timber operations have provided local employment; however, they ceased in Gola North in the early 1980s, and many unemployed logging workers now live and farm near the government forestry camp at Lalehun.

Second, commercial timber companies are interested in selective timber exploitation both inside forest reserves and in the unreserved forest areas around them ('salvage forest'), and in establishing local sawmills to process logs for industrial use or export. Several timber companies are managed by Lebanese businessmen, while other companies have recently moved to Sierra Leone from Liberia as a result of the civil war there. According to the 1988 forestry policy and regulations, all commercial timber negotiations must come under Forest Division scrutiny, even if they concern only salvage forest. Salvage forest deals are between timber companies and the people of the chiefdom, who should receive all the royalties. The government advises that these should be divided, with one-third going to the paramount chief, one-third to the affected landholders, and one-third to the 'chiefdom people', for example through development projects such as building roads and clinics. When negotiations involve reserved forest, forest policy states that the government and chiefdom should each receive half the royalties and the chiefdom's portion should be divided as before. In practice, both the government and chiefdom authorities find it nearly impossible either to secure reasonable royalty rates from timber companies, or to ensure that they keep their promises concerning chiefdom development. For example, in 1988 a Lebanese-initiated scheme which would have selectively logged over half of Malema chiefdom's salvage forest for a few leones per hectare was narrowly averted only with the help of a landholder's influential Freetown patron. Certain chiefs and MPs have gained from one-off payments from logging companies, but have subsequently found the timber companies' activities hard to control.

Third, there are some small-scale commercial timber operators who manage to work out of view, and therefore out of the control, of government or chiefdom authorities. Many of these are urban or Liberian strangers who negotiate private deals with landholders and use chainsaws to cut and process

PLATE 6.3: Village men operate a pit-saw to cut planks of *Terminalia ivorensis*, a common secondary forest species readily worked with this indigenous technology, for use in house construction or local sale.

logs for local or urban markets. Finally, at a smaller scale still is the intervillage trade in pit-sawn timber. This involves villagers in making timber sales either to local carpenters or to people who want to construct houses. Pit-sawing is much less damaging to the surrounding forest than mechanical logging operations, not least because no vehicles and logging roads are involved. However, most pit-sawn timber comes from trees maintained for the purpose in agricultural environments. The farmers who control such trees – predominantly male plantation owners – derive the most income from local pit-sawn timber sales.

Trade in non-timber forest products within West African countries is widespread and said to be increasing especially as urban growth and deforestation raise the demand for products from remaining forested areas (Falconer, 1990). Internationally, some wild plant products such as palm oil and kernels have long been exported from West Africa, while foreign and multinational drug companies exploit certain medicinal species. The marketing of non-timber forest products in Sierra Leone is less highly developed or structured than appears to be the case in Ghana and Nigeria. International exports are limited to palm products – a trade which declined in the 1970s and never particularly favoured the Gola forest area, since oil palms are ubiquitous in Sierra Leone – and the occasional export of *Physostigma* beans for drug manufacture by produce buyers (Davies and Richards, 1991). There is some trade in baskets, mats and medicinal products from Gola North to Kenema, although demand is restricted by the proximity of the town to the Kambui Hills forest reserve where many residents collect such materials for themselves. In contrast with non-timber forest products, the fuelwood trade is becoming highly commercialised to serve large towns (Cline-Cole, 1984; Kamara, 1986), and this provides an important source of income to local people living sufficiently near the roadsides from which sales are made.

Given the limited income-earning opportunities available from non-timber forest products, those who make most use of them are wives and young and/or poor men. The men and senior women with regular cash income, such as from cocoa, coffee and timber sales, tend to be less interested in these comparatively small revenues. But sales of seasonal fruits and seeds in the village are regular parts of the myriad small sources that make up wives' independent cash incomes. During the late dry season, for example, women often sell the seeds of *hela* (*Bussea occidentalis*) and *bɔbɔ* (*Irvingia gabonensis*), while fruits such as *ndawa* (*Parinari excelsa*) and *kpɔwuli* (*Sacoglottis gabonensis*) also provide occasional sources of needed money. Young men who do not yet have yielding cocoa/coffee plantations are the main manufacturers of baskets, mats and other household equipment to sell within and between villages, while the four men who regularly tapped and sold bamboo wine in Madina in 1988 were all strangers who had no regular cash-crop incomes. Chapter 8 explores the socially differentiated importance of forest-product incomes more fully, in the context of local and intrahousehold financial dynamics. Here, it is sufficient to note that results from Madina support the contention that women and the poor rely most heavily on incomes from non-timber forest products in the West African humid forest zone (Falconer, 1990; Okafor, 1981).

As forest products become commercialised, divisions of resource use by different social groups do not necessarily remain the same. Two examples will show how changes in income-earning opportunities from wild plants have been linked to changes in the division of labour for their collection and processing, and to shifts in women's and men's relative control over the products.

The first concerns fuelwood. Whereas women dominate domestic fuelwood collection and use, different divisions prevail where there are opportunities for lucrative roadside trade (Leach, 1991d). Here men frequently collect and package wood into bundles for sale, controlling the resulting income (Kamara, 1986). Because it is quite common for men to help out with domestic fuelwood collection, this shift has not involved men moving improperly into a sphere of exclusively women's work. In some cases fuelwood sale is a farm-household activity, making use of the numerous branches left strewn on upland farm-sites after burning. Even though wives may be called upon to help in fuelwood collection for such sale, the income is generally controlled by the farm-household head, and a wife's benefits from it are uncertain. Men's involvement has by no means excluded women from the fuelwood trade; village women continue to gather and sell some wood on their own account, while urban women are heavily involved in the intermediate and retail stages of marketing (Kamara, 1986). But men's ability both to call on their wives' labour and to stake claims over income by virtue of farm-household headship has allowed them relatively greater opportunities to gain from fuelwood commercialisation.

The changing market for palm oil and kernels provides a second example. Historically, gender-divided labour and control over the two main products of palm-fruit processing – red pericarp oil and kernels – has shifted along with changes in their relative market value. In the pre-colonial period, both pericarp oil and kernel oil were important subsistence products. Control over the pericarp oil was linked with the cutting of palm fruits, and thus lay with men, whereas women acquired control over the kernels as a result of their work in processing the fruit.[9] With the growth of the international trade in palm products in the early twentieth century, palm kernels – the main palm product exported from Sierra Leone – acquired considerable commercial value at a time when few other cash sources were available at village level. Men took over the palm-kernel trade, while the pericarp oil – only of direct-use value – became 'the woman's share of the profit' (Hofstra, 1937). Notably these men were primarily *mawɛɛ* heads, and at a time when production (of palm oil, as of rice) was organised in large *mawɛisia*. They controlled kernels partly by virtue of *mawɛɛ* headship, on the grounds that the revenue was necessary to support dependents. Men's control was also assisted by taking over the task of cracking palm nuts to extract the kernels (Hofstra, 1937) which had previously been performed by women. Senior men appear to have allocated this task to low-status male *mawɛɛ* members for whom, accustomed as they were to working with women (Chapter 4), it was less inappropriate than to high-status male patrons.[10]

Since the 1970s, palm kernel exports from Sierra Leone have declined (ILO, 1990). Pericarp oil, which has held its value for local use and marketing, is now relatively more valuable. Divisions of control over palm products have reverted to the pre-trade situation: the man who has cut the palm fruit can claim the pericarp oil, while women receive the kernels as a reward for processing. As palms are relatively scarce in the Gola forest area and as few people produce saleable pericarp oil surpluses, most women are allowed to keep the pericarp oil to cook. However, a wife has little recourse if her husband suddenly wishes to remove a large quantity of oil from her carefully budgeted supply to give as a gift. A woman who wants to trade in palm oil must do so with fruit or oil she has acquired through payment, purchase or a clearly understood gift; otherwise, if a husband or male kinsman was implicated, they could stake claims over the oil she produced.

Men are also less interested in the once-key men's task of palm climbing.

Palm-fruit cutting has ceased to open an important cash-generating cycle, and people now attach more significance to other aspects of male status, including farm-household headship and tree-crop ownership. Many men in Madina now claim that they do not know how to climb palm trees, and husbands no longer consider themselves obliged to do so for their wives.[11] Women, who continue to need palm oil every day for cooking, now find access to male labour a significant constraint on their processing opportunities.

As well as illustrating the gendered effects of product commercialisation, these examples show how disjunctions have emerged between women's concerns with the use of particular non-timber forest products, and their ability to exert effective control over them. Women are highly interested in processing and selling palm oil on their own account, for example, but their opportunities are limited by their lack of product control and of access to male labour. Similar issues will appear when we look at gendered access to products from particular places.

GATHERING PLACES

Contrary to common assumptions about forest-dwelling communities, the high forest itself is a relatively rare source of products for villagers living around Gola North. As Davies and Richards (1991) emphasise, more important gathering grounds in day-to-day life are fallow bush (*ndɔgbɔ*) on upland and in swamps, and land currently under annual or tree-crop cultivation. In general terms, Davies and Richards' (1991) surveys of forest-edge villages around Gola North found forest to be the source of food and raw materials on less than 20 per cent of the occasions on which these products were gathered. Of the 78 most frequently used species for all these uses, sources other than upland forest accounted for 60 per cent of recorded occasions of use. The reasons for this pattern relate to the ways that Mende wild plant product collection and use are integrated with agriculture;[12] in the managed environments on the high forest edge, a large number of useful species and products become available as a consequence of agricultural land-use practices. Villagers also selectively protect, preserve and encourage valued 'wild' plant species in cultivated and fallow land. These plants are thought of as 'semi-wild'; Mende say that they owe their origins partly to God (*ŋgɛwɔ*), partly to the farmer.

This general pattern of gathering places is repeated across several product categories, as both the study in Madina, and Davies and Richards (1991), surveys confirm. Where construction and equipment manufacture is concerned, poles in 6–10-year-old fallow bush are an ideal size for building farm huts and kitchens, as well as for making pestles and notched ladders; those used to build the farm hut, and often for other purposes, are taken from within the cleared farm site. As Davies and Richards (1991: 31) point out, the four most preferred pole woods, *Harungana madagascariensis*, *Musanga cecropioides*, *Margaritaria discoidea* and *Anisophyllea laurina* are all fallow, not forest, species. Davies and Richards' (1991) surveys of raw material use found that forest was the source on less than 20 per cent of occasions in Gbahama and Lalehun, and less than 5 per cent in Sembehun. Fallow bush accounted for 45–60 per cent of collection occasions, and swamp fallow for more than 25 per cent, in all three villages, with fields and plantations accounting for 2–5 per cent. As we shall see below, in Madina plantations appear to be a more important material-gathering ground than these survey results suggest. While this may reflect Madina's more plantation-oriented economy and land use, it also reflects the Madina study's focus on the contextual importance of particular environments for particular social groups.

While plant foods include the products of several forest trees, in Madina, especially, these are often collected in the plantations where these trees have been preserved. Bush yams can be found in forest, fallow, and plantation environments, but were collected in plantations in 62.5 per cent of cases (Davies and Richards, 1991: 44). Edible leaf vegetables are among the early colonisers of upland farm sites when the bush regrows after the harvest, and are sometimes preserved earlier in the year during weeding operations. Species of edible fungi grow in forest, fallow, farms and gardens, but the commonly used *Schizophyllum* is especially found in cultivated environments. Medicinal plants, as Davies and Richards (1991) show, are obtained from high forest somewhat more often than raw materials or food, but fallow is nevertheless the predominant source.

This practical distinction between frequently used farm and farmbush and more rarely visited high forest mirrors distinctions in other spheres of Mende resource use, such as food production. It helps to reinforce the conceptual distinction between bush (*ndɔgbɔ*) and forest (*ngola*). Most villagers would rarely think to visit high forest to obtain products they could find elsewhere, more because of the social than the physical distance involved. An expedition to high forest is considered 'special' partly because of the spirits (*jinanga*) and physical dangers one might encounter there, and partly because it is specialists (such as expert tree-fellers and hunters) who normally make such visits. Specialist herbalists do regularly visit high forest, constructing their reputations partly through their claims to do so safely and productively. Healing transactions begin when the cure-seeker pays the herbalist a token fee (*pili ndɔgbɔ hu*, literally 'throwing into the bush') to go and find the medicine. Herbalists claim to have special knowledge of the forest and the locations of rare leaves and bark, and to gain assistance from forest spirits who 'show' them the medicines. It is those medicines used for relatively rare and intractable ailments that tend to be collected in high forest, therefore. For most people, the role of high forest in relation to wild plant products is largely as a store for the future, and as a place to venture in the rare instances that the required quantity of a specified plant is inaccessible elsewhere.

The relative significance of different gathering places does not lie only in questions of product availability or of socio-cultural understanding. Questions of access and control, as related to labour, tenure and decision-making arrangements, are crucial determinants of plant preservation and collection patterns. In this sense, different environments form important gathering grounds for different people, and especially for men and women.

Labour arrangements

Labour arrangements in agricultural and domestic activities, and the issues of time and convenience connected to gendered work routines, make certain gathering places especially important to women at certain times of year. Special trips to collect wild plants, by women or men, are relatively rare. They are undertaken by medicinal specialists to look for rare plants, by people who need a large quantity of produce for an intended purpose (such as timber), or by those who need a product (such as fuelwood or twine) immediately and have no other cause to leave the village. More often, people collect wild produce in the course of their visits to the bush for other purposes, such as agricultural work, hunting or fishing, and from the places they pass through while on route to and from these other activities. This is not surprising given that people's time and energy are often limited, and accounts for the importance of gathering places in or near cultivation sites, and the fallow bush and plantations that everyone passes through between the village and the bush and farms beyond.

Women's ability to undertake long special gathering trips is especially constrained by the insistent low-level demands on their time, such as for food preparation, long drawn-out agricultural tasks, and childcare. Women seem especially reluctant to make long trips to the high forest and are particularly concerned to synchronise their wild produce collection with their agricultural work routines. It is for this reason that such a high proportion of gathered vegetables and fungi, for instance, are collected from farms and gardens which women must visit anyway for agricultural work, and in which they often establish additional 'domesticated' product supplies. Equally, late intercrop-harvesting trips to otherwise abandoned farm sites (Chapter 4) also become opportunities to collect wild vegetables from the re-growing bush. Women especially value the availability of wild produce in places that can be reached quickly and easily from their kitchens. In a survey of *fawa* (*Pentaclethra macrophylla*) seed gathering in the 1987–8 dry season, for example, 54 per cent of the women with *fawa* claimed to have collected it from cocoa and coffee plantations near the village. Most of the remaining 36 per cent who had obtained it from the high forest had been brought the seeds by a male relative. Nearly all the women who had not collected *fawa* said it was because they had lacked the time to search for it.

The time factor is especially significant for the products that women must

TABLE 6.3: Fuelwood-gathering grounds in different seasons.

Month of survey	Percentage of women whose fuelwood came from:		
	Farm	Bush	Plantation
April	38	16	46
August	69	11	20
November	54	12	34

Source: Three surveys in Madina; sixty women interviewed in each.

obtain on a daily basis, such as fuelwood. Table 6.3 shows how different gathering grounds take on different importance as sources of fuelwood in different seasons. Fuelwood becomes available each year when upland bush is brushed for rice farming, and preferred species remain to be collected among the charred branches left strewn across the farm after the burning stage of the agricultural cycle. The wood left when farms are cleared is the key source during peak periods of rice-farm work in August (weeding and bird scaring) and November (harvest). Fuelwood from plantations becomes important when women harvest cocoa there (November) and as a convenient local source for women occupied with village-based work in the late dry season (April).

Tenure arrangements

Gathering patterns also reflect tenure arrangements, which condition people's opportunities both to collect and to preserve products in particular places. Mende treat tenure over 'wild' plant products within the same broad conceptual framework as applies to agricultural activities. Plants and trees growing wild in uncultivated bush are considered integral to the territory (ndɔlɔ) 'held' by landholding families (at village level) and the paramount chief (at overarching, chiefdom level). Family heads bear broadly defined obligations to protect the wild plant resources within their territories, and can also grant others temporary rights to make use of them. For most foods, raw materials and medicines these rights are granted quite freely, even to non-family members. Family heads are also realistic about the possibility of 'policing' other's collection, so most products are acceptably taken without formal authority. Many people consider fallen tree products and tree parts, such as dead wood and fallen fruit, to be freely available to all. Thus practically speaking, people can gather such products in any uncultivated bush where they can find them.

Tighter control is kept over relatively scarce and valuable oil palms and timber trees. Mende say of these trees that sawa gbɔtɔngɔ lɔ na ma ('laws: there are many upon that'). To use them even family members are expected to notify the landholding family head, and non-members are expected to reciprocate for use rights with a gift in goods or labour. These arrangements are considered to help family heads to deter and resolve conflicts that might otherwise arise over the use of these valued resources; they also regulate who can use them. During the palm kernel trade, family heads were able to use such arrangements to restrict junior men's access to palms, helping them to retain their superior control over wealth and keeping male labour on *mawee* rice farms. Today (in the context of more individualised farm households and more important sources of wealth) these are no longer such important issues. But instead, allocating oil-palm use rights to non-family members has become a common way for family heads to create and consolidate patron–clientage relations, and to recoup rewards of goods and services from palm-users.

Similar arrangements apply to local uses of wild trees inside the forest-reserve boundary. The original forest legislation as negotiated with paramount chiefs in the colonial period allowed local communities continued rights to collect timber and non-timber forest products for local use. But given that many villagers continue to regard the reserved territories as 'family land', they apply the same understandings of wild plant control to them.

Just as the planter of trees or crops acquires exclusive rights to use them, so Mende consider transplanting or domesticating wild seedlings also to confer individual use rights. Individualised tenure over wild trees and plants can also be created by brushing away the vegetation around them. This is said to 'release them from the bush', which amounts to liberating them from a landholding family's territorial control. When bush is cleared for rice production the farm-household members temporarily gain exclusive rights to use any trees left on the farm until the end of the rice harvest. Farm-household members also have full rights to the fuelwood on a newly cleared farm, although people usually bother to uphold these only where fuelwood is harvested for commercial purposes (cf. Kamara, 1986). After the rice harvest, female farm-household members retain exclusive rights to collect the wild food and medicinal plants that grow along with the intercrops they continue to harvest there. These rights gradually diminish as the bush regrows. Cocoa and coffee farmers have exclusive rights to any trees preserved in their plantation for as long as they maintain it (and thus keep the trees released from the bush). Individualised tenure not only gives clear, indisputable rights to use products, which Mende consider especially important when products are to be sold or given to others, but it also allows the tree-holder, in turn, to allocate use rights to other people, and to benefit from goods, services and allegiance in return.

Mende also recognise nested rights in parts of trees, similar to the nested land-resource use rights associated with agricultural production. This is a common feature of African tree tenure (Fortmann and Bruce, 1988; Fortmann and Riddell, 1985), frequently leading to the right to plant or dispose of (fell) a tree being vested in different people from those who use certain of its products. For example, Mende wives acquire rights to use the fruit and fuelwood from trees that their husbands preserve in their cocoa and coffee farms. Farmers with individual control over raffia palms frequently grant short-term use rights to wine-tappers, in return for occasional material gifts or labour contributions. When some wine was stolen from one such tree in 1988, it was the holder of the use rights, not the tree-owner, who summoned the suspected thief to court.

Over and above tenure and resource use arrangements operating at family, farm-household and individual level are certain village and chiefdom level 'laws' (*sawa*). These apply primarily to resources that are considered relatively scarce, and are of several kinds. First, some regulations are intended to conserve resources in the supposed long-term interests of the community as a whole. For example, Madina residents and guests can be fined in the village court for felling palm trees, and chiefdom bye-laws stipulate that anyone who digs up a bush yam (*ngawu*) should replant the vine. Second, community-level arrangements regulate the use of trees with alternative uses. For example, in Madina town chiefs and elders prohibited the tapping of oil palms for wine in the 1970s, ostensibly so that scarce palm stocks could be preserved for their oil.[13] Third, temporal restrictions apply to the collection of some forest products. In many Mende areas palm 'poros' (administered by local chiefs with backing from the Poro society) forbid the cutting of palm fruit before a certain date (usually April) each year, to ensure that only properly mature fruit are harvested. In the past, these regulations helped to prevent male labour diversion from *mawɛɛ* rice farming before key male tasks were completed (Hofstra, 1937).

RESOURCE INTERESTS AND MANAGEMENT OPPORTUNITIES

Access to forest resources through tenure arrangements necessitates the creation of particular social and political relationships with people, and women do not have particular problems in creating the kinds of social relationships needed to gain rights of access to resources. But in reality, women do often face greater problems than men in securing the products they need, for several related reasons. Women have relatively greater needs to gather from convenient places. Gender divisions of labour and agricultural decision-making give women relatively less opportunity to preserve supplies of the products they value. Other resource-users' exertion of their land and tree-use rights can therefore reduce the availability of products women value in the places where they most value access to them. When conflicting resource uses are at stake, it rarely seems to be women's interests which are deemed to be of higher overall priority, or women who are able to stake their claims. The two cases considered below show how, in the context of changing agricultural land use, this can override and render insecure women's ability to acquire the products that they need, creating disjunctions between women's interests in wild plant products and their opportunities to acquire them. The continuing availability of products in less accessible places – including high forest – helps defuse such conflicts in favour of those who erode other's ability to acquire resources.

Cocoa and coffee plantations

When farmers establish and manage cocoa and coffee plantations, they preserve and domesticate economically useful trees amidst those used to shade the cocoa and coffee plants. Notably, plantations thinned from forest can house otherwise forest-dependent trees which provide food products, such as *Bussea occidentalis (hela)*, *Irvingia gabonensis (bɔbɔ)* and *Pentaclethra macrophylla (fawa)*. Plantations are also an important source of trees large enough for timber, which are otherwise unavailable in all but the longest-fallowed farmbush. Such trees offer the advantages of individualised tenure and a convenient position close to the village, but this is only for certain resource users.

The choice of which trees to preserve lies with plantation owners and caretakers. Whether men or (more rarely) senior women, they exhibit a similar set of priorities. Cocoa and coffee management needs take precedence, so certain trees are left for shading purposes, according to the local criteria discussed in Chapter 5: because they have the light, well-spread canopies considered to give ideal shade, or because they are suitably positioned.

Certain economically useful trees are always preserved, including oil palms, kola and preferred timber species. Many farmers in Madina have preserved *Chorophora regia* in their plantations and some have encouraged clusters of the timber tree *baji (Terminalia ivorensis)* to grow up to use for cash sale in local trade. One man in Madina gave these instead of cash donations to a community building project in 1989. Some plantation managers preserve further trees according to their particular interests. For example, a well-known herbalist in Madina maintained a range of medicine-yielding trees in his coffee farm, while a man who regularly manufactured tools and household items for sale had deliberately kept valued wood-carving species, including *Diospyros sp.*, *Hannoa klaineana* and *Nauclea diderrichii*.

Trees that plantation managers preserve primarily for shade also have other uses; notably 87 per cent of the trees enumerated during ecological surveys of plantations in Madina (Davies and Leach, 1991) had at least one local non-shade use and many had two or more. Both men and women make use of products from these trees fortuitously left by the plantation owner for other purposes. Other useful resources become available as bi-products of annual plantation management, such as the dead wood from coffee-pruning and under-brushing that women use as fuelwood.

However, plantation managers rarely seem to take women's particular product interests into account when deciding which trees to leave, and indeed will cut down tree species commonly used by women for fruit, oil seeds and products for cash sale if they are overshading the cocoa and coffee. Female plantation owners are no exception in this respect, first because they too give the main cash crops priority, and second because as Chapter 5 showed, they are senior women whose resource interests are more similar to men's than to younger women's. The individualised tree tenure that plantation owners acquire covers rights to control the use or felling of that tree, carrying no stipulation that others' nested use rights must be taken into account. Farmers normally fell *Parinari excelsa*, for example, because its fruits ripen at the same time as cocoa and therefore attract crop-damaging monkeys, even though women value the fruit to sell. In 1988 a farmer felled a *fawa* tree in his plantation from which women in the adjacent compound had habitually gathered seeds. Although this caused them major inconvenience, about which they complained bitterly in private, the women concerned brought no open palaver. The farmer, they pointed out, would simply say that there was plenty of *fawa* left in the high forest. This was true; it was the women's limited time that made forest *fawa* inaccessible.

Swamp fallows

Swamp fallows are a key source of non-timber forest products, especially for women. In swamps subjected to a regular cultivation and fallow cycle, a vegetation association of raffia palm and *Mitragyna stipulosa* becomes established. As we have seen, *Mitragyna* leaves are the main wrapping material, and raffia palm both a principal source of thatch and a vital source of fibres which women use to make nets and tie bundles. Swamp fallows also yield a range of leaf vegetables valued by women as sauce ingredients, such as *gbɔhui (Triumfetta cordifolia)*. However, women's access to swamp-fallow products is increasingly threatened by the growing agricultural land-use pressures on swampland. As Chapter 4 showed, these include increasing cultivation intensities for rice production and vegetable-gardening, and permanent conversion to tree crops and water-controlled rice production. 'Major' land-use decisions generally supersede rights to particular trees and plants standing on that land. Thus a farmer clearing a swamp forest for any of these other uses would not have to take account of other users' previous interests in products from that fallow. In the Gola forest area the claim that women could theoretically obtain products from more distant fallows still remains valid, although as pressures on swamps increase this situation is declining. In areas of Sierra Leone with higher population densities and intensive development of water-controlled swamp agriculture, absolute swamp-forest product availability has diminished, with serious consequences for women (Karimu, 1981).

In the light of these changes, places where women can acquire and maintain secure control over plant resources are of growing importance in their day-to-day lives. The areas behind their kitchens constitute one such place. Women domesticate wild tree seedlings (e.g. oil palm, and *Dialium guineense*, for fruit) here alongside planted fruit trees, maintaining individualised tenure over them. Women can readily perform the necessary protection from undergrowth with a cutlass for themselves because it is here defined as 'weeding', not 'brushing' (and thus men's work). A wide range of wild food and medicinal plants may also be transplanted into behind-kitchen areas, thus maintaining a convenient supply for quickly needed cooking ingredients or wound dressings, for instance. Women make use of readily available compost from their kitchen refuse heaps to keep these intensively cultivated places fertile and productive.

Space for kitchen gardens is limited and in heavy demand, so women make increasing use of vegetable gardens in bush-fallow land as a second kind of wild plant domestication site. Women who cultivate vegetable gardens either because they lack an upland intercrop site or to produce vegetables for the market also manage them as sources of 'wild' foods, medicines and products for sale. They transplant seedlings from swamp fallows to swamp-site gardens and from upland fallow to upland vegetable plots, and experiment with their transferability between agro-ecologically different sites.

CONCLUSION

This chapter has shown the central roles played by wild plant collection and use in Mende women's and men's lives. Amidst these, women's activities in acquiring and processing food plants are of central importance to subsistence. In this, Mende are not dissimilar to many African societies in which women play crucial gathering roles. But rather than accept 'woman the gatherer' as the natural, timeless role suggested by some studies of gender and the environment, women's activities must be understood in terms of dynamic gender relations. First, gendered concerns with particular wild plant products reflect socially divided work and responsibilities. Both genders collect food plants, for instance, but men's involvement is largely confined to staple and hunger foods whereas women's extends across a range of sauce ingredients, reflecting their respective food-provisioning responsibilities. Second, women's (and young men's) concern with non-timber forest products partly reflects their growing reliance on them as a source of cash income, given their limited access to 'major' income sources such as tree cash-crops. Third, gendered wild plant collection activities are evidently changing as people cope with and respond to new socio-economic and environmental pressures and opportunities.

As tenure and labour arrangements intersect with changes in agricultural land use and product cash values, women's gathering activities are being marginalised in certain ways. First as farm-household heads and plantation owners exert control over commercially valuable trees and managed environments, women are pushed towards the more occasional use of distant forest and fallow on one hand, and towards the more intensive use of gardens on the other. Such spatial shifts of women's activities 'inwards' towards kitchen gardens and 'outwards' towards uncultivated 'commons' have been noticed as a common feature of African land use systems under conditions of economic, demographic and/or tenurial change (Rocheleau, 1988).

Second, women have, in relative terms, 'lost out' from product commercialisation. As the cases of the fuelwood and palm-kernel trade showed, major economic benefits from product value increases have tended to accrue to those whose social positions – e.g. as farm-household or *mawɛɛ* head – placed them in a superior position to claim control over the income and others' labour. The case of timber trees and oil palms in plantations shows how greater opportunities to acquire control over commercially valuable trees accrued to senior women and men who control cash-crop production cycles. These gender-differentiated experiences of 'wild' tree commercialisation resonate with the changes surrounding the expansion of tree-cash crop production (Chapter 5). Conflicts of interest are presently expressed only through private struggles to find resources under subtly more difficult conditions. Increasing resource scarcity and an accelerated pace of market development may well be accompanied by more overt conflicts among spouses, within and between landholding families and in the courts. Resolutions will undoubtedly be generated in ways that depend heavily on the political status of the opponents – and in these processes women may well lose out.

These cases raise important questions about the concept of economically profitable 'extractive reserves', which aim to raise the value of products collected from the forest on a sustainable basis to increase the incentives of the resource-managing group to conserve the gathering ground. Clearly, product-value increases may be 'captured' by powerful groups rather than be shared, and may be manifested in the domestication and planting of trees in places subject to individualised tenure arrangements rather than conservation of their original forest extraction sites.

Mende are well aware that local social and economic life depends on the continued availability of certain forest products, and certain resource management arrangements, whether administered at chiefdom, village, or family level, help to conserve these for long-term social benefit. In 1990 dismay at Liberian refugees' felling of whole palms to obtain their fruit revealed Mende villagers' concern with the long-term status of their palm stocks. The adjustments to palm-access arrangements made by several village authorities to accommodate the refugees' demands[14] emphasised the resilience and flexibility of local resource management arrangements (Leach, 1992a). However, local institutions which control resource access are neither formed specifically for the purpose, nor is managing that resource their only objective. While they can respond to long-term sustainability concerns, they do so in ways shaped by other social and political concerns. Revealingly, 'laws' forbidding palm-wine tapping in Madina emerged in the context of increasing Islamic influence in the Gola forest area. While conserving palm-oil supplies, they also supported the interests and authority of those descent-group heads concerned to spread the Islamic alcohol prohibition that they themselves publicly uphold.

In contrast with villagers' resource use, commercial forest-resource use by outsiders – such as for timber – is difficult for local institutions to control. Excessively large numbers of short-term strangers, unfamiliar with local ways, can also overstretch local institutional control capacities. This was also shown during the 1990 refugee influx in the experience of communities near Gola West, many of which hosted three times more Liberian refugees than Malema chiefdom villages. Village and chiefdom authorities found it difficult to deal with this vast number of strangers and as a result the area lost many of its palms.

7

HUNTING AND FISHING

Fishing in local streams and hunting and trapping for bushmeat have long been important activities for villagers living around the Gola forest reserves. These forest products provide the main sources of animal protein for communities with limited livestock raising and limited access to purchasable alternatives. Only chickens and a few sheep and goats are kept, the latter for ceremonial purposes rather than routine consumption.

Animal-resource exploitation is often considered a key local pressure which can deplete forest wildlife populations and endanger rare species of national and international conservation interest. This chapter questions such stereotypes. It shows the significance of common species and non-forest environments to hunting and fishing for subsistence, and it shows that animal resources are managed as well as used by villagers. In these respects local animal resource use resembles the use of plant products considered in the last chapter. As for tree and plant products, the greatest threats to forest conservation stem not from locally managed activities but from external commercial interests which are difficult for local institutions to control.

The importance of hunting and fishing in Mende life extends far beyond their contribution to diet. After outlining Mende hunting and fishing techniques, and where and by whom they are applied, the second part of the chapter expands on the socio-cultural and political significance of these activities, especially for gender relations. On the one hand, men's hunting and women's net fishing are gender-separated domains of activity and control, within which relations between the members of each sex are created and maintained. On the other hand, specialist hunters and specialist fisherwomen operate in similar ways, reflecting parallels of status and interest between them. Looking at hunting and fishing helps our understanding of Mende gender relations. In turn, this social context is essential to understanding animal resource-using practices and the ways they are changing.

HUNTING, FISHING AND SUBSISTENCE

Various gender-specialised techniques are used to 'chase' (*kpe*) and trap animals and fish. Men hunt using guns (*kpande*) – mainly shotguns – and they set traps (*mani*) for small animals, either singly or in fences across known animal paths. In other areas, men used to hunt in groups using nets and dogs, but this appears not to have been important in Madina although today some children hunt with dogs as a game. Men occasionally fish the many small streams that flow near the village using hooks (*ndoli*) and lines, and in some other villages specialise in the use of weighted casting nets (*kamanti*), but Madina is too far from a sufficiently large river for this latter technique. Both men and women set pot-shaped fish traps (*mbumbu, hɔhɔ*) in stretches of current, and men sometimes barricade whole streams with fish weirs (*kale*) consisting of a stick and palm-leaf fence with several traps set into it. But the predominant and economically most important form of fishing is carried out by groups of women with scoop nets (*mbembe*) in shallow streams.

The hunting and fishing calendar is influenced by physical factors, such as rainfall and seasons, and by the farming calendar. Men shoot mainly in the rainy season, choosing moments when they are not heavily occupied with rice farming. Although gun-hunting is also carried out in the dry season, men say that it is often unsuccessful at this time because the hunters rustle dry leaves and alert their prey. The need to protect ripening crops ensures that more monkeys are shot between July and the end of the cocoa harvest than at other times of year. Traps surrounding the rice farm are primarily a crop protection measure and are usually in place from June until the end of the rice harvest. Women fish with nets only during the dry season because their techniques rely on trapping the fish in the shallow leaf-choked pools available then, and because women are least occupied with rice farm work at this time. Furthermore, many women fear to enter the deep, cold water of swollen rainy season streams (*nja vainga*). There is considerable seasonal complementarity between women's fishing and men's animal hunting with guns and farm traps. As women put it, 'During the rains men hunt, but in the dry season it is all up to us.' Non-farm animal traps and fish traps are an exception, as these are set throughout the year. Seasonal farm-labour demands hardly constrain opportunities for this, because farmers place and check their traps on the way to or from other work.

Diet, species and places

Both meat and fish are referred to as *ndahaiŋ*, the 'thing inside' the sauces eaten with rice. They should be added to every meal according to cultural notions of an adequate diet, and they are considered especially essential for meals for social gatherings, guests, and farm labour groups. People resort to alternatives – purchasing expensive non-locally dried fish, or substituting beans or edible fungi – only reluctantly.

Villagers living around the Gola forest reserves do not commonly consume rare forest mammals. Indeed, very few of the animal products that meet routine subsistence and social needs come from the forest at all. Fish is generally a more frequent contribution to meals than bushmeat, along with crustaceans and reptiles which are commonly caught during fishing trips. This is shown by data collected in Madina on the composition of the meals consumed by seven 'case-study' farm-households on a day each week between May and December (135 meals in total). On 38 per cent of the occasions on which wild animal protein was consumed, the source was from fishing. The recall surveys of forest food use carried out by Davies and Richards (1991) for a sample of households in Lalehun, Gbahama and Sembehun showed an even higher proportion of fishing sources: fish and crustaceans accounted for 38 per cent and reptiles for 22 per cent of the occasions on which an animal food source was used. Mammals accounted for only 37 per cent of occasions, with birds making up the remaining 3 per cent. Most of these fish are caught by women, who therefore play a central role in animal protein provisioning.

The relative importance of fishing is undoubtedly even greater than these figures suggest since both the Madina and Lalehun survey data derive disproportionately from the rainy season, thus underestimating the contribution of women's dry season net-fishing. Women express the importance of their activities in the face of men's unreliable food-provisioning: 'Sometimes men bring meat, but otherwise *ndahaiŋ* is our business.' Furthermore, women fish routinely and repeatedly, often net-fishing and trapping every day in certain seasons, since each yield may produce only just enough for the pot. In contrast, single animal kills which men bring may last for some time, but arrive much more rarely and irregularly. To preserve this meat for longer, women smoke it in baskets suspended above their cooking fires, taking what is needed for each meal. And in one case a fourteen-foot python, chopped into slices and so stored, filled one woman's cooking pot for over a week. But it may be a long time before the next animal is brought, and even then a man may choose to sell or give away the meat rather than hand it to his wife.

Bushmeat from mammal sources generally derives from relatively common species, and a greater proportion is obtained by trapping than by shooting. In the recall surveys carried out in the Lalehun area (Davies and Richards, 1991: 42), 40 per cent of the occasions of mammal use involved four species commonly trapped in and around rice farms: the cane rat or 'cutting grass' (*Thyronomis swinderianus, sewulo*), the giant rat (*Cricetomys gambianus*), and two species of porcupine (*Hystrix cristata* and *Atherurus africanus, sɛnje*). Another 34 per cent involved bushbuck (*Tragelaphus scriptus, ndɔpɔ*) and various species of duiker, mainly *Cephalophus maxwelli (tuawo)*, which are commonly trapped and hunted in bush fallow as well as forest. Primates accounted for 6 per cent of mammal bushmeat sources. In Madina, meal data collected from the seven farm-households suggest that primates account for a greater proportion of bushmeat sources: 48 per cent of occasions of mammal use. This difference may reflect the greater tree cash-crop orientation of Madina's economy and land use, and, consequently, more shooting of monkeys in conjunction with crop protection. It also undoubtedly reflects the particular situations of the sampled households, as three of these were headed by gun-owning cocoa farmers and two more had close kinship ties with regular gun hunters from whom they frequently received gifts of monkey meat. Nevertheless the primate species consumed in Madina, mainly Campbell's monkey (*Cercopithecus c. campbelli, lɔgbɔ*), spot-nosed monkey (*Cercopithecus p. petaurista, hokpalakole*) and the sooty mangabey (*Cercocebus sp, towei*), dwell predominantly in farmbush areas and around plantations. They are not forest-dependent primate species such as the red colobus and black and white colobus monkeys; these did not figure at all in the Madina case-study data. Indeed, rare forest-dependent mammals, whether primate or not, rarely figure in the diet of villagers around Gola North. Davies and Richards' (1991) surveys showed endangered species such as the chimpanzee, red colobus and bongo to account for less than 2 per cent of bushmeat sources.

Many of the commonly consumed species are crop pests. Campbells's, spot-nosed and sooty mangabey monkeys are notorious ravagers of cocoa and coffee plantations, and Mende who shoot and trap them there do so as much to protect their crops as to obtain bushmeat. Cane rats are highly destructive of rice, vegetable and groundnut crops. The fences farmers construct around their farm sites, with traps set into them at intervals, therefore serve the dual purpose of crop protection and bushmeat procurement. Especially where food crops are concerned, farmers complain that pest problems exceed their control capacities and cane rat populations are said to be increasing. This may result partly from the breakdown of large hunting drives once organised at the *mawɛɛ* level. It is also a likely result of recent land use changes, since the intensification of swamp rice cultivation has increased the area of grassy swamp fallow available to nourish cane rats during the critical dry season. There is much local interest in finding more effective cane rat control measures primarily for crop protection rather than bushmeat-consumption reasons, although the two concerns are clearly complementary.

Tenure arrangements allow villagers to hunt and fish in a range of different places, including the high forest. Mende consider all the wild animals and fish in the chiefdom to be 'held' by the paramount chief, who should receive specified portions of any large animals (*ndɔlɔhuaŋ*, or 'chiefdom

PLATE 7.1: A spring trap set into the fence around a rice farm to catch cane rats (*Thyronomis swinderianus*). Such common and pestilential species account for a much greater proportion of local bushmeat consumption than do rare forest mammals.

animals') killed. Landholding families are also considered to 'hold' animals, but only loosely because the creatures so often move between territories. Fish in streams and pools which cut across or border several family territories are sometimes said to be 'for' the whole village. Proprietary rights over animal resources are established only when they are killed or immobilised in a trap. People can, in principle, do this anywhere, although hunters and fishing groups tend to adopt habitual ranges and farmers understandably focus pest-control activities on their own farms. Conflicts over animal-resource use are normally arbitrated in the village court, although forest areas within the Gola reserves are supposedly subject to different arrangements. Forest-reserve legislation restricts some (but not all) hunting rights through a system of licences which should be obtained to shoot any of the larger and rarer animals. However, local people seem unclear about the precise scope of these state-reserve laws, and in practice pay more attention to customary regulations.

Not only do Mende subsistence animal resource uses contradict external stereotypes of hunting communities, they also fail fully to capture Mende ideas and practices about hunting and fishing. These address the socio-political importance, as well as the direct material value, of the chase. Discussions of hunting, for example, often lead into accounts of dramatic kills of large and dangerous animals such as elephants and leopards in the high forest by hunters with special powers. While such hunting is not, and arguably has never been, of great importance to local subsistence, the ideas and practices associated with it are of key socio-cultural significance to people–forest relations and to gender. It is to the activities of such hunters and their changing social importance that we now turn, before considering the parallel social importance of fishing to women.

HUNTER AND *KAMAJƆ*

Mende differentiate clearly between the 'ordinary' activities of trapping and killing bushmeat, which 'anyone can do', and the activities of 'real' hunters or *kamajɔ* (pl. *kamajɛisia*). There are twelve recognised *kamajɛisia* in Madina. They bring special knowledge and powers to bear on their hunting, enabling them to venture safely into the forest and hunt large and dangerous animals in ways which 'ordinary' people would not normally attempt. It is largely to *kamajɔ* activity rather than to routine subsistence uses that any local involvement in the depletion of large forest mammals is attributable. *Kamajɔ* activity is an exclusively male preserve which, at least in the past, assisted its practitioners to acquire important social and political positions. I will examine the knowledge, gender-exclusivity and socio-political opportunities associated with *kamajɔ* business in turn.

Kamajɔ knowledge and characteristics

While certain families claim innate 'gifts' for hunting which pass automatically from father to son, *kamajɔ* knowledge, powers and status must otherwise be acquired through training. The potential hunter attaches himself to an established *kamajɔ* as a pupil (*kaa lɔpɔ*, 'learning child'). *Kamajɛisia* refer to their pupils as 'small boys', regardless of their age. They describe the final medicinal leaf wash, which signals the completion of training, as making him into a 'man for himself', thus expressing a close association between *kamajɔ* and adult masculine status.

Hunters' physical skills include the ability to walk silently in the bush. Apprentices learn how to lay bait lines by breaking a line of sapling branches to encourage succulent new shoot growth, which attracts animals to a hunter, then lying in wait. Making nasal decoy calls which imitate the cries of young animals is also an acquired skill, remarkably effective in attracting duikers. The safe and effective use of a shotgun is perhaps the hunter's most basic skill. This links hunting with masculinity, in that the gun is linked explicitly with the phallus. When a hunter's gun broke during the course of fieldwork, a man commented to me that *i ya a nyahɛi naa* ('he has become a woman now'). People also link the act of shooting with male sexuality: acts or events that temporarily weaken a hunter's sexual power are thought to diminish the power of his gun. One man explained that a hunter should refrain from sexual intercourse before hunting because it 'takes something out of him' and 'makes him weak' – his shooting will fail.

Men emphasise that successful hunters need particular physical and emotional characteristics. They say that a hunter must have strength (*kpaya*) to survive alone, walk long distances, often at night, and carry carcasses. He should also have 'heart'. Mende talk of the heart (*ndii*) as the seat of emotions, and the phrase can refer to particular attributes, such as courage. Strength of heart as a whole, a capacity we might translate as 'emotional fortitude', is considered important for hunting. Elephant hunters kept the hearts of their kills to show that they themselves had the heart to match this strongest of prey.

Hunters often say that women are physically too weak to hunt. They sometimes draw an explicit contrast with fishing: 'Women only fish, which is not hard work.' Women do not necessarily agree, considering fishing equally tough in its own way. Although everyone acknowledges that there is much interpersonal variation in possession of 'heart', men use two different images of female emotions to claim women unsuited to hunting. The first is that they are too weak-hearted to hunt:

> The bush hog (*ndonde*) has a hot heart. If you have a strong heart you will kill it. But if you have a woman's heart and you hear it you will run away, or it will eat you.

The second image avers that women have 'more heart than men' but employ it recklessly. One *kamajɔ* even argued that women had the potential to hunt better than men, but that male hunters feared to give women guns in case they shot the men who displeased them.

Kamajɛisia claim to use numerous medicines (*hale*) to manage their relationship with the bush and its animals. Most of these are leaf or plant preparations that hunters apply to their bodies, hunting shirt or gun. Some of them make hunting more predictable: for example, certain leaves washed in water froth to indicate the location of prey. Others are used to draw animals to the hunter. Preparing a gun or light with *hale* is considered to improve its aim. *Kamajɛisia* also ingest or wash with protective medicines before hunting. The 'strongest' medicines allow a *kamajɔ* to become invisible or change into other animals, rocks or trees.

Kamajɛisia claim an ability to make useful alliances with bush spirits which, to most people, are unpredictable and possibly dangerous. They are said to 'know the forest', and are assumed to have special powers which make it safe and productive. They intimate that they have 'eyes' which allow them to commune with, and receive assistance from, bush spirits (*jinanga*) – especially the *ndɔgbɔjusu* which inhabits the 'deep bush'. They also claim exclusive ability to differentiate 'real' animals from disguised *jinanga* or witch spirits (*hona*), saying that, 'If you are a real hunter you can tell.'

Kamajɛisia set intricate rules of behaviour (*sawa*) for their activity and those who have contact with their medicines, explaining that flaunting these 'laws' not only reduces the efficacy of medicines, but can also make

PLATE 7.2: One of Malema chiefdom's well-know, but now elderly, *kamajɔ* hunters. He wears the shirt woven from local cotton which hunters prepare with protective medicine (*halei*), and carries a spear once fired from guns during elephant hunting.

them dangerous. Many hunters' laws are in fact part of complex symbolism which links ideas about hunting and gender. Some have the effect of conserving resources, revealing that hunters are aware of the need to preserve animal stocks over the long term. For instance, a hunter should not shoot a pregnant animal, or one with recent offspring. Many of the rules directly concern women and their sexuality. Some hunting medicines are claimed to 'spoil' on female contact: a prepared hunting shirt will lose its efficacy if laundered by a woman, for example. *Kamajɛisia* say that a pregnant woman who touches their medicines will miscarry, and that a woman who has sexual contact with a medicinally prepared hunter will experience prolonged menstrual periods and eventual early death. Such beliefs effectively exclude women from '*kamajɔ* business' by preventing them from using its 'means'.

Kamajɛisia strongly emphasise the need for secrecy when using their medicines, and are generally secretive about their work. They claim that secrecy is necessary if hunting is to be safe and successful. They tell stories (*njele*) of hunters who revealed their medicines only to find their confidant had a witch spirit (*hona*) who took on the guise of an animal and, knowing his 'means', sabotaged and nearly killed the hunter in the bush. They argue that a hunter should not reveal his intentions to townspeople before going to the bush because his enemies (*juei*) could exploit his vulnerable position to harm him with their own bad medicines (*hale nyamu*).

Secrecy further excludes women. Men with whom I raised the possibility of female *kamajɛisia* reasoned emphatically that it was unthinkable because women cannot keep secrets. This speaks to a more general view, widely ascribed to by men and elderly women, that female talk is uncontrolled. The idea is evident in the symbolic link between tongue and clitoris (both *nɛɛ*), and the symbolic restraint which clitoridectomy at initiation thus puts on talk as well as sexuality. Nonetheless, men argue that hunting medicines remain unsafe in female hands because they would undoubtedly be revealed. They suggest that women should not venture into the high forest on hunting trips because, 'You see things there which you should not tell in town.'

Women can endanger men's secrets by tempting men to revelation. Stories often attribute a *kamajɔ*'s downfall to a beautiful woman who lures him to reveal all during sexual intercourse. It is claimed that women's uncontrolled (extra-marital) sexuality leads both to reckless talk from hunters and damage to their hunting. For example, if a wife who knows her husband's hunting business takes a lover while he is hunting, his hunting medicines will spoil.[1] By contrast responsible and faithful wives can be safe and useful partners to *kamajɔ* business. As one hunter explained: 'When he is ready to go to the bush, the hunter gives his medicine to his big wife who must put it under a bench and sit on it.' Hunting discussions are therefore a significant context for the expression of Mende images of gender, and particularly of female character.

The 'special' knowledge that *kamajɛisia* claim to possess, and the secrecy with which they surround their work, should be understood in socio-political and historical context.

Hunting and socio-politics

Political culture and leadership roles have long been associated with hunting in the Gola forest area. Elephant kills and hunting incidents often appear in local oral histories. Many villages are reported to have been established on the site of an elephant kill, where a hunter distributed meat to followers who subsequently helped him to found a new territorial descent group. For Mende, elephant-killing legitimates both conquest and the political power of elephant-slayers turned chiefs (Hill, 1984). Five of the seven main landholding descent groups in Madina today trace their origins to a *kamajɔ*. Neither hunter-founder stories, nor claims that present political leaders were once hunters, are necessarily precise accounts of reality. As Hill (1984) suggests, they may be recounted as part of histories which, in large part, validate contemporary political structures, acting as important markers symbolising settlement foundation and leadership acquisition. This makes it virtually impossible to untangle the 'truth' of hunters' past socio-political roles. Nevertheless, other aspects of oral accounts suggest that hunting also had genuine practical value and was therefore useful in creating and consolidating socio-political relations as well as validating them.

Hunters often became patrons to groups of followers during the nineteenth century (Abraham, 1978). Not only could they offer their clients protection from wild animals and provision with meat, they also promised protection as successful warriors. Warfare and hunting required similar skills and attributes and similarly used the forest as a locus for fighting. Hunting often preceded war in the careers of important leaders.

Because they wandered in the forest, hunters were uniquely suited to, and played a key role in, finding new territories. Their searches for game led them to existing communities to conquer, and to suitable sites for new settlement. Hunters were therefore especially likely to be the 'firstcomer founders' of new territories. Among later arrivals, men with established reputations as hunters were more likely than others to be accorded importance, granted control over sub-territories and the right to establish a separate descent group, as opposed to being incorporated as clients into their patron's group. Thus hunters often came to head various levels of nested territorial and kinship structures, supporting the likely historical veracity of accounts tracing descent-group origins to a hunter.

Elders suggest that *kamajɛisia* continued to occupy important and specialised positions during the colonial period. In the 1940s, renowned Madina *kamajɛisia* used to fire their guns at the village entrance on occasions of large kills, and celebratory dances and songs ensued. The songs sung for hunters often explicitly associate '*kamajɔ*' with 'big man'. For example:

Ye ma hinwaini lɔ mu lima
We are going with these big men
Ma kpakpa komani lɔ mu lima
We are going to stick (animals) in the stomach

While some *kamajɛisia* became chiefs or *mawɛɛ* heads, others hunted as 'professionals' and brought meat for a patron. As a 'noble business', hunting allowed *kamajɛisia* a higher status than other *mawɛɛ* members and relief from the bulk of farm chores. Furthermore, hunters had access to social and material resources which reduced their dependence on a *mawɛɛ* head's patronage, and could assist even those who began in a low status kinship position often to become *mawɛɛ* heads eventually. First, *kamajɛisia* could acquire clients and make useful alliances by dispensing meat as patronage. A hunter was expected to inform the people of the chiefdom and invite his kin to help prepare the meat and receive a share of it. Hunters did not have exclusive rights over all their kills, since the paramount chief was entitled to a portion (foreleg, hindleg and elephant tusk) of those large animals (elephants, buffaloes, large cats), considered as *ndɔlɔhuaŋ* or 'country meat'. *Kamajɛisia* were therefore part of a hierarchy of control over resources and the people dependent on them, in which they deferred to the paramount chief but could acquire authority over those to whom they distributed meat.

Hunters who made important kills could also gain the notice of politically influential men and enter into useful alliances with them. Such 'rags to riches' tales recount, for instance, how a *kamajɔ* in Mogbaima worked on the rice farm of a distant relative when he was young. One day he heard about an elephant that had wandered across the Liberian border and succeeded in shooting it. He took a leg to the paramount chief who gave him a symbolic ten leones, a piece of shirting and a gun. He started to hunt for the chief and to work with the big men of the chiefdom.

Hunters were respected for their socially constructive role in removing animals that were considered dangerous and threatening. Mende are much more ambivalent about elephants, leopards and chimpanzees than conservationists. On the one hand, Mende attribute characteristics and powers to such animals (and indeed many others) which are in some senses sympathetic and useful to people. Elephants, for instance, as Richards (1992) argues, are considered by Mende to have given them numerous 'hints and clues' about living productively with forest ecology. This included showing them important local rice varieties, *hɛlɛkpoi*, named 'elephant dung' after the origin of the first grains that people found and domesticated. Informants in Madina express similar ideas, and an elderly man went so far as to accredit elephants with the origin of rice generally. But on the other hand, certain animals, including elephants and leopards, are also acknowledged as dangerous. Many Mende fear the high forest for its animals, and in some senses welcome the decline in their numbers that hunters' activities and high forest loss contribute to.

In the past, *kamajɛisia* had superior access to economic resources. This both gave them an unusual degree of economic independence from *mawɛɛ* heads, and helped them to acquire dependents. People in urgent need of money – such as to pay house tax – might bring gunpowder to a *kamajɔ*. The hunter who transformed the small investment in firing material into meat that could be sold for cash could subsequently exact labour and political loyalty from his indebted client. *Kamajɛisia* seem to have acquired wives without heavily indebting their labour and services to elders. Their access to cash allowed them to pay the brideprice for themselves, and families would offer their daughters gratis to well-known hunters because of the political and economic benefits such alliance would afford them (Crosby, 1937).

Finally, *kamajɛisia* acquired control over the labour and allegiance of the young men they took as apprentices. Hunters usually describe apprenticeships as occupying two to three years, during which the 'learning boy' gradually progresses through a set of stages, learning first practical and then 'medicinal' skills. However, biographies show them to have constituted patron–client arrangements of a more general and enduring kind. 'Learning boys' performed farm work and other services for their teachers, and sought their political support and help in acquiring wives as well as their hunting skills. Hunters often maintained groups of four to six 'learning boys' for ten years or more before declaring them fully trained. For example, one man joined a group of four apprentices in Tungia. He did 'everything' for the hunter: 'We made rice farms, we washed his wife's clothes.' He eventually returned to his home town after fifteen years.

Although *kamajɛisia* themselves often describe secrecy as necessary to ensure safe, effective hunting, the foregoing discussion suggests that the auspices of *kamajɔ* business are not only – or even primarily – important to hunting itself. Bellman has suggested in relation to secret societies in the region that 'the contents of secrets are not as significant as are the doing of secrecy' (1984: 17). Through hunting under certain auspices *kamajɛisia* use secrecy to preserve their status in relations of authority, and their superior access to economic, social and political benefits.

If *kamajɛisia* are 'special' relative to other members of society in the context of hunting, what of their relationships with each other? *Kamajɔ* organisation in and around Gola North shows many characteristics of closed associations or 'secret societies', although these have no specific name and are constituted much more loosely than is described for peoples of Mande origin further north (cf. Jackson, 1977). Hunting itself is carried out by individuals or by two or three people, when apprentices accompany their teachers. But a wider network of shared knowledge created through past apprenticeships, kinship and patron–client ties links *kamajɛisia* throughout the Gola forest

area, cross-cutting descent group, village and even chiefdom boundaries.
Kamajɛisia are often more concerned to emphasise their unity and distinction
from non-*kamajɛisia* than differentials of skill and status among themselves.
In some senses they consider all trained hunters to be of equal status,
forming a cooperative unity *vis-à-vis* the dangers of the forest.[2] In the past
kamajɛisia, indeed, are said to have communicated with each other in a
special, secret language, and to have united to organise ceremonies associated
with the killing of large animals, or at the funerals of famous hunters. Even
today, they sometimes group as a corporate body, especially when rules
concerning bushmeat resource management are at stake. For example, in
1988 the twelve *kamajɛisia* in Madina summoned a man to the village court
for stealing a duiker from another person's trap, and when the town chief
and elders found him guilty the *kamajɛisia* demanded part of the fine on the
grounds that the culprit had offended '*kamajɔ* honour'.

CHANGES IN HUNTING

As this last example showed, '*kamajɔ* business' is still very much a presence
in villages around this part of the Gola North forest reserve. But at the same
time *kamajɛisia* perceive new limits to their activities and to the respect
(*baa*) they receive, especially from young people. These attitudes and the
substantive changes that partially underlie them relate to recent increases in
bushmeat procurement for the market, and corresponding changes in the
social organisation of hunting. As *kamajɔ* activity has declined, new forms
of hunting have emerged, carried out by hunters with very different social
characteristics.

Kamajɛisia in Madina say that they hunt less often now than in the past.
Indeed, only five of the twelve *kamajɛisia* in Madina still actively sought
large animals in the forest using medicines in 1988, and then only occasionally;
the others confined their hunting to trapping and shooting smaller and
pestilential animals around farms and farmbush like 'ordinary' men. *Kamajɛisia* claim two causes for this decline: first a decrease in the availability of
forest prey and second a decrease in the time available to look for it. Both
probably have some practical validity, although the political and symbolic
importance of hunting makes *kamajɔ* accounts difficult to interpret: understandably, they tend to exaggerate a glorious hunting past.

First, *kamajɛisia* are clear that populations of some of the larger animals in
Gola North – notably elephant, pygmy hippopotamus, leopard and the larger
antelopes – have declined over the last few decades. This has reduced the
productivity of their hunting, and encouraged some to feel that it is no longer
worthwhile. As one *kamajɔ* said: 'Once you would go hunting and come back
with ten or twelve animals. But now you are lucky if you shoot even one.' And
another: 'When I learned to hunt, there were plenty of elephants. Now it is not
worth looking for them; they are too hard to find.' *Kamajɛisia* recognise their

own role in this, explaining, for example, that: 'Too many kamajɛisia have hunted here,' and that: 'Hunters set pitfall traps for hippos along the river, and now they are all gone,' a role which, it must be re-emphasised, other community members consider constructive as far as dangerous animals are concerned. They also accurately blame the major contributory role of the non-local hunters whose activities are discussed below. The decline in elephant numbers is locally attributed as much to elephant emigration 'away, behind the water' (across the Moro river into Liberia) as to elephant killing *per se*, concurring with ecologists' observation that these animals tend to retreat from areas of heavy hunting pressure. However, ecologists have recently suggested that the elephant population of Gola North has never been large, only ever consisting of the fringes of a population from the Lofa-Mano area of Liberia (Davies, 1987: 52). It seems likely that elephant kills were always rare; indeed, hunters acquired social prominence through them partly because they were unusual and notable occasions. Small animals undoubtedly contributed to the patronage resources that kamajɛisia acquired and distributed, as well as providing most of the bushmeat eaten on a day-to-day basis.

Notably, colonial administrators' accounts often substantiate local views of past animal abundance. Major Pearse, for example, observed while on a tour through the Gola forest in 1909 that:

> Elephants are found in the forests all along the frontier South of Malema . . . Leopards are fairly plentiful, but very rarely seen . . . Duiker and bush goat are numerous in some parts . . . Nearly every village or town passed through between Malema and Ba had a supply of elephant smoke-dried meat in it. (Pearse, 1909: 9–10)

However, such officers were easily misled by ignorance of the social organisation of hunting; as elephant meat was often distributed chiefdom-wide, for instance, all this dried meat may have come from a single kill.

Second, kamajɛisia claim that they now have less time available for long expeditions to search out forest animals. The social and economic changes in agriculture that Chapters 4 and 5 documented have contributed to this. With the shift from large mawɛɛ-based production groups towards small farm-households, hunters' opportunities to work as 'professionals' while other mawɛɛ members accomplished farm work have disappeared. Most kamajɛisia are now heavily physically involved in rice production, while many also have cocoa and coffee farms to maintain. As one kamajɔ explained, 'Once hunters were just hunters. But now we all try to do everything.' Again, because of the socio-political importance of hunting, kamajɛisia might be expected to exaggerate the extent to which they did this and nothing else before. Nevertheless, perhaps more than in the past kamajɛisias' day-to-day hunting is now very like other men's, predominantly of relatively common species in and around farms and farmbush.

Hunters also find 'kamajɔ business' less rewarding in social and political terms. Money increasingly replaces meat distribution as a medium to create and sustain networks of political patronage and support. This has reduced the superior opportunities to acquire authority and control over other people that once accrued to *kamajɛisia* by virtue of their animal killing, although many still have such control in their capacity as descent-group heads and chiefs, and *kamajɛisia* are still valued for their unusual ability to engage safely with the high forest. Furthermore, as one hunter explained, 'Now there are plenty of money men': hunters are no longer unusual in their ability to subsist and acquire wives independently of a patron, and other people place less value on a hunter's ability to acquire money for them. I knew of only one man who asked a *kamajɔ* to shoot for him in 1988; other people in immediate need of cash sought loans from traders or tree-crop farmers. Correspondingly, *kamajɛisia* say it is difficult to secure apprentices today. Not only are young men 'more interested in money and diamonds' than in learning *kamajɔ* skills, they can also find the resources to avoid long-term dependence on a hunter-patron. Only three of Madina's hunters had 'learning boys' in 1988, and these were taught through occasional visits rather than residential arrangements in which the hunter had direct and exclusive access to his pupil's labour and services. In this sense, *kamajɛisias'* complaints of decreasing respect from the young speak more generally to tensions as 'junior' people acquire the means to compete more evenly with their seniors in the play for power and wealth, albeit within the materially poor conditions of life in modern Sierra Leone.

As *kamajɔ* activity declines, new forms of hunting are emerging to serve growing commercial markets. The bushmeat trade in the Gola forest area is expanding rapidly, and operates at two levels. First, there is a growing small-scale trade within and between forest-edge villages and short-term diamond camps. Second, and on a much larger scale, dried bushmeat is exported to urban markets in Kenema and Freetown and, until 1990 when the trade was halted by the civil war, across the border into Liberia. Commercial hunting in and around Gola North is nothing new. It is said that the first trading contacts with the coast, perhaps as early as the seventeenth century, involved the exchange of ivory and leopard skins for gin and firearms. Hunters from both the Sierra Leonean and Liberian sides of the Moro river negotiated arrangements with chiefs to hunt elephants for trade right through the nineteenth and early twentieth centuries (Davies and Richards, 1991: 58). But whereas this trade seems to have been relatively well-organised by local authorities, and indeed often to have involved *kamajɛisia* themselves, many of today's commercial hunters have quite different social characteristics and their activities are much more difficult for local institutions to control.

While some young village men are involved in the small-scale inter-village bushmeat trade, modern commercial hunting is dominated by strangers to the villages around Gola North. Some of these are individual professional hunters, mainly of Liberian or Guinean origin, who establish more or less temporary residence in Gola North villages for commercial hunting purposes. There were several such stranger-professionals operating from Lalehun in 1990–1 (Davies and Richards, 1991); there were no such hunters resident in Madina at the time of the study, but several were based in the smaller, southern forest villages of Malema chiefdom. Other commercial hunters operate in gangs, often based in the urban centres of Sierra Leone or Liberia. These gangs dominate the long-distance bushmeat trade, especially to Liberia. They tend to be well-equipped with powerful weapons – including machine guns – and to hunt on a large scale; indeed, there have been reports of militarily-armed and organised Liberian groups killing elephants in the Gola reserves. These large-scale commercial hunters rarely operate with the full permission of chiefdom authorities. If they negotiate arrangements with local paramount chiefs at all, it is usually on a private share-of-profit basis, but they often enter local territories with no such 'permission'.

Commercial hunting represents a much greater threat to conservation interests, and especially to forest-dependent mammals, than does hunting for local subsistence. Continuing pressure on the diminished elephant populations in the Gola reserves comes from commercial hunting gangs. The long-distance bushmeat trade also exploits several forest-dwelling primate species, especially the rare, red colobus monkey which is a preferred food in Liberia and valued for long-distance transport because it dries exceptionally well. Chimpanzees are also taken by long-distance traders, who shoot their mothers so that the young can be sold as pets in urban areas. However, the bulk of commercial hunting relies on relatively common species (Davies and Richards, 1991). Of non-primates sold locally and in urban markets, small duikers – especially the common Maxwell's duiker – predominate. Cane rats trapped around rice farms account for much intra-village and village-diamond camp trade. Primates are very important in Liberia-oriented and urban trade, accounting on average for just under half of bushmeat sales on any day in Kenema market, for instance (Davies and Richards, 1991). Some of the primates that dominate urban trade – like those consumed locally – are Campbells' monkeys, spot-nosed monkeys and sooty mangabeys, all of which thrive in farmbush as well as forest and are cocoa and coffee pests.

The predominance of monkey meat in modern bushmeat trade and consumption deserves special note. Villagers say that monkeys were rarely consumed, let alone sold, during the early part of this century. Monkey-hunting began to increase with the expansion of tree-crop production because of its compatibilities with pest control. It received a boost from national policy in the 1950s when, in response to estimations that 15–20 per cent of the cocoa crop was being lost annually, monkey drives were organised and a bounty paid for each monkey killed; some 250,000 monkeys were killed in

nineteen years (1948–67) (Are and Gwynne-Jones, 1974). While it is question-
able whether this led to reduced crop losses, it certainly encouraged large-
scale monkey-hunting and commercial sale. Monkey consumption is also
becoming increasingly popular as public Islamic prohibitions are challenged
by social change and ethnic intermixture. Especially in urban areas, roast
monkey and monkey soup are increasingly popular as roadside snacks and
wedding foods. In villages around Gola North, as we have seen, monkey
meat is now a common part of the local diet. Commercial hunters favour
monkeys because they can be shot with more certainty, ease and speed than
other animals. As well as being shot by stranger-professional hunters, monkeys are the principal prey of the young village men who sell bushmeat
locally. These young men shoot monkeys in their own or other's plantations
with firearms that they have inherited, bought with tree-crop earnings or
borrowed; the complementarities with crop pest control mean that gun-
owning tree-crop farmers are happy to lend guns to be used in their own
plantations.

Mende ideas about monkey hunting and its suitability to different people
contrast strikingly with their ideas about other forms of gun-hunting. This
contrast in modern local thought is eloquent expression of the tensions felt
as a result of the changes in hunting linked to the growing bushmeat trade.
Monkey hunting, in many senses, now epitomises commercial hunting in
local thought. The young men and stranger-professionals who engage in it
do not occupy the established positions in social and political relations that
kamajɛisia and descent group elders do; rather, they are precisely the groups
whose money-earning enables them increasingly to challenge such positions.

Mende draw no explicit associations between monkey-hunting and male
sexuality. Nor do they consider it appropriate to 'big men', and unlike other
forms of gun hunting, monkey shooting carries few associations with masculinity. Instead, I often heard both men and women refer to monkey shooting
as the suitable work of 'those young men who want to make small money
for themselves', and as proper to 'small boys'. Kamajɛisia themselves draw
the clearest distinctions between monkey hunting and other gun hunting.
They claim that killing monkeys is not kamajɔ business. No medicines are
used, and no training is involved. As one kamajɔ put it: 'Monkey hunting is
different. Any young man who had a gun could kill monkeys. You just go
out into the bush, and you see monkeys, and you shoot. That's all.' And
another: 'There are two kinds of hunter, hunters of ground meat who use
medicines, and monkey shooters.' When kamajɛisia themselves shoot monkeys, which they sometimes do to protect their cocoa farms and to meet
urgent needs for cash, they do not employ medicines or surround the activity
with secrecy. Kamajɛisia explain that: 'Even a woman could shoot monkeys.'
No women in Madina, to my knowledge, have recently done so, but the idea
is not inconceivable.

Kamajɛisias' attitudes towards the status of monkey hunters seem to be associated with their own threatened status. Monkey hunting is associated with tree crops, modern social values, and wealth-acquiring young men and strangers. The processes through which these have emerged are precisely those that threaten *kamajɔ* authority over the young, both as hunters and as *mawɛɛ* heads and elders. In dissociating themselves from monkey hunting, *kamajɛisia* also dissociate themselves from these changes. In labelling monkey hunting suitable to 'small boys' and 'women', they preserve the association between *kamajɛisia* and 'men'. *Kamajɔ* business seems to have acquired new associations with 'traditional' authority, and its discourse provides a means for elders to maintain their social distance from the men who newly have the economic means to challenge them.

Do Mende distinctions between *kamajɔ* business and monkey shooting also speak to changing gender relations? Hunters recognise the possibility of women shooting monkeys, in stark contrast to their exclusion from *kamajɔ* business. Perhaps men's emphatic upholding of *kamajɔ* business is important for maintaining a balance of power between the sexes. But in local eyes this reflects on difference and complementarity more than it does hierarchy. While women were excluded from the social and political rewards of hunting, it would be wrong to assume that women are overly impressed by men's hunting abilities or see their exclusion as 'subordination'. Rather women are – and have long been – occupied with fishing, a serious business of their own.

WOMEN'S NET-FISHING

Women set out in groups to go fishing around midday throughout the late dry season, dressed in their most worn and easily removable clothing. They return, laughing, dirty and bedraggled, just before dark. Most net-fishing does not bring the large one-off rewards of men's hunting. Women embark upon fishing with the same-day's food needs in mind, rarely catching a sufficient surplus to store, sell or distribute widely as gifts or patronage. But economic need only partially accounts for why women go net-fishing several times a week, some even every day. Like gun hunting for men, women's group-fishing is an important social activity through which they create and maintain relationships among themselves and with members of the opposite sex.

Just as Mende associate hunting guns with masculinity, *mbembe* – the scoop net used by women together with a fish carrying-basket, *piyɛ* – is a powerful female symbol. Women make *mbembeisia* themselves from palm leaf-fibres twisted into string, and spend much sociable time in their preparation during the early dry season. A young girl acquires her own *mbembe* around the time of her initiation, and this is considered a significant marker of her adult female status.

PLATE 7.3: A women's dry-season fishing group at work in a stream near the village, using scoop nets (*mbembe*).

Net-fishing involves knowledge in which women specialise. Various techniques involve different skills and forms of group cooperation. Women's principal fishing technique is to prop all the nets around a chosen pool while they clear it of leaves, branches and palm fronds. Two or three women sometimes work together to explore holes in a log or tree trunk in the water, positioning their *mbembeisia* to trap escaping fish. Women search holes in the mud banks, and drag their nets along the stream bed, both individually and in coordination. They lift and check their nets for fish periodically, shaking them to expel leaves and twigs. Women are skilled at assessing the point in the dry season at which different stream waters have lowered enough to permit their techniques, and at matching different techniques to different water flow conditions. They also know the behaviour and habitats of the various local fish species in detail; for instance, in certain places they search mud banks for *ngɔkɛi* (*Tilapia sp.*) and are ready to move quickly to catch them when they 'jump'. In other places they drag their nets to catch the *hale* (small catfish) and *bɛbɛ* that inhabit the mud in the stream bed. Women are also well aware of environmental changes that affect these habitats; upstream diamond-digging can disrupt fishing, for instance, while silting can be caused by soil erosion from short-fallowed land.

For all its complexity, however, the knowledge surrounding women's regular group-fishing does not involve medicines or secrecy, and it is passed on without formal teacher–pupil relationships. In this it contrasts with men's *kamajɔ* business, and, as we shall see, with a second sort of group-fishing employing poisons. Most women say that they learned net-fishing while young by watching female relatives. Sande initiates are taken fishing during their period of confinement in the bush, accompanied by women from the village, but even senior society officials admit that the girls learn few new technicalities. The main 'lesson' which Madina's 1988 Sande cohort learned seems to have been that fishing is a women's activity, and one to take part in and enjoy as a group. The necessary exclusion of men from these Sande-governed fishing trips, and the loud songs used to warn them away, emphasised to the initiates that, even in 'ordinary' life, fishing is an activity to be carried out separately from men.

Group organisation contrasts strongly with the solitary independence of male hunters, but is integral to the character of women's net-fishing. Women usually fish in groups of between six and ten, sometimes combining these into a party of twenty or more. During 1988 I found that four or five groups of women regularly assembled to fish. Their membership centred on co-wives, mother-and-daughter pairs, or women with proximate kitchens, and often included kin or friends from elsewhere in the village. While these groups were not rigidly constituted, most women preferred to fish with their regular companions and would only join a different group if it contained a close friend or relative. The techniques themselves rely on group coordination and cooperation. A woman can rely on certain benefits from a collective fishing trip because, although women consider each as entitled to the fish she catches, successful women will contribute to the basket of a group member who catches very little. Heavily pregnant women are often helped in this way since they cannot bend easily to catch for themselves. Women also value the support of a group in facing fishing dangers, such as snakes in the water or encounters with the *jinanga* that inhabit deep meanders. Most fisherwomen, unlike male hunters, do not talk of status gains to be made by meeting such dangers alone.

The social benefits that women derive from collective fishing expeditions clearly include enjoyment. Fishing occurs at the time of year when bellies are full and spirits tend to be high. It is invariably accompanied by singing, teasing and the telling of bawdy jokes. Fishing also provides a refuge from men. In the peace of shady streams women discuss husbands and lovers, share personal concerns and air grievances in ways they do only in other exclusively female places, such as the Sande bush and women's sleeping houses (*pɛlɛ wa*). Finally, through fishing, women reinforce personal relationships that are important to other spheres of their daily lives. Mende make explicit links between fishing and companionship (*mbaa*), so, for example, story tellers who want to emphasise that two female characters were friends often explain that 'they used to go fishing together'. The women whom an individual joins for fishing are often those she joins for other collective activities – such as rice harvesting – and with whom she cooperates in the reciprocal giving of goods and services.

Group-fishing is therefore a context for cooperation and solidarity among women. In allowing women to separate from men and engage in forms of talk and action that promote cohesion among themselves, even everyday fishing resembles group activities organised under the auspices of Sande (MacCormack, 1979). In turn the Sande-like aspects of group-fishing seem to contribute to men's non-participation. Women make no 'laws' to exclude men from everyday fishing and say, if asked directly, that 'men can fish with us if they like'. Men usually claim that net-fishing is not worth their attention; that compared with hunting and trapping fish and bushmeat it is tedious and unproductive. But men also seem to feel their participation inappropriate, and behave with awkward reserve or joking bravado if they encounter a women's fishing group. Notably on the occasions when women and men fish together, there is little sense of female cohesion, and women behave with more reserve.

These joint fishing occasions arise when fishing, normally a matter for individuals and small groups, is subjected to village or supra-village level control. In some villages, chiefs and elders administer laws (*sawa*) that forbid regular fishing in sections of stream in which fish are known to breed or grow prolifically. This has the effect of protecting breeding grounds and stocks of young fish, thus enhancing the long-term sustainability of fish stocks. Such laws are often publicly justified on the grounds that the fishing would anger the *jina* associated with the water in question or, as in the case of a group of deep pools in Lagula, Madina's main stream, that the fish there embody ancestral spirits. Restrictions may be lifted on two or three designated days in the year, and on these days village men as well as women flock to the stream. Madina's catfish breeding pools are entirely protected but the first heavy rains of the year flush mature catfish downstream into pools and swamps. When this happened in May 1988, men and women combined in a mass fish-harvest: the women used nets and the men hacked the fish with cutlasses. These catfish, many of them 40 or 50 cm long, fetched up to 60 leones each when sold. Women and men alike recognise that community controls are in everyone's long-term interest, and are quick to support the fining of anyone who breaks them. But the large, one-off harvests so created invite men's involvement to the extent that women are denied the exclusive control they have over the rewards of regular fishing.

Although women are unable to exclude men entirely from either village-wide fishing activities or 'ordinary' group-fishing, there are fishing occasions on which women do have this exclusion capacity. These arise when fish poisons are employed.

Fishing with poisons

Some women begin to use fish poisons (*tawu*) towards the end of the dry season. When poisons are used the knowledge and organisation involved in fishing can contrast starkly with 'ordinary' women's fishing trips, and have much in common with men's *kamajɔ* business.

The mechanisms behind the use of fish poisons are simple and locally widely known. A pounded plant material, dispersed in the water, anaesthetises the fish into a stupor – women say that they become 'drunk' – which allows them to be caught easily with the usual techniques, or even picked by hand from the water surface. *Tawuisia* include the fruit of *yɔkɔmei* (*Blighia welwitschii*), the black pod known as *gbojɛnjɛn*, the bark of *mbɔlɔ* (*Piptadeniastrum africanum*), and *nda-lawu* (leaf *tawu*) which some women plant as an upland farm intercrop. The fruit of *nduvu* (*Raphia hookeri*) is considered highly effective, but it is used with caution because of its high toxicity.

Only five women employed fish poisons during 1988. All were influential 'big women', who had acquired high status through a combination of age, kinship and/or achieved authority in patron–client relations. One was a descent group head, two were senior Sande officials, and two were middle-aged widows who headed farm-households. They embellished their finding, preparation and use of *tawu* with many of the attributes with which *kamajɛisia* surround their use of medicines.

Big women speak of the *tawuisia* as medicines, saying that *hale lɔ na ma* (there is medicine on that), and talk of them secretively. They make special expeditions into the bush to find the materials, and intimate that spirits assist them. Big women do not easily pass on their knowledge of exactly how to secure and prepare the poisons. They teach others on a one-to-one basis, similar to – although less enduring than – hunting apprenticeships, and often exact a fee from their pupils. None of Madina's initiates learned about fish poisons in the Sande bush, but two were, however, taken out especially to be shown the use of *yɔkɔmei* by a senior society official soon after their coming-out.

Tawu fisherwomen describe the strict rules of behaviour that must be obeyed if the poisons are to work successfully. For example, the woman who pounds the *tawu* should refrain from eating or washing her face beforehand, and no-one should spit or urinate in the stream once the poison is in place. Some of the rules emphasise sexual separation: a pregnant woman should not use *tawu*, the woman who spreads the poison should not have had sexual intercourse the same day, and no men should be present during any stage of the fishing.

The intra-group dynamics of *tawu* fishing differ from those of women's usual expeditions. There may be no group at all: 'big women' often make their *tawu* fishing into a solitary activity, akin to male hunting. When the owner of the *tawu* allows a group to accompany her, she asserts her leadership over it. She directs the movements and techniques of the other women closely. She uses a much larger net (*vɛi*) that symbolises her superior contextual status and, suitably positioned, allows her a superior share of the fish. Finally, she exacts a contribution of one or two fish (*kɔji*) from each member at the end of the trip, in recognition both of their gain from her poison, and of her authority over the expedition as a whole.

Tawu fishing is undertaken only occasionally, but it can produce catches three or four times larger than regular fishing trips. *Tawu* fisherwomen treat their catches less as a regular contribution to daily diet than as a resource that can be dried and stored, sold, dispensed in gifts or fed to a social gathering. This resembles hunter's acquisition and use of bushmeat more strongly than it resembles women's use of collectively caught fish.

In contrast with the cooperative solidarity that characterises 'ordinary' group-fishing, then, the social organisation of *tawu* fishing is stratified. Other women become the contextual subordinates of the poison owner who controls the knowledge and means to make the poisons efficacious. This also reflects aspects of women's secret society organisation, which involves hierarchies between senior officials, non-officials and initiates as well as uniting women in solidarity (Bledsoe, 1984). The link between poison-fishing and Sande is sometimes explicit as, for instance, when senior women suggest that their *tawu*-using powers derive from Sande medicine.

There are, then, remarkable parallels between the behaviour of poison fishers and of *kamajɛisia* within their respectively female and male forms of 'chase'. Both make similar uses of medicines and secrecy, and both affirm and reinforce their authority over junior kin, clients and learners through their 'chase' activities. A similar point has been made about the leaders of sex-specific secret societies:

> By acting as strategic managers of relations between the sexes, Poro and Sande elites have more in common with each other than with lesser people whose sex they happen to share and who are, in fact, valuable prizes to be negotiated for in the competitive political arena. (Bledsoe, 1984: 467)

CONCLUSION

As gender-specific activities, hunting and net-fishing are of crucial importance to gender relations. Their practice strengthens not only solidarity between the members of each sex, but also ideas of gender difference and separation, and of complementarity and interdependence. Hunting and fishing offer different opportunities for acquiring control over people and resources, although Mende do not evaluate the activities in a hierarchical way. Each activity, however, is hierarchically stratified; in hunting, between *kamajɛisia* and apprentices, 'ordinary' hunters, and monkey-shooters, and in fishing between those who control poisons and those who do not. The chase (whether as hunting or fishing) is one of several activities through which patrons (*numu wa*) acquire and maintain control over clients, and the similar behaviour of 'big men' and 'big women' within their respective forms of chase reflects their parallel status and interests. But such status and interests remain parallel and do not overlap. When such high status performers are involved, hunting and fishing becomes exclusive to each gender. By contrast it is not inconceivable for men to join women's 'ordinary' fishing trips, or for women to trap or shoot monkeys.

Two rather different conclusions about animal-resource use emerge from this chapter. First, concerning its subsistence aspects, it is clear that conservationists need be little concerned that Mende are heavily dependent on rare forest wildlife for food. Local dietary concerns centre on fishing and on relatively common, even pestilential, species. Villagers consider many of these animals over-abundant, while maintaining arrangements to manage and conserve supplies of those they consider potentially scarce.

The second conclusion concerns the socio-political aspects of the chase. Clearly, it is not just people's immediate material concerns that shape local organisation, practices and attitudes around hunting and fishing. The *kamajɔ* activity that involves Mende with rare forest animals has always been understood and motivated primarily in socio-political rather than subsistence terms. '*Kamajɔ* business' remains integral to Mende notions of forest-settlement history and to descent-group politics, while the gender-specific forms of social organisation and specialist power embedded in hunting and fishing continue to shape relations among and between men and women. As we have seen, these dimensions of social and political life importantly affect how Mende consider animal resource use and the ways it is changing.

The changes discussed in this chapter relating to increases in tree cash-crop production and the growing trade in bushmeat have both social and ecological implications. As the practice of *kamajɔ* hunting declines, so does an important context for the expression and affirmation of ideas about masculinity and authority, as well as the pressure from *kamajɛisia* on large forest prey. At the same time, monkey shooting in plantations, to protect crops and supply local bushmeat markets, is increasing. Taken together, these changes suggest that the practical emphasis of villagers' own hunting is shifting still further away from the forest towards common species in agriculturally managed environments; from a high status forest activity to one centred on plantations, farms and crop protection, more like the 'garden hunting' described elsewhere (Linares, 1976). But the growing bushmeat trade also brings intensified hunting pressures to the forest in the form of externally organised, well-equipped hunting gangs. It is these resource users, rather than the forest-edge villagers around Gola North, who constitute the principle threat to forest-dependent fauna in the immediate future.

8

MONEY, FOOD AND MANAGING

Chapters 4, 5, 6 and 7 have shown Mende villagers to have a diverse range of direct concerns with the management and use of forest resources. These concerns are social and political as well as economic, because of the ways that resource-management processes themselves implicate and shape relations between people. And they guide strong, though diverse, local interests in the current and future status of the forest-resource base. Given that local concerns over forest-resource use are guided in large part by their capacity to provide food and money, an understanding of forest-resource use must also comprehend the social relations within which food and money themselves are distributed and consumed.

In the context of the changes in land use documented in earlier chapters, the cash economy has become increasingly important to Gola forest villages and their resource-using activities. The changing relationship between tree cash-crop and food production, especially, has enhanced local dependence on wider economic and political processes, and the depressed Sierra Leone economy as a whole, to meet day-to-day subsistence needs. As money now plays a greater role in local-level provisioning and socio-political relationships, money shortages, more than ever, contribute to insecure supplies of food and other necessary goods. Day-to-day struggles to cope and to 'manage' are now a dominant part of most people's lives, and these struggles themselves entail particular forms of forest-resource use in local coping strategies.

People's experiences of the management and use of money and food are strongly gender-differentiated, and are today affected not only by well-accepted local principles but also by tensions and ambiguities that recent socio-economic changes have served to accentuate. Money is addressed first. The chapter begins by summarising the income sources available to different people from forest and non-forest sources. It explores women's and men's financial contributions within kinship and patron–client relations, showing how such contributions help structure social and political relations on which people depend for wealth, status and security. This provides an essential context in which I examine financial and food-provisioning arrangements between husbands and wives, now of great relevance both for day-to-day survival and for marriage relations. The last section turns to the use of cooked food as a resource. The chapter serves to emphasise that external conservation-with-development interventions that affect village economies, such as road-building and marketing schemes, have a social as well as an economic context. They lock into and reshape existing socio-economic processes and tensions, and their operation and efficacy cannot be understood without considering these.

MONEY AND MANAGING

Incomes and investments

Gola forest villagers derive money from both forest and non-forest related sources. Today almost everyone earns some form of cash income, although the activities involved and the cash flows they generate vary by gender, age and socio-political status. Agricultural incomes derive from sales of both tree crops and annual crops. Since the expansion of cocoa and coffee production in the Madina area, tree-crop sales have become the most important income source for the men and 'big' women who have plantations, although their proceeds have diminished substantially along with falling prices since the 1970s.[1] Other women and young and stranger men do gain some income from gleaned, gift and appropriated cocoa and coffee, and from occasional sales of fruit from other tree crops, but for these people sales of annual crops are more significant. Rice, today, is rarely sold from the area around Gola North. Women and junior men now sell groundnuts and cassava, and women, especially, rely heavily on intercrop and other vegetable sales to earn money. Some villagers also do paid labour for others. 'Big' men and women rarely do this, but other men earn occasional daily wages for brushing tree crops and annual crop land, while occasional payments for harvesting and processing crops add to women's incomes.

West African forest communities are commonly noted to derive more income from sales of non-timber forest products than from agricultural activity. This is said to be the case for people in the Cross River area of Nigeria (WWF, 1990) and around the Korup Park (Republic of Cameroon, 1990). Around the Gola North reserve, incomes derived from such directly forest-related sources appear to be relatively less important. In surveys carried out by Davies and Richards (1991: 24) in twelve sample villages, in which 1670 people declared an average of 3.1 income sources each, 'forest-related' activities (e.g. hunting, herbalism) accounted for only 3.6 per cent of income sources in forest-edge villages and 3.4 per cent in villages further from the reserve boundary. Of the 180 people declaring forest-related incomes, only seventeen were women (Davies and Richards, 1991: 26).

The case studies and detailed participant observation undertaken in

Madina, however, suggest that such surveys may underestimate the roles played by non-timber forest products in certain social groups' incomes. Most women sell gathered fruit, seeds, leaves or processed products (e.g. soap, oil or fishing nets) at some point in the year. Although the sums of money so generated are individually too small and too occasional for women formally to declare them as 'income sources', they contribute significantly to the range of sources that typically comprise women's incomes. Furthermore, they are often obtained at opportune moments, thus playing important roles in women's coping strategies. Equally, while it may be only specialist male hunters, wood-carvers and so on who declare forest-dependent incomes, many other men sell occasional bushmeat, rattan, palm or wood products to meet urgent cash needs. Nevertheless, as Chapter 6 noted, wealthier villagers with secure access to other income sources – such as tree-crop revenues – tend not to rely on forest product collection for sale.

Off-farm incomes that do not depend directly on forest products include specialist activities such as blacksmithing (carried out by three Madina men), carpentry (by two Madina men) and masonry (by one Madina man). About half the village's male population also periodically seek money from diamond-digging, joining the temporary, shifting populations of the diamond-digging camps that quickly grow up where local diamond discoveries are made.[2] For women, preparing and selling soap from commercial ingredients and snack foods provides occasional income, and about half the women in Madina trade on a small-scale in items such as salt, stock cubes, palm oil and dried fish. They buy in weekly periodic markets in Jojoima and Laoma and sell for a few leones mark-up in Madina. About ten village women and men trade on a larger scale in cocoa, coffee, palm oil and rice. Like the external produce traders who visit the village two or three times a week in the dry season, they buy produce from villagers and sell it to buying agents in larger towns.

Income sources contrast between those that are 'lumpy' and intermittent, and those that involve the repeated acquisitions of smaller quantities of money. Bulk tree-crop produce sales, bushmeat sales and diamond earnings are of the first type, whereas vegetable and forest food sales, labouring and small-scale trade lead to repeated small earnings throughout the year. Aggregating the sources suggests gender-distinct earning patterns: men's incomes tend to be acquired on a lumpy, intermittent basis, whereas women's incomes derive from a much wider range of scattered sources in smaller but more regular quantities. As women put it, they acquire money 'little by little' (*klo-klo*). A few senior women, especially those who control tree cash-crops, experience income rhythms similarly to men; and conversely, some men, including the young and recently arrived strangers who lack access to cash crops, have an income pattern more like women's. These contrasting patterns, as we shall see, are significant for the ways financial responsibilities are divided (cf. Leach, 1991b).

Limited incomes and pressing expenditure needs make saving difficult, but the different income patterns also give people different opportunities for this. Those with relatively 'lumpy', intermittent incomes try to keep some of the revenue acquired in the dry season to meet hungry season needs, and to save for the future. Women and young men, who acquire cash little and often, have fewer saving opportunities. Those who do accumulate money rarely save it as cash: this depreciates very quickly in Sierra Leone's inflationary conditions and is considered socially difficult to store, as it invites claims from kin and problems from those jealous of others' fortune. People prefer to make socially acceptable investments that hold their value, and they often choose relatively liquid forms of investment which can be realised as rapidly changing social and economic circumstances dictate (cf. Berry, 1989). Commodities such as rice and palm oil, which have held their economic value and can be traded for profit, have become common investments. Men and women both invest in small ruminants and chickens. These assets can be sold quickly, and chickens are also useful to feed guests and, if necessary, in sacrifices (sara). Goats are also important in sacrifices, as well as secret society business, marriage and funeral arrangements. Savings groups are another common means of keeping money: tree-crop owners sometimes create family (mbonda) level groups, while both women and men organise rotating savings/credit associations (osusu) in which each member contributes an agreed sum every week, which members take turns to receive. At least three of these operated in Madina during 1990–1. Most importantly, people with money 'invest' in other people by giving or lending it to them or contributing to social occasions.

As it is Gola forest villagers with access to tree-crop and diamond sale or trade revenues who tend to be the most prosperous, prosperity is now less a prerogative of age and high kinship status than in the past. Until the 1960s, in the context of land use centred around large household upland rice farms, only a few high status mawεε and descent-group heads could acquire large sums which they used to support large groups of wives and dependents. Since the 1960s economic opportunities such as tree crops and diamonds have made it easier for junior men to compete with them in economic terms. Attitudes towards house construction illustrate the tensions which this 'evening up' of economic opportunity has generated. In the mid-1980s several younger men in Madina had sufficient resources to construct zinc-roofed houses, but feared to embark lest their senior kin think them disrespectful and attempt to 'put them down' with bad medicine (hale nyamu). People reflect on these tensions, asking rhetorically: 'We have money here, but how many new houses do you see?'

Women's income-earning opportunities have changed less than men's over the last few decades. A few 'big women' now have regular access to tree-crop revenues, but most have limited cash earnings. Expansion of their

trading, forest product and vegetable sale activities is constrained partly by
economic difficulties in acquiring starting capital, and partly by limited
markets. Local demand for products is small, while the poor communications
to the Gola forest area have restricted the growth of rural-urban trade. In
Malema chiefdom, dramatic but short-lived increases in local marketing
opportunities occurred in association with the localised 'diamond boom' at
Bandajuma in 1988, when the patrons of digging groups began to buy food
for their workers. The influx of refugees from Liberia in 1990 had the same
effect (Leach, 1992a). Some women intensified their vegetable sale and trading
activities to meet this demand, indicating their interest and ability to do so
on a more regular basis should marketing opportunities improve.

Wealth differentials are not stable. In the hazardous physical, economic
and political climate of rural Sierra Leone money can be gained and lost
quickly and differentials are fluid, even reversible (Richards, 1986). A farmer
with substantial agricultural revenues one year may find his or her yields
devastated by pests or disease the next. Macro-economic instabilities, including rapid price changes and inflation, allow both for the rapid depletion of
cash stores and for the lucky speculator to reap windfall profits through
trade. Mende admire those who can pull off a risky economic or political
venture; gambling is a regular feature of village life which finds its counterpart
in the competitive, unpredictable arena of the village court.

Furthermore, wealth differentials now exist only within generalised poverty. Money has become more important to food security, especially as with
land-use changes on the forest edge, staple food production has declined
(Chapter 4). It has become increasingly important to social arrangements, such
as for marriage and funerals, and people now also aspire to a range of purchased
material items and services including clothing, household equipment (e.g.
metal buckets and kerosene lamps), public transport, education and 'Western'
medicines. Just as the importance of money has grown, so its value seems to
have diminished. The price of imported goods has risen dramatically in the late
1980s as a result of the country's declining foreign exchange position and the
economic reforms encouraged by international agencies (ILO, 1990). Services
are less easily available and are increasingly expensive. For example, Madina
houses one of the three government clinics in Malema chiefdom and villagers
must now pay not only for expensive drugs (under the government 'cost recovery' scheme) but also for the additional money the dispenser must charge to
survive and pay for transport to fetch the chronically-scarce medicines. Similarly, primary education is supposed to be free but parents must pay for books,
uniforms and the 'supplements' that teachers demand to substitute for the
meagre salaries the Ministry frequently fails to pay. Government taxes are low,
but frequently augmented by additional demands from state authorities.[3]
Sierra Leone's deepening recession since the early 1980s has forced everyone to
downgrade their expectations of possible incomes and expenditures.

People's financial dealings and experiences are conditioned not only by their income opportunities and cash needs, but also by the social possibilities and dilemmas that surround the use of money. Initially, I will consider financial issues associated with creating and maintaining kinship and patron–client relations. Then I go on to look at the arrangements between husbands and wives that are now central to 'managing' on a day-to-day basis.

Money, kinship and patron-clientage

In villages around the Gola North reserve a wide range of financial expectations is now associated with social relations of various kinds. These money transfers are not merely moral obligations; they also structure the relations of both power and security. Men have a range of obligations as members of patrilineal descent groups. For instance, they are expected to meet requests to help with family contingencies such as illness, and to contribute to occasions such as members' funeral ceremonies and secret society initiations. Senior members often receive requests from younger relatives for help with school fees, marriage payments, fines and court fees. Caretakers of family tree-crop farms who do not immediately share out the revenue are supposed to use it to 'help' the planters' siblings and children. Women also contribute materially to occasions such as initiations, funerals and naming ceremonies within their natal families. Adult children frequently 'help' their mothers, fathers and guardians with small gifts and financial assistance. Mende expect children to show gratitude and 'goodness' to those who have raised and 'trained' them, and financial contributions have become part of this (Bledsoe, 1990).

Transfers of money are also associated with wider kin relationships. Young men and women can appropriately seek material help from their maternal uncles, either as a person (*kenya*) or as a group (*kenyeisia*), for instance, and commonly thus gain assistance with secondary school fees and economic ventures. The creation and maintenance of marital relationships also imply specific financial duties, extending beyond those between husbands and wives themselves. A wife's parents often demand bridewealth, which today most men try to pay for themselves. This normally includes a substantial immediate cash payment, after which the son-in-law is expected to make periodic gifts to his wife's parents and to assist them in times of difficulty. Husbands are also expected to contribute to a wife's family ceremonies; for example, if one of her parents dies, a son-in-law is supposed to provide a goat at the funeral.

Other financial transfers are associated with patron–client relationships. A patron (*numu wa*) is expected to provide clients with economic assistance (including money to help with court fines, clothes, food, bridewealth, etc.) and political support, in return for rights to the clients' labour, political allegiance and other services. A stranger-father (*hota kɛɛ*) is considered generally responsible for the well-being of a stranger–client, which extends, for example, to assistance with fines and court fees. Money transfers are now central to the acquisition and maintenance of patron status, since dispensing money to kin and others is a way to create ties of indebtedness with them which the giver can recall, whether in labour, other resources or political allegiance. As one man reflected: 'Here in Mende, I would not want you to have more money than me; instead I want to have more than you so that you are always coming to me and asking for things.'

The notion of being 'for' or 'behind' a patron who provides necessary support permeates other social relations, and in this sense kinship and patron–clientship are not easily separated; a senior co-wife, a father or an older sibling may be a patron figure. In conditions of political and economic insecurity socio-political relations of this kind take on greater importance. Modern reasons for people to need patron figures include contacts with higher authorities or schools, support against charges trumped up by neighbours and protection from hunger. Patron–client relations provide durable, though not necessarily egalitarian, social and economic security for clients, and can act as a 'safety net' for the otherwise vulnerable (cf. Richards, 1986 and 1990).

Contributions to group occasions such as funeral ceremonies and secret society initiations are just as important for power and security as are transfers to individuals. Actual or aspiring patrons often contribute especially generously to these since this enhances their reputations and ability to call later on the services and resources of those who attend. For everyone, such contributions affirm an individual's identity as part of a family or village-level group, helping to ensure future access to its support, and rights such as to residence, land and resource use. For instance, a woman usually sustains strong links with her natal family, both as a source of personal support in the short term, to ensure support if her marriage founders, and to assure her rights to land and residence if she later returns to live there, perhaps on widowhood. Women who have married away from their natal homes are helped in this by the Sande society, which supports a woman's rights to make return visits to the place of her initiation.

The modern importance of money to socio-political relations contrasts with a past in which *numu wa* roles were more strongly linked to high status activities involving the high forest. As we know, important patronage roles once accrued to descent-group heads who founded new forest settlements, to *kamajɔ* hunters and to healers – people seen to have specialist knowledge of the high forest and superior capacities to deal with it – as well as to other manipulators of *hale* such as secret society leaders. While these sources of power are still significant, they have diminished in the face of changes in land use and social organisation, at the same time as money-related patronage opportunities have increased. Lending money is an especially important way to create and sustain patron–client networks since the creditor has both direct leverage over the debtor until the loan is repaid, and can take unpaid debts to court, enabling the creditor to extract a fine and enhance their own reputation. These money-based opportunities are more easily available to middle-aged and younger people who, given modern, more individualised forms of production and land use (Chapters 4 and 5), can often build up resources through farming or trade. Increasingly, younger people who have access to money achieve success in the competition for clients. Principal lenders of money in Madina in 1988 included three men under thirty-five years of age and a long-established stranger. A forty-year-old man, of no significant status in 1988 but quietly building up resources through diligent tree-crop farming, was by 1991 commonly regarded as a *numu wa*.

Arguably, the increasing relative importance of money has enhanced women's relative patronage opportunities; yet questions of resource access and control frequently limit women's ability to build up economic resources. Thus in Madina, a few confident women of high-ranking lineages and secret society status are as involved as men in family and village politics. Two other late-middle-aged women have built up resources through tree crops and trade, and now regularly loan money. Most younger women confine their involvement in patron–client type relations to a smaller circle of kin. They find it more difficult to build up the resources needed to attract and keep clients on a larger scale. Furthermore, at least while of childbearing age, a woman is in some respects a legal minor, expected to defer to the authority of a husband or male relative, and this limits women's credibility both as patrons and valuable clients.

Indebtedness is by no means confined to long-term resource-poor villagers, nor is it a permanently reproducing cycle, as fortunes can reverse over relatively short periods (cf. Richards, 1986). Most credit is obtained from those interested in lending to create and sustain patron–client ties. Men often need loans to balance conflicting pulls on their resources: to buy rice during the hungry season, to meet unexpected demands from kin, or to spend on social investment and litigation, a situation that befalls elderly family heads more than younger men because their 'senior' position means they receive a heavy share of unavoidable demands to help with family difficulties. Men commonly take cash loans from village patrons or produce traders, either with an arrangement to repay after a fixed period or, if the debtor is a tree-crop owner, on the agreement that the creditor will take part of his farm in pledge until the sum is repaid. Produce traders also offer loans of a bag of rice in the hungry season, to be repaid with a bag of cocoa at harvest. Outsiders often think such interest rates usurious, but they are less so to Mende who interpret credit transactions as part of networks of patron–client obligations.

Women are often interested in credit for private enterprises (e.g. to pay male labour to brush swamps, and buy inputs to trade) but also to purchase food and clothing for themselves and their own children. Women's access to credit from such sources is limited since they do not usually have tree-crop farms to pledge, and patrons are unwilling to lend to them since they are less desirable clients than men. *Osusu* groups in which credit is extended within small, mutually trusting groups constitute many women's sole credit source, but the amounts are limited, restricting their ability to expand activities such as trade. All these 'informal' credit sources have tended to prove more resilient and appropriate to local social and political conditions than the 'formal' credit schemes that government and donor agencies have introduced to rural Mende areas (Johnny, 1985). Most of the village-level thrift and credit societies established with government support since the 1940s have broken down amidst factional rivalries, while credit schemes associated with large donor-aided Integrated Rural Development Projects have mainly benefited wealthy and politically influential villagers.

Understanding how broad kin and patron-client relations strongly influence the calls on an individual's money and resources is crucial for understanding financial relationships between husbands, wives and children.

MONEY AND MARRIAGE

Financial arrangements within marriage

As cash crops and the bushmeat trade have impinged on direct subsistence production and collection activities, money has become more important to day-to-day provisioning. In the past, many of the economic arrangements relevant to such provisioning revolved around the *mawεε* level of social organisation. But corresponding to changes in the organisation of production and land use (Chapter 4), many financial and food-provisioning arrangements are now associated with a grouping usually consisting of a husband, his wife/wives and unmarried children, perhaps with additional dependents, kin or clients. Equally, single women and men may find themselves financially self-supporting. Thus relations between husbands and wives are now of key importance in day-to-day arrangements over money, and are hence worth considering in their own right. However, this should not be considered a stable trend towards a 'conjugal household'; just as in farming, the degree to which spouses are a unity or separate, and between resource flows to spouses and wider groups of kin and clients, are matters of unresolved tension.

As in most parts of West Africa, there is no notion of a pooled conjugal budget. Mende husbands and wives have always maintained separate income streams and expenditures, whether in cash or kind. Mende have clear ideas about how certain provisioning responsibilities should be divided. A married man should ensure that his wife/wives and children are provided with staple food, by meeting farm-household production expenses and, as is common today, purchasing supplementary rice. He should provide clothing, by purchasing at least one 'double lappa' of cloth for each wife each year. A husband also expects to take responsibility for long-term investments such as house construction. Wives are expected to provide the sauce, purchasing ingredients such as salt and extra vegetables. They meet expenses associated with their private farming and trading activities which, as Chapter 4 showed, have increased as household production has declined, and they meet additional expenses associated with their own children. Women often pay for their children's education.

There are powerful incentives for a man to try to meet his obligations. First, doing so reinforces his image as patron and provider, of 'holder' of dependents, and strategic planner. These images are currently strongly associated with adult masculinity; failing in these duties to wives and dependents implies failing as a man. Second, claims made by a wife in relation to food and clothing have legal backing. She, or her parents, are entitled to issue a court summons against a husband who fails to meet them. A fine can be levied, and if the case leads eventually to divorce, the wife is supposed to receive the greater share of divided properties. Cases that have occurred in the area give husbands who repeatedly fail to meet their basic obligations a realistic reason to fear that their wives will leave them. However, neither court summons nor separation are as common as might be expected.

There is a range of more ambiguously divided expenditures. These include relatively new expenditures for which there is little precedent, such as clinic medicines, kerosene and imported consumer goods. Ambiguity can also arise where cash is used to meet responsibilities once met in kind. For instance, men's and women's responsibilities for palm-oil provisioning are relatively clearcut when associated with the division of product rights in a production process (Chapter 6). But responsibilities are less clearcut when oil is bought with money that either a husband or a wife could provide. As money becomes increasingly important, responsibilities have become divided more in relation to money flow than to item; men tend to take responsibility for bulk purchases and long-term needs, which suits their more 'lumpy' incomes, and women use their repetitively acquired incomes, including small forest-related sources, for smaller purchases and day-to-day needs – which can nevertheless have long-term implications, as in the case of education. In this context the quantity in which commodities are purchased affects the clarity of rights and responsibilities over food-provisioning. Men usually expect to meet their food purchase obligations by buying rice by the bag and palm oil by the four gallon tin. Such bulk purchases are also the most cost-effective during the early part of the year. If further purchase becomes necessary in the hungry season, limited cash availability, the expense and the scarcity of these commodities usually means that they must be bought cup-by-cup (rice) or pint-by-pint (palm oil). Equally, hungry season staples such as cassava are also purchased in small quantities as needed.

Responsibility for these purchases made little by little (*klo-klo*) is more ambiguous, and men are sometimes able to redefine them as 'small things' (*haŋka mumuisia*) which are appropriate for women to provide. When one husband described expenditure responsibilities, he said: 'I buy rice and oil, and leave the rest to my wives.' Yet this referred only to his purchase of a bag and kerosene tin of each, not to the repeated small quantities that his wives were buying throughout August, September and October.

Currently, when either men or women contribute towards these ambiguous expenditures, it is understood as 'help' (*gbɔ*): as a voluntary contribution rather than a duty. In some senses they are less 'voluntary' for women than for men, both because women cook, and must, in the last instance, make sure there is food in the pot, and because women bear more direct and immediate responsibilities for children's welfare. Mende attribute roles to both spouses in the upbringing and training (*makɛ*) of any children in their care.[4] But it is women who perform the bulk of day-to-day childcare, and wives who, in polygynous marriages, must defend their welfare and interests *vis-à-vis* co-wives' children. In this respect women's concerns should not be considered as merely 'domestic'. Women are especially concerned that their children should advance, socially and economically, not least because of the security that contributions from well-placed children can bring them in later life. Fosterage and marriage into important local families and apprenticeships to hunters and Islamic teachers through which socially and ritually valued knowledge is acquired are among the ways in which parents seek to assist their children's advancement. Today, some see education, and the knowledge of English and Krio, and the access to urban jobs and contacts that it may bring, as an important key to their children's future. Women are often concerned that their children's school fees should be paid regardless of their husbands' opinions. Thus like men, women have long-term concerns and ways to deal with them.

Amidst these ideals and ambiguities, conjugal financial arrangements are very varied and subject to a great deal of more or less explicit bargaining. Not only are there tensions over who should provide for which joint needs, both husbands and wives must reconcile these claims on scarce resources with their range of expenditures on kin and clients. Table 8.1a and b and Table 8.2 illustrate how some of these dilemmas were resolved in practice among the seven groups of husbands and wives followed as case studies during 1988. They show the modern importance of the purchase of basic foodstuffs, the varied ways in which 'ambiguous' expenditures were divided, and that in some cases wives even took over supposedly well-defined male responsibilities such as the purchase of clothing.

While husband–wife conflicts over money are not infrequent, people's financial relations vary. Mende distinguish harmonious marriages from those in which there is nothing but palaver over economic affairs. Personal issues

TABLE 8.1: Husbands' and wives' contributions to food expenditures.
(Source of supply to a sample of meals, seven households A–G)

(a) STAPLE FOOD

	Farm-household production	Percentage of meals in which source was:		Obtained by wife Rice (cup) or cassava
		Purchased by husband		
		Rice (bag)	Rice (cup)	
A	19	—	33	48
B	50	—	25	25
C	100	—	—	—
D	—	20	30	50
E	14	36	21	29
F	39	13	—	48
G	26	13	—	61

(b) PALM OIL

	Own production	Percentage of meals in which source was:		Obtained by wife
		Purchased by husband		
		By tin	By pint	
A	33	6	22	39
B	—	—	54	46
C	—	100	—	—
D	—	—	56	44
E	—	69	—	31
F	39	11	—	50
G	—	13	—	87

TABLE 8.2: Husbands' and wives' contributions to non-food expenditures.
(Seven households A–G during one year; H=husband purchased most or all; W=wife(s) purchased most or all; H–W=both purchased)

	Wife's clothing	Children's clothing	Kerosene	Soap	Medicine
A	W	W	H–W	W	H–W
B	W	—	H–W	W	W
C	H	H	H–W	H–W	H–W
D	H	H	H	H–W	H
E	H	—	W	W	H–W
F	H	W	W	W	H–W
G	—	—	W	W	H–W

and characteristics are undoubtedly influential: people's generosity and tolerance vary, and some spouses are manifestly more affectionate, concerned
for each other's welfare and interested in each other's opinions than others.
But these are difficult bases from which to generalise, and it is important
not to obscure in personal questions the more 'structural' issues that underlie
such differences.

Spouses' relative ages and stages in the 'developmental cycle of domestic groups' (Goody, 1958) are more general sources of difference. A young man who acquires a first wife may be highly concerned to support her well but have difficulty in doing so, especially if he himself still depends on a senior relative's support. Young, single wives often receive little 'help' from their husbands, therefore, and are among the women most concerned to retain ties with their natal kin for security. As both partners gain in age and resources, they become more easily able to fulfil their respective responsibilities, so mature, monogamous marriages are most likely to appear 'cooperative'. Husbands and wives may pool resources for particular projects (one couple agreed to put all the proceeds from a jointly constructed fish-trap fence towards palm oil, for example), and bargain explicitly over the fulfilment of ambiguous responsibilities: for instance, each agreeing to pay half the cost of medicines for a sick child. The addition of a further wife little disturbs arrangements if the new wife is much younger. The new wife defers to the senior wife, who continues to manage resources with her husband.

When a polygynous marriage involves several wives of similar age, a husband is likely to restrict his contributions to the minimum. To avoid overwhelming demands on his resources and possibly provoking co-wife jealousies, a husband often leaves his wives to furnish virtually everything (beyond basic food needs) for their own children. In these circumstances, and especially when individual wives also cook for their own children and pay for their education, the relevant 'unit' for much of day-to-day life is an individual woman and her own natural or fostered children.

Both older widows who re-marry younger husbands, and women from high-ranking descent groups who are married 'up' to by incoming strangers, have greater authority and experience conjugal finances quite differently. One such wife in Madina controlled her husband's tree-crop revenue as well as her own trade earnings, using this money to organise and plan for all their food and clothing needs. The economic position of older women is further improved by their diminished responsibility to support young children (although Mende grandmothers commonly foster children for younger relatives) and by help from their adult children.

Relative wealth also influences financial arrangements. Wealthier couples seem to experience less tension over the possible directions of resource allocation. Mende often say that poor households are more prone to palaver. Overall resource scarcity can provoke a husband into making only minimal contributions, even sometimes failure to provide staple food; and many wives are not tolerant of such failings. As Whitehead (1990) argues, impoverishment in interaction with the terms of the 'conjugal contract' is often manifested in gender conflict in Africa.

These tensions and variations were especially obvious during two recent 'shocks' to Madina's economy. First, in May 1988 about 30 per cent of the married men in the village departed to dig diamonds just when hungry season rice purchases usually begin. They mostly kept their cash to meet their personal needs while at the digging camp, claiming that they would buy rice as soon as they found diamonds. As their wives had predicted from the outset, however, most men neither found diamonds nor bought rice, and women were left to buy food themselves throughout the hungry season. Only a few elderly women succeeded in keeping their husbands' resources directed securely towards hungry season needs, either by persuading them not to take part, or by insisting that financial help was given on frequent return visits to the village. Second, in 1990 the influx of refugees and returned family members from Liberia imposed a heavy burden in feeding and hosting 'strangers'. Although women and men shared the general view that this was both necessary and socially and politically valuable, husbands and wives often disagreed over whether food and money should be given out or retained in particular instances (Leach, 1992a). For example, one wife was angry when her husband refused to buy rice and clothes for their children, yet subsequently purchased food for four refugees who were helping him prospect for diamonds.

Tensions and variations in direct financial transfers from husbands to wives are similar to those affecting marital expenditure negotiations. It is considered appropriate for men to give the women who cook for them 'chop money' (mɛhɛ kɔpɔ) to 'help' with the purchase of essential food items, especially during the hungry season when food prices peak. A man might also give a gift of produce or money during dry season crop sales to the women (e.g. wives, daughters, sisters or nieces) who have worked on his cocoa and coffee during the year. Third, men occasionally contribute to their wives or female relatives to assist their private activities (e.g. paying swamp farm labour or the cost of her transport to visit kin) or in association with kinship obligations and family ceremonies. Such contributions are irregular, unreliable and not obligatory. They have become symbols of affection, whereas making regular contributions ('payments') of money to women is socially sensitive (Todd, 1971).

Elsewhere, the extent to which men and women variously gloss similar redistributive flows as 'redistribution' or 'payment for domestic services' is a moot point. Guyer shows that for the Beti of Cameroon women construe the second interpretation while men keep their contributions discretionary, and 'justify their right to be erratic providers of cash' by emphasising the first (1984a: 105). In Madina, all flows of money within marriage are considered as gifts (kɔ), emphasising that the relationship is not bound by ties of contract. Men are anxious not to give money regularly, saying, for example: 'If I always gave them money they would be always be panting behind me,' or 'I don't give my wives money every day. If I did there would be none left. I just give it when I please.' They claim that women are uncontrolled in their demands for material resources, just as in their talk and sexuality (Chapter 7).

The ideational complex that links tongue with clitoris and clitoridectomy with restraint seems to underlie this notion of female behaviour. Men consider it advisable to protect their finances either by giving only occasionally, or by clearly demarcating boundaries between when they will and will not give. A man who gives liberally often declares a boundary around 'special circumstances', claiming, for example, that he is giving money regularly to a wife to buy food in July and August 'because it is the hungry season'.

Polygynous men also find it difficult to give money to their wives lest the act be interpreted as favouritism. A husband can justify more regular contributions of 'chop money' to his senior wife (*nyaha wa*) than to her junior mates, because she is more responsible for purchasing ingredients for joint meals. Senior wives often present themselves as restrained and reasonable in their demands, emphasising their status differences from their co-wives. Such women often help manage their husbands' resources to mutual benefit. A wife's village networks can help a husband to buy rice in the hungry season, for example. Usually the only rice then available for sale is that which other wives have appropriated from their farm-household stores, and which can therefore be obtained only through private arrangements between women. A husband often rewards his wife for such services with additional financial contributions to her private endeavours.

Husbands and wives do not know the full extent of each other's resources and expenditures. It is accepted that men and women keep their financial affairs private. While this can lead to ambiguity and suspicion, too much openness is also thought to invite problems. Wives often suspect husbands to be withholding resources, spending them on co-wives, or depleting them unwisely such as on 'unnecessary' litigation or social investments. Keeping cash stores and flows private is considered to maintain marital harmony partly because such flows remain hidden, rather than being brought into the open where they might invite palaver. Keeping finances private also helps people control the boundaries and directions of resource flow. Both husbands and wives can avoid certain expenditures by claiming that they have no money. Women are especially concerned that their crop sale and trade earnings will be drawn into expenditure on 'joint' needs by their husbands and co-wives if they are known to possess them. Similarly, privacy helps control the financial give-and-take with kin. While men and women often perceive social and political advantages in giving money to kin, in certain contexts such claims can be an unwanted drain on resources and public knowledge of one's cash resources invites such unwanted claims. If people must 'store' money, they do so privately. Local saving and investment strategies, which avoid cash storage, partly respond to the need for control over cash flow. Wives treat *osusu* savings groups partly as a way to save money safely away from husbands' and co-wives' claims, and they also store much of their 'money' not as cash but as resources which can be exchanged for it as and when needed, which enhances their control. For example, a woman might sell groundnuts to buy palm oil, and gardens and intercropped upland farms are treated as stores of crops to be fetched and sold as required.

Financial arrangements and marriage

The tensions over conjugal financial relationships associated with poverty have implications for gendered attitudes to marriage and its stability. While some women whose husbands have money are financially assisted, and some senior women are well-placed to gain access to their husbands' resources, other women, for reasons we have discussed, are not. The day-to-day economic situation of such married women may be little different from that of single women. Many resent this state of affairs, which they perceive as eroding a once-just balance. As one wife emphatically complained: 'The Mende men here do not help us at all.' Another complained that 'X is bad, he will not give me cloth, he will not buy food.' Wives of plantation owners especially resent being expected to work for their husbands for so little in return. In the past, they say, men 'had the plantations for us', in the sense that they supported their wives from the revenue. Observing current husband-wife relationships, elderly women reflect on past days when: 'Our husbands held us well.' Now, they say: 'All the good ones have died.'

Even when husbands' failings constitute a clearcut infringement of conjugal obligations, it is fairly rare for a woman to initiate a major 'house palaver' or summon them to the village court – a process that might end in divorce. First, wives often see little hope of upholding their rights against the interests of their husband and his family. Political influence partly determines the outcomes of court cases, and the village court is dominated by middle-aged and elderly men. A woman is likely to win only if she has strong family backing – which she may lack, especially if she has married out. One woman explained that she could not summons her husband in Madina as she is only a 'small child', i.e. a politically unimportant person; but that he responded quickly to threats from her elder brothers during a visit to her natal village. The Sande society will also support a woman's rights in court on occasion, although such support is often biased to women living in their natal villages, under the protection of the particular Sande elders who initiated them (Cunningham, 1991). Second, most wives lack the resources to be confident of meeting fines ensuing from village court proceedings; in recent village history only women who have amassed significant resources from tree crops or trade have successfully divorced their husbands. Third, women are often under parental pressure not to press for divorce. If parents have received bridewealth, they will have to refund it, while there is risk of losing rights to the couple's children, which is of concern to parents as well as to the woman herself.

Husbands face dilemmas. On the one hand, failing to support wives and children reflects badly on them, but on the other, many are glad to be assisted by wives who take over responsibility for day-to-day needs. For this, men value increases in their wives' incomes, but fear that wives may become financially more powerful than themselves; that, as one man put it, 'my wife will pass me'. Men fear that such wives will become disrespectful and neglect them. In response, husbands and others often 'look badly' on a woman who does too well, for example in business, saying that she is behaving inappropriately like a wealthy, 'gentrified' person (*kpatɛmɔ*).

Similar dilemmas affect relationships between younger and older people. Parents often complain that their adult children no longer help them, even when they have assisted their upbringing and marriage arrangements; that they are ungrateful and disrespectful. Perhaps elderly people have always felt this way. Yet adult children are now in a bind, struggling to support their own dependents as well as to fulfil obligations to parents and in-laws. Parents are also in a bind, keen that adult children should fulfil obligations to their spouses and children, but also concerned that they themselves get less help as a result. Some parents seek a resolution to this dilemma in encouraging their children to seek urban marriages and jobs, hoping that this will bring economic as well as social success. But today visits and remittances from urban-based children tend to be rare and small, partly because life in Sierra Leone's urban areas is also an economic struggle. This encourages other elderly people to consider urban-based children even more disrespectful than rural, and to prefer their children to remain nearby.

Amidst these dilemmas, both unassisted married women and single women cope by relying heavily on their own crop sales and trade, on networks and exchanges with kin and other women, and on a range of 'covert' strategies. These coping strategies, partly necessitated by changes in resource use on the forest edge, in turn involve using forest resources in new ways.

STRATEGIES FOR MANAGING
Food receipts from networks

Women are involved in exchange networks to obtain a wide range of food items. Earlier chapters have discussed these exchanges in relation to natural resource-using processes and product rights, but they are also of great importance in coping with food shortfalls. First, individuals who visit kin in another village, or return from such a visit or a day at market, should bring a 'greeting present' (*njoyo*), or receive one (*magbatɛ*). These gifts are often food items, and they commonly include wild plant and animal products. Second, women can request foodstuffs from other women in town, and the early evening round of visits to other kitchens to assemble missing ingredients before cooking is an integral part of women's lives. Most women maintain a flexible circle of female kin and friends whom they can approach, expecting

TABLE 8.3: Food-provisioning through gifts and networks.
(Sample of meals, seven households A–G. Includes both cultivated and wild
products)

| | Percentage of meals in which item was obtained as a gift: | | | | |
	Staple	Oil	Vegetables	Meat/fish	Salt/maggi
A	33	6	28	14	10
B	21	—	22	67	—
C	13	8	28	78	40
D	36	32	36	—	29
E	40	8	40	40	—
F	18	5	18	29	10
G	8	—	21	—	13

to return the favour at some future time. Sometimes, women deliberately
build up the number of favours owed to them, 'investing' in the network,
by repeatedly giving to or doing things for other women, so that they are
well-placed to call in their debts when they need a particular item. The
importance of fishing and wild plant collection to women lies partly in the
inputs they provide to these networks of gift exchange. Certain women, by
virtue of age, kinship status and moral leverage over younger relatives,
receive considerably more than they give. One senior wife, for example, met
a large proportion of her palm oil needs in 1988 through gifts from the
trading supply of her daughter. Table 8.3 indicates the relative importance of
such gifts in women's day-to-day meal provisioning.

'Covert' strategies

Many women in Madina, both single and married, use 'covert' strategies to
acquire resources. First, they subsist partly on favours from lovers. Second,
they obtain and sell resources from their husbands and male kin without
explicit authorisation. Literature on gender and resources rarely considers
such 'covert' resource acquisitions, perhaps because ethnocentric biases con-
demn these apparently 'illegitimate' activities on moral grounds. However,
the activities appear differently if they are viewed in a cultural and socio-
political context, and in the light of the dilemmas of daily economic life.

In Chapter 5 I discussed the discreet appropriation of cocoa and coffee
from the tree-crop farms of husbands and male kin as a way for women and
young men to resist and compensate for the lack of rewards for their labour.
Women also treat the sale of appropriated crops as a substitute for absent
receipts from men, and as a means to resist a situation they resent without
openly challenging it. As one woman said: 'Clothes, soap and medicine for
our children – if we don't steal how will we manage these things? the
Mende men here do nothing.'

Although particular instances may be cleverly concealed, men are usually aware that their wives and dependents take their resources. However, they are prepared to 'forget' (*lema*) – i.e. pass no comment on – these doings, for several reasons. First, the anathema of payment (*pawa*) as a form of transaction between close kin seems to imply, by opposition, relatively high tolerance for 'taking undercover'. Men consider it a means to allow dependents some reward without engaging in inappropriate 'contracts'. Indeed, the relationships within which people tolerate 'stealing', and the styles of language with which they describe it, suggest that it is an appropriate manifestation of social closeness. Both women and men refer to it as *huma* (theft) or *kafa hinda* (trickery business), but only jokingly.

Second, men acknowledge that the expenditure responsibilities that they offload on to their wives often exceed their wives' financial means. They claim to tolerate 'theft' as it is more convenient than facing wives' incessant demands for money, or risking co-wife jealousy. As one man said: 'I would rather they stole than were always behind me for money'; and another: 'Of course she steals; that is how she buys our palm oil!' Third, 'stealing' also seems to resolve tensions between the directions of men's income flows. Women, who appropriate a proportion of tree-crop revenue for subsistence needs, keep this safe from diversion into men's political activities. While men might consider this to counter their interests, their awareness that some revenue has been safely appropriated also 'lets them off the hook' of concern to balance marital versus wider expenditures. Men successfully maintain the rhetoric of being 'in charge', while allowing their wives quietly to manage operational budgets. Equally, men acknowledge that their senior wives' appropriation and sale of household rice can have mutual benefits. A wife's rice sales secure her place in female networks which her husband too might depend on if rice needs unexpectedly to be purchased for consumption or seed.

On several occasions during 1988 women asked me to write letters on their behalf to their lovers in distant towns, to request financial assistance with farming or trade. Close female friends regularly confided to me sums of money they had received from lovers. Mende strongly associate 'loving' (*pue, pue gbua*; extra-marital sex) with material gifts (Lahai, 1971: 55), so involvement in an affair offers a significant source of economic benefit to a single or married woman.

Gifts depend on who, and where, a lover is. Some women receive small, repeated gifts from a lover in the same village (an unmarried man or another woman's husband), whereas those involved with one or several men in larger towns receive larger, more occasional gifts in response to visits or written requests. Wives sometimes acquire lovers among the temporary strangers who visit forest villages for activities such as hunting, or among the diggers at local diamond camps, which they visit on Fridays under the guise of doing 'market business'. Quantitative data is obviously difficult to obtain, but cases suggest that while a woman is involved in an affair her receipts from her lover are likely to exceed her receipts from her husband, and perhaps from trade and crop sales.

In some circumstances husbands consent to, and even connive in, their wives' love affairs. These can be socio-politically advantageous, since a man can acquire his wife's lover as a client by taking him to court for adultery and then agreeing to forgo the charges (cf. Bledsoe, 1980b). Husbands are also prepared to 'forget' (*lema*) their wives' affairs when these bring routine economic benefits. One husband expressed his knowledge candidly when, in the *naïveté* of early fieldwork, I talked to women about their incomes in his presence: 'You shouldn't ask my wives questions like that in front of me because they get money from their boyfriends!' A husband accepts that a lover's contributions usually go straight into expenditures on food and house-hold items and thus partially release him from the burden of providing from his own resources and dealing with co-wife jealousies. He may also acknow-ledge the useful labour a wife's lover gives her. When toleration is in mutual interests, both men and women refer to lovers as friend (*ndiamɔ*), a conveni-ently ambiguous and non-committal term since it is also a word for friend in the non-sexual sense. Men avoid places where women are known to discuss their lovers, such as while fishing, harvesting rice and in their kitchens and sleeping houses: places and activities that importantly reinforce solidarity among women.

Men do not always wish to connive in or ignore either crop-stealing or wives' extra-marital affairs, however. They can construe crop theft as damage to their property, an offence punishable in court, and they can construe wives' affairs as an infringement of their exclusive rights to their wives' sexual services, underwritten by customary marriage law and the Sande society (Bledsoe, 1984). They sometimes wish to do so, whether because of jealousy, personal reasons or resource control. The choice of whether to discover – to draw the boundary between forgotten and openly illegal act – is a powerful form of leverage for husbands and patrons. Women therefore need to 'hide' their activities from their husbands, not because the activities are, in themselves, illegitimate, but to keep control in their own hands.

Women's attitudes towards their husbands' lovers tend also to centre on material concerns, but to be more directly negative. A married woman often fears that if her husband takes a lover he will deplete family resources by giving her money and expensive clothes. Some securely married women therefore hold in disrepute the young single women who pose the greatest threat as potential lovers of their husbands. Nevertheless, most women support and assist each other's 'covert' activities, and have developed a range of sophisticated ways to do so. For example, they organise crop-harvesting and processing activities among themselves to assist crop appropri-ation. Women who share 'big houses' (*pɛlɛ wa*) assist each other to meet lovers; the elderly women in the house recognise the knock of a suspicious husband and refuse to let him enter. Many women prefer *pɛlɛ wa* residence for this reason, as well as for the female company and solidarity it offers. Many husbands disapprove of it for the same reasons. Today it is mainly widows, unmarried and separated women and co-wives who sleep in the *pɛlɛ wa*, the latter taking three-day turns to sleep in their husband's room. Single wives sleep with their husbands every night, while men who can afford to build their own houses prefer their wives to sleep in a separate room inside it.

FOOD AND COOKING

Considering the use of money as a resource highlights aspects of gender relations relevant to forest-resource use. On the one hand, different women's and men's social and economic needs to use and exchange money help to shape their interests in the forest-resource using activities that can generate it. On the other hand, cash transfers are integral to creating and maintaining the kinship, patron–clientage and marital relations that people draw on in forest-resource management and use. The same is true of food. Whereas the discussion of food in this and earlier chapters up to now has concentrated on the acquisition of food items, the focus is now on gender issues in cooking and using cooked food.

Cooking

Cooking (*ngili*) is one of the most gender-exclusive tasks in Mende life. People talk of it as 'women's own work' (*nyahanga ti nda yɛngɛ*). As a child, a girl learns to cook from her female relatives, and Mende ways are re-emphasised in the Sande bush school. It is acceptable for young, unmarried men sometimes to cook for themselves, but a mature man does so only when no women are present, such as while hunting or diamond-digging.

In the past, women often cooked communally as a *pɛlɛ wa* group to feed all the members of a large *mawɛɛ*. Today, a woman's daily cooking obligations are to her husband, children and – in the agricultural season – to a (small) farm-household. She feeds her own children and ensures that her husband and his dependents or clients receive at least one meal a day. She cooks for visiting kin, guests and for day labourers on the household farm. The main rice meal of the day is usually cooked in the evening (*kpɔkɔ bɛi*, evening rice). Farm workers are fed at midday (*kɔndɔ*, a meal for labourers), and women may cook additionally, or reheat leftovers, in the morning (*ngɛnda mɛhɛ*, morning food). Modern cooking arrangements are reflected in expectations about kitchen-building. Whereas women once cooked in large, open buildings associated with their large sleeping houses, today a husband must build a separate kitchen for his wives. Most kitchens are lockable thatched buildings of wattle and daub.

Men and women almost always eat from separate dishes. Between June

PLATE 8.1: Kitchens are a preferred place in the village for women of all
generations to socialise and care for children, as well as a locus for cooking,
processing and storage activities.

and November they often do so in the farm hut. When in the village,
women and children usually eat in the kitchen, and carry the men's food,
neatly covered, for them to consume in their houses or when they are
working. Withholding food is an effective statement of a wife's dissatisfaction
with day-to-day marital relations, and a common form of leverage through
which women seek – and often succeed – to influence their husbands'
behaviour.

Cooking and eating arrangements are not confined to a regular 'household' or 'cooking pot' unit; they are varied and flexible, as they respond to
a variety of social and economic interests and expectations. First, people
expect to share food with a wider circle of kin and friends. Mende consider
eating 'one food' (*mɛhɛ yila*, i.e. food cooked and/or served in a single pot)
to express love and friendship, and refusal of offered food signals a broken
relationship. Mende commensality is only ever among peers, however; father
and son, husband and wife or host and stranger, would hardly ever eat from
one pot. Anyone who is dishing out food or eating is expected to call a *mu
mɛhɛ mɛ o!* (let us eat) to others nearby. These expectations diminish only at
the height of the hungry season, when people cook privately in their farm
huts and accept that others' food may be too scarce to distribute. In town,
there are two flexible food-sharing loci at virtually every meal. Women
invite women from nearby kitchens to eat from their pot, and men share
with other men. Four brothers who shared a house, for example, habitually

ate together four times each evening from the pans brought by each of their wives in succession, rather than eat their 'own' rice alone.

Second, in polygynous marriages, women meet their joint responsibilities in a wide variety of ways. It is considered ideal for co-wives to cook together in a single pot (*fɛi yakpe*), as this indicates their cooperative and cordial relations. Co-wives who cook together explain that: 'We do it through love' and that: 'We are all one.' Only a few uphold this ideal, however. When there are large status differentials between the women involved, domestic arrangements are often hierarchical. A senior wife often devolves cooking tasks on to the youngest wife, perhaps explaining that she is 'training' her. Elderly women offload tasks on to their daughters or daughters-in-law. Co-wives who anticipate quarrels over casual arrangements often take turns to cook, either on a weekly basis or according to each wife's turn to sleep with their husband. In the latter arrangement, a wife is the responsible food giver just when she is best positioned to press her personal interests with her husband. Wives may compete for a husband's favour by attempting to provide larger, better quality meals than their co-wives. In certain other co-wife groups, each wife cooks separately, so the regular 'cooking unit' consists of a single co-wife together with her own children. Each wife expects to feed her husband, who may therefore receive several platefuls at each meal. But even when co-wives cook in unity or turns, a wife often wants to cook separately and additionally for her own children to give them extra food or to prepare weaning foods for the young.

Third, women also make inter-kitchen arrangements. Many of these are irregular, egalitarian and friendly. On a particular day, friends from different kitchens might decide to cook jointly in order to spend time together and pool ingredients to mutual advantage. Other arrangements are longer term, and less egalitarian. For example, one senior wife encouraged her married daughter to come from her husband's compound to cook with her every evening during the hungry season, to feed both husbands. The older woman thereby gained access to the rice that her daughter's husband had bought for his wives; she was, by this point in the hungry season, otherwise eating only cassava. In managing their day-to-day food-provisioning roles, therefore, women often move between the kitchens of a number of conjugal units other than their own.

Fourth, women pursue a wide range of individual interests through food and cooking. The distribution of cooked food forms part of the coping strategies that they now resort to more than ever. Women often use cooked food to reciprocate directly for goods given or services performed, sending a pan of evening rice to a female friend who has helped her during the day (by looking after a child or helping with farm work, for instance), or a man who has performed an unpaid task for her, such as bringing fuelwood. By giving out cooked food a woman can build up the number of people who owe her favours, which she can call in when she needs them. Women expect to cook for members of their own families who visit, and value this to maintain supportive links with them. Gifts of food are also important in establishing and maintaining extra-marital affairs. A woman who is 'loving' with a man in the village generally keeps a pan of rice in her kitchen after serving out and sending her husband's food to him, which she later shares with her lover.

As cooks, women are entitled to relative autonomy to distribute food as they wish. A man who is over-inquisitive about whom his wives are giving to is considered to invite palaver. Most men therefore refrain from interference, and leave the control of daily cooked food budgets to their wives. Women's opportunities to pursue personal food distribution interests are affected by their positions in co-wife hierarchies, however. The head wife, who oversees cooking arrangements, can more easily arrange to cook herself when she has additional interests in mind, whereas younger wives are often more restricted in pursuing their own food-giving projects by cooking arrangements, and hesitant to do so under the watchful, and potentially disapproving, eyes of their seniors.

Women can sometimes reorganise kitchen-sharing arrangements to suit their preferences rather than modern marriage-based ideals. A wife sometimes prefers to share a kitchen with a friend or female relative than with her co-wives. Many women consider individual kitchen space to be highly advantageous, as it allows private cooking interests, tool and crop storage, and socialising to be pursued undisturbed, and some co-wives consider separate kitchens the only possible way to avoid constant argument. A senior wife or elderly woman can often persuade her husband or a male relative to build her a new kitchen or divide the existing one. Failing this, a woman can move out of a conjugal or mother–daughter kitchen to share with another woman, or cook in one kitchen but store crops and spend time in another. Table 8.4 presents a static snapshot of the kitchen arrangements in Madina in 1988; in reality they are fluid and dynamic.

Women do not confine their kitchen-based activities to single kitchens, however. They carry out a wide range of domestic activities beyond cooking itself there, including crop-processing, tool-mending and childcare, and kitchens are women's main place for daytime talk. Since they spend several hours in and around their kitchens every day, they establish constant, intimate ties of proximity with women who have kitchens nearby. These ties often become the basis of informal cooperation in tasks such as food-processing and crop-drying, agricultural labour and savings groups, and exchanges of food ingredients and vegetables.

TABLE 8.4: Kitchen-sharing arrangements, 1988.

Composition	No. of kitchens
Conjugal unit only:	
Monogamous	10
Polygamous	8
Co-wife alone	8
2 conjugal units	8
Conjugal unit and single woman	7
Co-wife and single woman	4
Single woman alone	2
2 or more single women:	
Mother and daughter(s)	4
Other	5

Cooking for ceremonies

As well as having day-to-day significance, cooking and the distribution of cooked food are also important to wider kinship and socio-political relations, and to the affirmation of different levels of 'community'. Food is a crucial element in the political hospitality offered to strangers and guests. It is important to welcoming potential clients, a meaning which offers of food to refugees from Liberia often took on in 1990. It is also considered important to feed visiting patrons and influential contacts, as the large plates of rice lavished on visiting officials from development and conservation projects demonstrate. Food-sharing, usually from huge communal platters, is also a central part of ceremonies associated with funerals, initiations, sacrifices (*sara*) to ancestors, and communal labour. Many of these activities are concentrated in the dry season, when food is most plentiful. Sharing food at initiation ceremonies can reinforce gender solidarity. When consumed in association with funerals and family sacrifices, food-sharing emphasises the contextual unity of family members. 'Community' at village level is emphasised by food-oriented arrangements in which the whole village takes part, such as in association with village-level ancestral sacrifices or communal labour for village projects.

Cooking for such occasions is usually the privilege of women of contextually high status. For example, the women's leader is responsible for organising food for town labour groups (*ta yɛngɛ*) and visitors to the whole village. Senior women organise cooking for their natal kin during family sacrifices, and elder sisters cook for their brothers at funeral ceremonies. Cooking for major social events involves such women in resource uses and decisions well beyond the confines of their own homes. Town-level duties involve negotiations with the chiefs over arrangements and to obtain rice from the village store, and with townspeople to collect prearranged food and financial contributions to the occasion. Family-level duties involve a woman in decision-making with descent group elders, and both levels involve recruiting junior town or family members to assist.

CONCLUSION

People draw on a wide range of social relations in the acquisition, control and use of money and food resources. This makes it impossible to understand the local economy by focusing on particular social units, such as kitchens or 'households'. In as much as these exist, important activities and relationships constantly cross-cut their boundaries (cf. Guyer and Peters, 1987; Leach, 1991b). Nor is it possible to understand women's use of money and food by isolating current female activities for analysis, as some studies of women's socio-economic and environmental roles do. Instead, people are embedded in nexuses of specific opportunities and obligations associated with kinship, friendship and patron–client relations, and their experiences depend on their ability to manage and draw on these effectively. This applies equally to different women and men, although there is considerable variation in their needs and in the claims and relations on which they are able to draw. In the context of the land-use changes on the northern edge of Gola North, I have drawn attention, for example, to the growing disjunctions between women's limited cash incomes and high expenditure needs, and to the increasing ambiguity surrounding men's provisioning responsibilities and contributions. Whereas older women derive support from their adult children and some wives are assisted by natal kin living nearby, other women cope by investing on their own accounts in subsistence activities and social networks, and by resorting to strategies such as covert resource appropriation in the ambiguous spaces between what is and is not publicly acceptable.

These social networks and patron–client relations are central both to people's security and to their acquisition of wealth and status. The monetary economy is not leading to the disintegration of these 'wealth in people' relations; instead, money is increasingly an input to and medium for them. Money has, however, altered the opportunities for certain groups of people to acquire independence from others' control, and acquire clients for themselves. Financial acumen now rests alongside high-status forest-related activities as a means to attract and keep followers, and this has added to tensions in village life, whether between older and younger people or men and women.

This chapter has shown how the resource-using activities presented in earlier chapters are currently integrated within monetary and consumptive relations. Annual-cropping, tree-cropping, and wild plant and animal use are all at least partly oriented towards acquiring money and food, and certain aspects of these become clearer when seen in terms of people's concerns over 'managing'. Current socio-economic struggles shape such recent resource-use practices as hunting for the market, sales of local timber and non-timber forest products, and the cultivation of cassava, groundnuts and vegetables. Money and food-use also shape (and are shaped by) natural resource management relations, as when patrons make claims on their financially indebted clients' agricultural labour, or when sharing food at a family sacrifice to ancestors reinforces people's common membership of a family (*mbonda*) group and their acceptance of its head's authority, of importance in land and other resource-tenure arrangements.

Means of 'managing' which reduce villagers' direct dependence on local forest-resource use have also been suggested in this chapter. These include income-earning opportunities that do not draw on forest resources, such as in trade, and the substitution of imported food and goods for items produced using forest resources. They include 'migrating' economically, if not physically, away from the local forest-based economy, such as by securing remittances from urban contacts, by fosterage and by educating children. They also include involvement with non-local people to use forest resources in new ways, such as in diamond-digging, commercial hunting to supply long-distance bushmeat markets, and employment in logging companies. The balance between these various sources of livelihood, and the kinds of resource management involved in each, play a major role in shaping current and future pressures on the forest and forest-edge environments. In the conclusion we shall see some of the ways that Gola forest villagers reflect on such alternatives and their implications for forest futures which are at once social and environmental.

9

CONCLUSIONS:
FOREST RESOURCES, FOREST FUTURES

Women's and men's lives in the Gola forest area have changed considerably over the last few decades, as resource-management practices have intersected with local and wider processes of socio-economic change. Yet amidst this dynamism, and across the diverse resource-use situations considered in Chapters 4 to 8, some common themes recur. Both the continuities and the changes in this Mende analysis have implications that extend well beyond the Gola forest area, not least into the realms of policy discussions concerning people-oriented conservation and gender and the environment. It is my concern, in this conclusion, to draw out these themes and implications. I begin with specific substantive and analytical issues, and move on to examine some specific conservation and rural development interventions in this light, focusing on those already tried or considered in Sierra Leone. But in the end I shall argue that conservationists must also engage with local people at a more general level, in terms of the idioms within which continuity, change and the future of forest life are locally debated.

RECURRING THEMES

The importance to local subsistence of bush fallow, rather than high forest, has been a persistent theme of earlier chapters. Whether for agricultural production or in obtaining useful wild plant and animal products, Mende make most regular use of environments already 'captured' and managed within a rotational bush-fallow cycle on upland or swampland, or incorporated into long-term use as plantations or gardens. Much non-timber forest product collection takes place in conjunction with agricultural activity, in cultivated or fallowed places managed to enhance the availability of such products. Many of the products that Mende value derive from common farmbush species, from plants that readily colonise farm sites, and from animals which are crop pests. It is farmbush resources whose management and use dominates day-to-day socio-economic life; where tenure and ecology are skilfully manipulated. The central importance of farmbush to local subsistence starkly contrasts with the focus of conservationists, whose interests are shaped by very different agendas, on the high forest. As Davies and Richards (1991) point out, whereas foresters and conservationists have long viewed the conversion of high forest to bush fallow in negative terms, this shift may, on balance, be positive from the perspective of local subsistence.

The high forest is also important in Mende life, but in very different ways. As we have seen, Mende villagers treat forest partly as a store for occasional and future subsistence use, and as a valuable buffer to resource inaccessibility in managed environments on the forest edge. Most importantly, however, the high forest is central to the creation and maintenance of local authority and power relations. Contextual specialists engage with high forest in ways ordinary people do not, whether as *kamajɔ* hunters or poison fisher-women, herbalists, the founders of new settlements and territories, or the expert fellers of large forest trees. In their activities these people reveal the powers and abilities to deal safely and productively with high forest possibilities and dangers. Their protective, mediative or productive activities in the high forest are essential for society as a whole; they deter dangerous wild animals, they establish useful liaisons with forest spirits, and they enable society's expansion into new territories. In so doing, such people become patrons to people in society, playing key roles in local politics whether concerning chieftaincy, descent or the secret society organisations so central to local governance.

Amidst these persistent themes concerning people-environment relations, Chapters 4 to 8 documented numerous specific changes in resource management and use. Gola forest villagers have interacted with their environment amidst shifting local socio-economic and ecological conditions, and changing pressures from the wider political economy. These processes of change have introduced new interests, opportunities, difficulties and dilemmas to which people have responded in creative ways. These responses have led to changes in patterns of resource management and use, whether in the realms of food production, cash cropping, hunting and gathering, or the distribution of money and food. Evidently, Mende have responded effectively to many new ecological and resource-management challenges over the last few decades. Local knowledge and skills have flexibly incorporated new activities such as swamp-vegetable gardening and tree-crop plantation management. Tenure arrangements have accommodated a range of new cultivation practices and the introduction and expansion of commercial tree crops. Local institutions have successfully controlled the use of many resources which Mende have come to value, enabling the instigation of conservation measures where necessary. Contrary to the suggestions of some studies of 'common property resource' management, the primary purpose of such institutions is not managing natural resources *per se*; this is just one of numerous organisational activities of family, descent group or village authorities, and natural resource control is integrated with these.

Gola forest villagers do nevertheless face certain environmental problems and natural resource scarcities. Increasing pressures on swamps are creating access difficulties to cultivation sites and to valued swamp-fallow products. Certain animals are becoming scarce. Extending the upland cropping period may carry negative implications for fallow recovery. Incipient local concerns about environmental sustainability are, to a certain extent, buffered by the continuing accessibility of high forest. In Mende areas further north near Bo, where there is greater population pressure and reduced forest availability, local people show concern about the evident shortening of fallow periods, the invasion of savanna grasses and the loss of useful wild products. Such concerns may well increase in future in the Gola forest area, especially as population densities rise. But it is clearly insufficient to assume that they are shared equally and similarly across a 'community'. Social differentiation in resource access and control is just as relevant to people's experiences of environmental change as to the processes contributing to it.

There are significant differences between women's and men's opportunities in resource management and use in the Gola forest area. These arise because of the ways resource-using processes intersect with social relations. Previous chapters have shown several persistent aspects of Mende social life and of ideas about gender which are of crucial importance to the structuring of gendered resource-use interests and opportunities. These include secret society organisation, which supports ideas of the role complementarity of women and men who are 'different' but not hierarchically compared, and which offers the members of each gender separate power bases and support networks. They also include ideas about the characteristics and capabilities of the sexes, reproduced in a division of labour in which certain tasks are exclusive to either women or men. Ideas and practices associated with 'wealth in people' or patron–clientage constitute a third persistent theme. While both women and men may create relationships of obligation and dependency with other people, they do so for different reasons and in different ways. Women's opportunities are constrained partly by the fourth set of issues: descent and marriage arrangements. Ideals of patrilineality can easily be drawn upon against women's control of kin groups, inheritance and residential arrangements, while women's marriages and childbearing potential are central to local politics. Women have little control over their own marriages and in many contexts count as legal minors while of childbearing age.

To acquire, maintain and make effective use of resources, and in negotiations over how they should be used, Mende villagers draw on various kinds of claims arising from their positions in nexuses of social and economic relations. In many situations, women have a more limited range of claims on which to draw, and less autonomy and influence than men within the power relations that affect resource management. We have seen numerous manifestations of this. For example, women's lack of access to others' labour, and the claims made on their labour by men, have shaped and constrained their agricultural and tree-planting activities. Women have had a limited ability to command control over new activities, crops and products, or to resist male 'encroachment' on their own activities when their profitability increases. Women have also tended to lose relative to men in situations of conflict, competition, and ambiguity within and between resource uses. Thus, for example, women have lost access to upland intercrop-planting places when this interest conflicted with men's swamp rice-farming decisions. They have found it difficult to uphold their tree-crop inheritance claims amidst the competing claims of others. And they have been unable to avoid taking on new expenditure duties amidst the current ambiguities surrounding marital financial arrangements.

Along with recent historical changes in resource management have gone shifts in the range of specific social and economic claims open to men and women. These have in turn influenced gendered resource interests and opportunities, and hence patterns of environmental use. For example, among the conditions that have led women increasingly to cultivate private swamp rice, vegetables and upland crops are changes in farm-household organisation, linking food-provisioning and farm labour contributions more closely to husband-wife relations, and men's involvement in tree cash-cropping, making husbands' contributions to rice-farm households more unreliable. Women's opportunities to engage in tree cash-cropping on their own account are restricted by men's claims over their wives' labour for producing their own tree crops, by residential arrangements linked to marriage, by definitions of tree-crop 'brushing' as a male task, and by women's limited access to other men's labour. Instead, while men have concentrated on tree crops, women have taken over more of the work involved in household food production. They have focused their increasing independent production activities on food and cash-generating vegetable, groundnut and cassava crops, producing these in ways and places that help them cope with labour difficulties, and that help them make effective use of their kin and friendship ties with other women to gain and maintain control over land resources, labour and products. Women's gathering and wild plant domestication activities, too, have focused on these field and garden environments, in the context of men's superior opportunities to manage plantations as sources of the products they value. Evidently, then, processes of gendered resource access and control shape overall patterns of forest-resource management and use. For this reason rainforest resource use, and the issues of sustainability and productivity in local people's relationships with rainforests raised in Chapter 1, cannot be properly addressed without an understanding of gender relations.

The analysis in previous chapters also allows some reconsideration of the 'gender and environment' perspectives discussed in Chapter 2. In their general directions, the historical shifts I have documented would seem to support those theories that link a decline in women's resource position to the penetration of cash crops and a 'feminisation of food production' (cf. Boserup, 1970; Shiva, 1989). Indeed, Boserup's (1970) thesis has been applied directly to explain the gender effects of cocoa and coffee development in Sierra Leone (Klomberg and Van Riessen, 1983). However, this theory falls short in several ways in accounting for the changes documented in earlier chapters. First, the changing social division of agricultural involvement has not followed neat male–female lines. Certain men – principally young men, strangers and poorer farmers without tree crops – have maintained their labour involvement in rice production and are, like women, now highly concerned with the production of root crops and hunger foods. Among women, it is junior co-wives, widows and divorcees (as opposed to older and senior wives) whose labour inputs and independent agriculture have most increased, since such women have least access to men's resources and least opportunity to devolve their labour burdens on to others.

More generally, this book has shown how other kinds of social difference – such as age, origins, descent position or socio-economic status – interact with gender to shape people's resource management and control claims. In certain cases this leads to parallels of interest and opportunity between different groups of women and men. Earlier chapters have repeatedly shown that 'big' women and 'big' men have much in common as regards resource management, whether in plantations, rice production or hunting and fishing, even if they acquired their patron status in different ways. Young men and wives of childbearing age also share a range of interests and opportunities, as do male and female strangers. This serves to emphasise that Mende women are by no means a homogeneous category. Gender interacts with many other variables in shaping people's positions in social relations and their range of claims relevant to resource access and control.

Second, it would be wrong to attribute to women the defenceless acceptance of processes that deny them resource access often implied in historical-materialist theories. In relation to the food/cash-crop dilemma and in other cases we have seen Mende women's resistance of situations they resent, either publicly in the village or family courts or in 'covert' ways. In other cases, women have coped by seeking alternative means of resource access, usually through their independent activities and social networks. Such coping strategies have tangible effects on both patterns of and equity in environmental use, and as such need to be addressed. Notably, however, women can be denied effective access to formal channels to voice their complaints by precisely the same processes that restrict their resource access in the first place. In this respect the institutions that can assist women to uphold their claims *vis-à-vis* men's, notably the Sande society and women's natal kin, are extremely important. These also provide vital alternative sources of support to marriage. It is not surprising that women invest so heavily – socially and economically – in these institutions.

This analysis of Mende forest resource use also confirms the limited use of the two other 'gender and environment' approaches outlined in Chapter 2. Women's environmental interests and activities clearly cannot be understood in isolation from their relations with men, as some 'women and environment' positions imply, for it is these very relations which have, time and time again, been shown to condition what women are doing and why. Nor do women's environmental concerns arise from their 'natural' involvement with an unchanging domestic domain, as studies that highlight women's fuel and food-procurement roles often suggest. Mende women perform such tasks because of social, not natural, divisions of labour. And to the extent that their day-to-day domestic duties are a persistent feature of women's lives and environmental use, they fulfil them in changing ways that are integrated with their productive work, involvement with the cash economy and long-term social expectations. Women's collection of fuelwood in conjunction with new tree-crop plantation work obligations as discussed in Chapter 5, or their distribution of cooked food to maintain supportive female–female and inter-lineage relations as discussed in Chapter 8, provide but two examples.

Nor has the ecofeminist view that women are closer to 'nature' than men proved helpful in understanding Mende women's interactions with their forest environment. Indeed, if we were to adopt the analytical categories of 'female', 'male', 'nature' and 'culture', associating the forest with nature or with 'the wild', the inverse would appear to be true. It is Mende men who seem, more often, to be associated with the 'wild' high forest in their roles as hunters, seekers of distant forest products or fellers of forest trees. It is Mende women whose lives seem to revolve more closely around the 'tamed' spaces of garden or cleared farm site, and who themselves are tamed sexually through clitoridectomy and socially through the metaphorical silencing that the symbolism of tongue=clitoris implies. But such an analysis would grossly oversimplify complicated Mende perspectives. In as much as high forest carries connotations of untamed nature in Mende thought, it also carries many other highly cultural meanings, for example as a site of ancestral worship and a 'store' of sites for future settlement. Equally, Mende link masculinity to many highly 'tamed' aspects of life as well as to male forest roles, considering men as appropriate lineage authority figures and household-planners and providers. Maleness is strongly linked to certain forms of 'domestication' as well as to apparent 'wildness' (cf. La Fontaine, 1981). Just as categories such as male, female, nature and culture are polysemic in Western thought, offering a matrix of contrasts that can be differently drawn upon at different times (Strathern, 1980), so they are for the Mende.

This book has strongly supported Agarwal's (1991) criticism of ecofeminist analyses for stopping at the level of ideology; as she argues, 'women's and men's relationship with nature needs to be understood as rooted in their material reality, in their specific forms of interaction with the environment' (Agarwal, 1991: 10). But the problem with many ecofeminist and other culturalist analyses is not just that, in focusing on ideas, they neglect material questions of resource control; it is also their assumption that these dimensions of gender can be analysed independently. However, just as ideas about gender shape resource-using activities, so these acts in turn shape ideas about gender. We have seen, for example, how women's fishing and men's hunting reproduce Mende ideas about the characteristics of the members of each sex. We have seen how Mende notions of gender complementarity were annually reproduced in the upland rice-farming cycle, and how palm-tree climbing and tree-crop ownership have shaped definitions of masculinity. Resource-using processes are, as Guyer (1984b) has argued in relation to agricultural production, symbolic means of validating social and cultural arrangements. If ideas concerning gender are historically persistent, this may be less because they are timeless cultural ideals than because they are repeatedly reaffirmed in day-to-day life.

Appreciating the interdependence between ideas about gender and the environment, and resource-using processes, also alerts analytical attention to the ways in which changes in material conditions can challenge those ideas. Changes and dilemmas in gendered farming relations, for example, challenge the Mende ideas about gender that were annually reproduced in the upland farming cycles of the past, since the concentration of women's work in an independent labour process to produce an independently controlled product, rather than a sequence of male and female tasks which results in a joint product, does not so easily support ideas of male and female interdependence and complementarity. The decline in men's kamajɔ hunting activity in favour of hunting forms less strongly identified with male capabilities and characteristics has diminished the contexts in which such ideas of masculinity were expressed and affirmed. And the growing importance of money suggests a growing substitutability between men's and women's resource-sing activities, challenging the ideas of gender difference reproduced when men and women work in separate and complementary spheres of environmental interaction.

Mende gender ideologies do not yet seem to be undergoing major shifts in response to these challenges from forest-resource use. To a certain extent the challenges are buffered by broad continuities in other spheres of Mende gender relations, for example in the domain of secret society initiation and activity. But as earlier chapters have shown, certain aspects of gender relations show signs of fragility, and people's apparent attempts to reassert older-established values account for certain features of modern forest-resource use patterns. And as we shall see, the implications of changing patterns of resource control for the meanings of gender recur in the terms in which Mende themselves reflect on the future of their forest lives.

What implications does such an analysis carry for rainforest conservation policy, especially for 'people-oriented', conservation-with-development approaches? It is useful to reflect on some of the specific interventions under consideration, as outlined in Chapter 1, in the light of the Mende analysis. I want to do this by examining some specific policies and projects in southern and eastern Sierra Leone, some of which have explicit conservation and/or forestry objectives, others which have more general rural development objectives but potential applicability to conservation-with-development. Difficulties and issues that have arisen with these interventions are more readily comprehensible in the light of the discussion in previous chapters. The Gola forest analysis also suggests ways in which such interventions would need to be oriented to meet local concerns in general, and gendered ones in particular. Broader issues will also emerge from the review of specific interventions, and from the book's analysis. These concern who controls conservation-with-development processes, and the terms in which conservation debates are couched. From this discussion of conservation approaches and the foregoing gender analysis, the book concludes by showing the kinds of idioms of local debate which conservationists must attempt to comprehend if they are to work effectively with the plurality of local interests.

PEOPLE-ORIENTED CONSERVATION: INTERVENTIONS
Swamp rice

The development of water-controlled swamps using permanent earth and/or cement structures has long been promoted as an agricultural development strategy in Sierra Leone. There is extensive debate as to its relative merits. As well as supposedly improving rice productivity (by raising yields and allowing several crops per year of 'improved' short-duration rice varieties) swamp development is thought to enable agricultural intensification and provide an alternative to shifting cultivation on uplands, thus reducing pressure on forest use (Government of Sierra Leone, 1989). In practice, swamp development in Sierra Leone has proved difficult to sustain, and abandoned water control structures are common. Richards (1986) and others (e.g. Dries, 1989; Johnny et al., 1981) have forcefully argued that this strategy is ill-suited to local resource-management conditions and concerns, and the analysis in this book both supports and adds to their arguments.

First, swamp development is problematic in the context of issues surrounding labour mobilisation. It requires heavy male labour inputs to establish water control structures, as well as relatively sustained, steady male and female labour in structure maintenance and transplanting during subsequent years. Most labour-scarce Mende farmers face difficulties in this. Indigenous swamp management strategies are well-suited to farmers with limited labour access. As Johnny et al., (1981) argue, those farmers with access to sufficient labour for successful swamp development commonly remain more interested in upland farming, where brushing and tree-felling is linked with male authority, and assembling groups to meet highly peaked labour demands is a means to create and consolidate patron-client ties. Second, the narrow focus on raising rice production conflicts with local resource management priorities. As we have seen, Mende ideally cultivate swamps as part of catenary site-use sequences, valuing the intercropping possibilities and the opportunities for agro-ecologically and temporally adapted rice varieties on associated upslope sites (Richards, 1986). They also obtain a range of useful non-timber forest products from indigenously managed swamp fallows. Permanent swamp development removes these possibilities.

Swamp development has proved especially problematic from a gender perspective. Female farmers find it especially difficult to secure sufficient male labour to build and maintain water-control structures (Johnny et al., 1981). Women's workloads have often increased as husbands have claimed their labour for the increased rice-transplanting involved in 'improved' swamp cultivation. Women have lost access to intercrop-planting sites when their husbands undertake swamp development, just as this has happened when men focus narrowly on swamp-farming according to indigenous methods. And women rely especially heavily on the use of swamp-fallow products, and suffer as swamp development reduces their availability.

Agroforestry

The problems with swamp development have encouraged some Sierra Leonean agricultural development agencies to look more closely at opportunities for improving the productivity and sustainability of upland agricultural use. In the context of forestry and conservation concern, there is currently much interest in finding appropriate agroforestry techniques that combine tree-planting or preservation with annual crops. As well as assisting the sustainable intensification of current rotational bush-fallow use, it is thought that these could help provide economically useful tree products such as fuelwood, reducing people's need to take these from forest areas.

The analysis in this book confirms that agroforestry is nothing new for Mende. Combining trees with crops, whether by tree-planting or preserving wild seedlings, and whether by interplanting or sequential combination (as in rotational bush-fallow) is well-grounded in local knowledge and practice. Equally, Mende have long relied on such indigenous agroforestry systems to obtain useful tree products. Much of the agroforestry research attention in Sierra Leone currently focuses on exotic tree species, and on the design of entire tree-crop systems such as alley-cropping, designed to replace those that farmers are already using (Allieu, 1990). But if agroforestry is to meet local resource-management needs and interests, it is important to work with farmers in the use of locally valued indigenous species, and to build on existing local practices such as in kitchen gardens and plantation management (Davies, 1990).

This book has also drawn attention to a range of important resource access and control issues affecting local agroforestry and women's and men's involvement in it, relevant to conservation-oriented agroforestry developments. First, local agroforestry practices such as in cocoa/coffee plantations respond to prevailing labour conditions, allowing for low-intensity management inputs during labour-scarce periods. Systems such as alley-cropping, with relatively inflexible labour-timing requirements, might prove problematic in this respect. For upland management, conservationists rightly consider that working with farmers to upgrade local fallow-management techniques, enriching fallows by preserving and/or planting soil-enhancing and economically useful trees, may be more appropriate (Davies, 1990; Davies and Richards, 1991).

Second, agroforestry involves gender-divided tasks, land and labour use, and product control. We have seen the contrast, for example, between cocoa/coffee plantations in which women work for their husbands but do not control the crop products and have little opportunity to preserve the wild trees they value, and kitchen gardens in which women have control over decisions, processes and products. And Chapter 5 showed that when control over trees is disputed, they may be left unmanaged. The varied claims over resources that different women and men can stake are therefore crucial to the ways agroforestry is managed and whom it benefits. As has been shown elsewhere in Africa (Rocheleau, 1990; Francis and Atta-Krah, n.d.), the feasibility and equity of new agroforestry activities depend on how they are introduced into this nexus of gendered opportunities.

Extractive reserves

As in agroforestry, gender issues recur in relation to the conservation strategy of 'extractive reserves'. None of these have yet been established in Sierra Leone explicitly for conservation purposes, although the extraction of non-timber forest products from the country's forest reserves has long been part of forestry policy. As elsewhere, extractive reserves are now considered a key strand of forest conservation-with-development, and there is discussion of orienting village marketing projects already established by NGOs towards non-timber forest products to increase their economic value. This book's analysis suggests, however, that increasing product values will not necessarily have the intended effect of encouraging local people to conserve the bush and forest in which they grow. Equally sensible responses would be to domesticate the species concerned into gardens or plantations, or to clear the surrounding vegetation so as to 'release them from the bush' and hence establish individual tenure over them, as already happens among the Gola forest Mende with certain timber trees and palms.

Furthermore, product value increases do not necessarily work to the benefit of the group previously using the resource, undermining the suggestion that extractive reserve developments are necessarily beneficial for women and the poor (e.g. Falconer, 1990; Hecht, Anderson and May, 1988). First, their relative access to the resource may diminish if, for reasons such as task definitions and limited control over land and labour, they cannot establish individual tenure for themselves and lose out to others. Second, their income from the resource may diminish if changes in the commercial value of products lead to the renegotiation of social control over them. The case of historical changes in palm-product control showed, for example, how certain men have drawn on claims over labour, on their positions as *mawɛɛ* heads, and on their performance of certain tasks to acquire control over whichever product – palm kernels or pericarp oil – offered greater financial rewards.

Women's vegetable gardening

Observing that economic development processes frequently work to the detriment of women, The Sierra Leonean government has adopted 'women in development' as a policy focus (within the Ministry of Rural Development, Social Services and Youth) and in the late 1980s established a Women's Bureau. In conjunction with donor agencies and through NGO activity, 'women's projects' have multiplied, many of them focusing on income generation. Vegetable-gardening projects are a common type of women's rural development intervention. They are considered a potentially appropriate intervention for 'people-oriented conservation', contributing not only to improving local (women's) livelihoods on the forest edge, but also to processes of agricultural intensification to reduce pressure on the forest.

The experience of vegetable-gardening projects shows the problems in conceiving of women as a homogeneous category, and in ignoring their socio-political relations and diverse institutional involvements. Agencies commonly assume that the most appropriate organisation for such projects is a 'women's group', headed by a village women's leader. The latter is usually an older woman from a high-status descent group, often a Sande official. But while village women are used to uniting under her authority to perform women's share of 'town labour' (and perhaps in Sande), this is not necessarily the most appropriate level for organising 'cooperative' vegetable production, sales and revenue management. Women of different ages and social positions do not necessarily share either the leader's or each other's interests and opportunities. Socially influential women may be less interested in gardening, while hierarchies can develop to the detriment of younger or in-married participants. As this book has shown, Mende women unite in numerous other smaller groupings to cooperate in different socio-economic activities, such as *osusu* savings groups, fishing groups, farm labour groups and particular networks of kin and friends. These might provide more effective forms of organisation in projects. When CARE implemented a vegetable-gardening project in Madina, for example, women, left to organise their own labour and financial management structures, successfully divided into three groups of seven to ten women corresponding to habitual cooperation and exchange networks (Leach, 1991a).

Sierra Leonean experience also shows that separate women's projects do not necessarily yield the intended benefits to women, nor do they necessarily guarantee them access to needed resources and decision-making power. In many cases, the cash-income benefits of women's farming projects have been 'captured' by men who have been able to claim control of the commercially valued products. This seems to happen more often when the project activity concerns crops and places used by both genders, such as upland cassava or maize, than for vegetables and kitchen/swamp gardens where there are strong precedents for female resource control. In other cases, publicly known increases in women's incomes as a result of their project involvement leads to renegotiations of husband–wife expenditure responsibilities, so that a woman's increased income is absorbed, for example, in newly acquired expenditure demands on children's food, once provided by men. Labour issues also affect women's benefits. In one NGO-funded women's farming project in Moyamba district, for example, the women's group expended much of the project loan funds on hiring male labour to brush their site. Many of their husbands became involved in an (unfunded) men's group which started to cultivate a nearby site. These men not only brushed their own site free for themselves, they also called their wives to help weed and harvest the men's crops, reducing the women's time to work the women's project site. Not surprisingly, the men's eventual yields were much higher than those of the 'women's project'. Such examples emphasise that women's activities do not proceed in isolation from men's and that the gender relations between them operate in a project context just as outside it.

Wildlife conservation

Where wildlife is concerned, discussions in Sierra Leone have long recognised that much of the local killing of animals for bushmeat takes place in the course of crop protection. Waldock, Capstick and Browning (1951) emphasised the need to focus efforts on the control of crop pests in agricultural areas, while constituting game reserves in thinly populated ones. The government pursued the former between 1947 and 1962, for example, when in response to cocoa-pest problems a bounty was offered for killing monkeys and monkey drives were organised. However, it is unclear how far this actually reduced crop losses. Northern donor and research influence has encouraged game reserve establishment as part of wildlife conservation efforts since the late 1960s. Although several schemes are in hand, wildlife conservation and reservation has generally proved difficult to enforce, at least partly because the Government Wildlife Conservation Branch[1] remains small and ill-equipped.

These policies are just as relevant in the context of today's concerns with rainforest conservation. The analysis in this book supports Davies and Richards (1991) who emphasise that working with farmers to upgrade local pest-control techniques would serve both local people's subsistence concerns and conservationists' interests in further reducing high forest hunting pressure. Improvements to local fishing would also serve conservation-with-development interests, given its crucial importance to local subsistence. Attention to gender issues would clearly be crucial in any such development given the gender complementarity of women's and men's respective fish and bushmeat provisioning, and the importance of women's group fishing to female solidarity. These could easily be undermined, implying the need for careful attention to women's involvement in fishing, and to the institutions – including Sande – which help them to control it.

Local people would probably not see the establishment of a forest wildlife reserve as a threat to their immediate subsistence. But the importance of high forest *kamajɔ* hunting to local socio-politics suggests the importance and advantages of involving local people in this aspect of conservation. As mediators between society and forest animals, throughout Mende history, it would seem obvious for *kamajɛisia* to be so in a conservation context. Since in local eyes *kamajɔ* engagement with the forest and its animals has always been more significant than killing *per se*, the idea of hunters turning protectors might not seem incredible. In conjunction with local chiefs, *kamajɛisia* have also controlled institutions of tenure and knowledge around forest hunting. In conservation activity, they could well become the most effective wildlife guides and controllers of animal exploitation in reserves.

While *kamajɛisia* play a crucial role in governing local animal resource use, however, neither they nor the chiefdom authorities have been able to control commercial hunting so effectively. Hunting for the urban and Liberian markets is both the greatest current threat to forest-dependent mammals, and the one least subject to local institutional influence.

Forest reserves and revenue control

As in the case of hunting, the Mende analysis has shown the effectiveness of local institutions in controlling many resource-management and use activities, and the distribution of benefits from them. But certain other forest resource-using activities are much less easily controlled. This distinction is crucial for conservation activities centring on forest-reserve management.

Sierra Leone's forestry policy recognises that local cooperation in forest-reserve protection and management requires local communities to receive some share of the revenue. Accordingly, the 1988 Forestry Act re-emphasised the principle that royalties paid by timber companies should be divided between government and chiefdom (via the paramount chief), and attempts to ensure that reasonable rates are paid. In the context of strict nature reserve protection associated with people-oriented conservation, such revenues might derive from research fees or 'ecotourism'. Local reserve protection is especially important, given the weak enforcement capacities of the Sierra Leonean state. This book's research suggests that effective local institutions exist to manage such revenues, and that these can respond more effectively to the plurality of local needs and interests than outside-imposed institutions. This does not mean just the authorities at chiefdom or village level. As Chapter 8 showed, indigenous financial management depends on a range of other institutions, including small savings groups (e.g. women's *osusu*, family groups) and patron-client relations, and all these might have a part to play in people-oriented conservation interventions. These have proved their superior appropriateness, resilience and flexibility in the context of rural credit in Sierra Leone (Johnny, 1985), even if donor agencies have often been reluctant to support them on the grounds that they are 'inegalitarian' in Western terms.

Several of the activities currently placing most pressure on high forest-resource use do, however, operate largely outside community control. In addition to commercial hunting, these include logging operations by commercial timber companies, and diamond-digging. It seems unlikely that unsupported, local authorities could acquire greater influence over them in a conservation context. All of these tend to be instigated by outsiders, and to be established with quite different economic, and political and institutional interests from local activities. Some local people have benefited, whether from employment or, in the case of some chiefs, by accepting private payments for assisting their activity. But local authorities find them difficult to regulate. There might be a role for conservationists to work in conjunction with local institutions towards the better policing of such activities.

PEOPLE-ORIENTED CONSERVATION: APPROACHES

Beyond the specific interventions themselves, these examples of Sierra Leonean experience raise some broader issues concerning conservation and rural development approaches. In particular, they make it clear that rural development interventions intersect with dynamic social and political processes. It would be naïve to imagine that outside interventions operated on a blank societal slate, or transformed one situation into another according to preconceived objectives (whoever defines these). Rather they 'lock into' and shape the ongoing processes through which people manage resources and deal with social relations, providing new resources and bases for claims that are rejected or incorporated in ways congruent with local idioms of understanding. Thus just as gendered labour relations manifest themselves in women's farming projects, as shown above, development project loans are commonly incorporated by village patrons into the sets of resources they use to support their clients (Richards, 1986). Outsiders' natural resource-management proposals are locally interpreted and considered within local idioms of ecological and socio-political understanding. For example, women in Madina considered the supposedly 'improved' hybrid vegetable seeds and row-planting practices offered by an NGO project to be agro-ecologically and economically disastrous compared with their customary intercropping and plant moving-and-transplanting practices. But they undertook them anyway since, as one put it, 'they [the project staff] are big people, and they might help us in future'. In other words the participant women considered themselves to be investing in a patronage network as much as 'vegetable gardening'.[2] In short, local social processes and concepts are highly resilient. Flexible and accommodating as they are, they are not amenable to wholesale subversion or transformation by outsiders.

The resilience of local social processes and idioms of understanding raises dilemmas for people-oriented conservation. This resilience may appear as an advantage to conservationists when local processes lead – either on their own or in interaction with development interventions – to outcomes that accord with conservation objectives. But such outcomes are neither assured, given the contrasting origins of local and conservationist agendas, nor predictable by outsiders, given the dynamic nature of local processes. Equally it is important to recognise that the very local social processes and institutions which help promote environmental sustainability may work against social or gender equity as defined by outsiders. The idea of building in 'compensations' or building on 'complementarities' between differently defined local and conservation objectives becomes muddy and difficult to handle once we appreciate the extent to which all development (whoever defined the original objectives) is incorporated into local processes. Seeking social or environmental solutions in a narrowly defined 'empowerment' of 'communities' or 'women', also becomes problematic when resource management is appreciated as embedded in nexuses of relations and dynamic social processes. It is difficult to identify who precisely is being empowered and to determine the resource-use implications of this.

In short, it is illusory to imagine that conservation policies can be tailor-made to combine 'strategic empowerment' with 'strategic sustainability'. 'Fine-tuned' conservation-with-development interventions, for example, might build on overlaps between the interests of particular social groups and conservationists, or address the specific problems of a particular social group, but the social and ecological outcomes will ultimately depend on how such interventions articulate with the dynamic processes which already condition resource allocation and use. In this light, I should like to conclude by moving away from specific resource issues towards some broader perspectives through which villagers around the Gola Reserves reflect on their forest futures. Local idioms of debate address recent changes in socio-economic and gender relations in locally-relevant ways.

An important idiom through which Mende reflect on their changing lives in a forest environment brings together notions of 'wealth in people' with the differences between 'open' and 'closed' places. This local conceptual framework integrates many of the specific natural resource-management issues considered in this book; it also provides terms of debate in which Mende consider broader issues concerning the relationship between people and high forest, and would consider conservation-with-development interventions intended to alter that relationship.

For Mende, successfully dealing with the high forest is considered partly as a source of power for local patrons (*numu wa*). Whether as *kamajɛisia*, herbalists or tree-fellers, those who interact with high forest, performing vital protective, productive and mediative functions, attract others to become and remain 'for' or 'behind' them. Chiefs and family heads, who 'hold' people and territories, maintain their authority partly through their claimed links with those who interacted with high forest in the past to found new settlements. By performing such forest-related patronage roles, these people emphasise their difference from those who are their clients and who engage only with farmbush for subsistence-related purposes. In short, interactions with high forest are a medium for patron–client relations, and those who mediate between high forest and society also build followings in society.

As Richards (1992) has found, Gola forest villagers also liken the high forest itself to a patron. Society has, in local thought, grown up under the protection of the forest. People think of themselves as 'behind' it, in the sense of clients dependent for their economic and social progress on the possibilities and resources it may provide. As Richards (1992) points out, this local viewpoint contrasts with conservationist emphases on 'saving the rainforest', which suggest that the forest is the client that society, as patron, should protect.

Forest and political patronage are, indeed, closely linked for Mende. The patronage roles of the high forest only come to be of benefit to most members of society through the activities of forest-related patrons who act, in effect, as brokers. Patrons play central roles when the support of the high forest needs to be drawn upon more heavily, as when hunter–founders located new forest-settlement sites for expanding communities in the past, or when expert forest tree-fellers enable new areas of forest to be incorporated into the bush-fallow cycle and day-to-day subsistence.

Those who derive authority from high forest activities acquire prominence in socio-political relations more generally, in local institutions and in arranging how natural resources are managed and used from day-to-day in village, farm and fallow environments. Many of the ways in which Mende conserve resources they value for the future depend on the authority of chiefs, family heads and hunters. Questions that conservationists might ask about the sustainability of natural resource use are thus, for Mende, inseparable from questions about these people's relative authority.

Socio-economic change is bringing new opportunities to the Gola forest area, challenging both the control held by forest-related patrons and people's dependence on the high forest as a patron. Mende often reflect on such changes and their implications by drawing a contrast between 'open' and 'closed' lifestyles and places. 'Open' and 'closed' each conjure up a range of ideas for Mende which can plausibly be linked. Openness can imply knowledge of a wide outside world; the presence of roads, transport and markets; diverse economic opportunities; numerous strangers; speaking Krio; Islamic and Christian values; and 'modern' (European-derived, *puu*) foods, things and styles of behaviour. Closed places, lacking these attributes, can be linked with lifestyles based on farming and forest-resource use; foods such as local rice, wild foods and red palm oil; talking Mende 'deeply' and properly; and the values expressed through ancestral sacrifices and secret society activities. These various attributes of lifestyles and places can be drawn upon comparatively. Thus a small village in the forest near the Moro river is 'closed' compared with Madina, but Madina and its ways of life can be considered 'closed' compared with the forest diamond camps, with their milling strangers and thriving markets. None of these are as 'open' as urban areas such as Kenema, where there are roads and transport and people eat and do 'modern' things.

In Mende terms, forest-dependent lifestyles and forms of authority derived from interactions with high forest are linked with closure. The opening of places brings two sorts of possibility, with different implications for people-forest relations. On the one hand, openness brings people, things and kinds of behaviour that would tend to undermine forest-related patronage, and local control over natural resources. It brings money-making opportunities through which more people can acquire control over clients, perhaps superseding *kamajɛisia* and family heads. It brings large numbers of short-term strangers who are difficult to control and accede less easily to local governance. And it brings new forest-resource uses, such as commercial logging, hunting and diamond-digging, which local authorities cannot easily control. On the other hand, openness brings new ranges of choice and socio-economic opportunity that would allow people to reduce their dependence on the patronage of the forest. These include opportunities to earn cash income locally, such as through trade or employment in local services, reducing direct dependence on natural resources for subsistence. And they include opportunities for education, seasonal urban employment, and remittances from urban kin, thus allowing 'migration' (economically if not always physically) away from forest-based lifestyles.

Closure and openness thus suggest two contrasting approaches to forest conservation, both of which would seem logical in Mende terms. The first, retaining closure as it were, would emphasise support to forest-related patronage roles and local-level resource-management capacities, so as to enhance the forest's capacity to support local livelihoods. The other, emphasising openness, would imply that the clients of the forest and of forest-based patrons should look elsewhere, to other activities and patrons. As Richards' (1992) informants put it, they would 'come out from behind the Gola forest'. The open-closed idiom also provides a local means to interpret intermediate conservation-with-development approaches. For example, support to local institutions to manage 'extractive reserves' sustainably while creating new marketing opportunities for their products, might be seen by Mende to combine aspects of closure with aspects of openness.

Crucially, any such change in society–forest relations also implicates the changing relations between people in society. People reflect on these within the open-closed idiom, showing varied opinions that reflect their different social and economic positions. For example, young people often express their wish that Madina would open up so that their independent cash-earning opportunities would increase, and more traders would bring imported European goods. Young men and their parents hope to gain from their employment in commercial enterprises such as logging, should the village open. Aspiring patrons value openness because it brings more strangers who are potential clients. Everyone links openness with desired improvements in health care, education and transport services. Yet openness can also represent unwelcome tendencies for young people to become more independent, disrespectful and 'concerned only with their own business'. Those whose authority is grounded in high forest interactions, descent or secret society activity can perceive it as threatening. *Kamajɛisia* complain that the Gola forest is opening to young men who just want to shoot monkeys for money, and do not respect *kamajɔ* business. An elderly Madina family head appropriated medicine prepared by a specialist to promote village diamond excavations, because, others said, he wanted to 'keep the village closed' so as to retain his superior leverage over kin. Meanwhile, everyone recognises that life in Sierra Leone's most open, urban places is becoming harder, amidst the country's economic difficulties. In closed forest areas, the opportunities to subsist and affirm social ties through natural resource use, community ceremonies and strong secret society business provide valuable alternatives which, at times, everyone actively seeks. Thus the open-closed idiom expresses dilemmas that everyone faces. No-one is always on one side or the other; rather everyone is living a sometimes precarious balance between 'open' and 'closed' worlds.

The open-closed idiom also expresses dilemmas in gender relations. Certain women become and remain patrons through means linked to the closed forest world, whether as descent group heads, Sande officials, or poison fisherwomen. But closure also supports socio-political arrangements that restrict many women's opportunities to acquire wealth and status, such as control over women in marriage, forms of authority and resource control based on patrilineal descent, and task divisions that exclude women from high-status activities such as hunting. Openness brings more opportunities for women's independent acquisition of wealth and status. Men can feel threatened, and as one put it: 'Husbands who were born here and have not been out fear that women who go out frequently on market business and speak Krio will overtake them and become disrespectful. Many men do not want the village to open because of this.' While many women value such social and economic opportunities, they also link them negatively with hus-bands' growing tendency not to 'hold their wives well'. Women continue to value the gender complementarity embodied in 'real Mende' forms of rice-farming and forest-product use in more closed places, and the vital support of the Sande society and its officials. Thus women's interests are not squarely linked either with openness or closure; each, for women, represents huge ambiguities.

I suggest that if conservationists are to work effectively with local com-munities, they must be cognisant of local terms of debate such as these which link changes in people–forest relations with changes in rural society, and attempt to work with them. Such discussions reveal local priorities and problems. The extent to which they raise local dilemmas rather than clearcut answers reinforces the need for conservation-with-development planning itself to be a process of discussion, working gradually towards resolutions, rather than based on the assumption that community needs and interests can be straightforwardly identified and enabled. Local terms of debate are also more sensitive to the plurality of local perspectives. The extent to which people's opinions are differentiated and contextual reinforces the need for such planning processes to allow multiple views to be represented. Women's interests may be marginalised – in conservation-planning as in everyday life – because they lack the power and channels effectively to express their concerns. Supporting their ability to do so may mean less ensuring that women 'participate' in village meetings, than working with and building on the diversity of institutions, channels and socio-economic arrangements through which women can and do press their interests in day-to-day life.

Local terms of debate also reveal the highly politicised nature of the issues that conservationists deal with. Forest-resource use is the very stuff of local politics, and of the relationships between local society and the state. There is no escaping the fact that conservation, which implies intervention in these relations, is a very political issue (Anderson and Grove, 1987). It touches, too, on concerns of the most personal kind, as local discussions link people–forest interactions with changing relations between older and younger people, or husbands and wives; with what it means to be a woman or a man.

In losing control over the capacity to decide their use of forest resources, people therefore lose control over their lives in much more fundamental ways. And in the end the question of control must lie at the heart of people-oriented conservation. Many divergent interests will continue to affect rain-forests, and local people and conservationists may continue to have different priorities. It would be naïve to imagine that such differences could ever be entirely resolved. People-oriented conservation should not be a search for an unattainable consensus, nor is it about the precise ways in which forest resources are managed. It is about control over the process of discussing and deciding forest futures, and about enhancing local women's and men's capacities to do so on their own terms.

APPENDIX I

Research Methods

This appendix briefly describes how my study of gender and resource use in the Gola forest was organised and the main methods it used. The basis of the research was village-level fieldwork using social anthropological methods, but it was necessary to situate this in a wider socio-economic, policy and historical context. I spent three periods in Sierra Leone during the course of the research – fifteen months during 1987–8, and one month in 1990 and again in 1991 – and each contributed in different ways.

The first, main fieldwork period was originally undertaken for my doctoral dissertation on gender relations and natural resource use (Leach, 1990). Following three months of language-learning, living with a Mende family in Bo, I was resident in Madina, my main Gola forest study village, for a year. My choice of village was guided partly by the desire to work in one of the larger settlements around Gola North, and partly by the advantages, in terms of comparisons and coverage, of working in an area not covered by Davies and Richards' (1991) Lalehun-based study. The encouragement offered by Malema chiefdom's (now late) paramount chief and the warm welcome offered by the villagers themselves confirmed Madina as a suitable site. Although most of my work was carried out here, I gained an understanding of life in the chiefdom's smaller forest villages through several week-long treks with overnight stops, and periodic stays of several days at a time in Misila, a small forest hamlet.

I had my own house and kitchen in the centre of Madina which I shared with my research assistant, a young woman from another part of Mendeland. She initially helped me to learn and translate Mende but as my language proficiency increased, her role instead became one of survey assistant and companion. The main fieldwork method was participant observation, supplemented by interviews and surveys. Throughout fieldwork, managing my own domestic life inevitably meant participating in and learning about the myriad exchanges, negotiations and processes through which Madina women and men manage theirs. Participant observation of other productive and resource-using processes followed seasonal rhythms. I arrived in the village in January and during the dry season spent much time on women's fishing trips, which helped me to be accepted and to establish friendships with women. I also studied hunting in Madina and Misila. The firm designation of hunting as 'men's business' presented this part of the study with practical and ethical difficulties. Having debated whether to attempt it at all, I eventually obtained most of my information from a few men who became close friends, and drew heavily on my identity as a white outsider (*puu-mɔ*), rather than as a woman, to do so. From the start of the rainy season in May, I focused attention more closely on seven farm-households whose members I had come to know well. Accompanying each farm-household or selected members on a single day each week, I took part in whatever range of activities was on the day's agenda. A large proportion of my data on annual cropping, cocoa and coffee production, and timber/non-timber forest product use derives from these days. I collected samples of gathered plant resources and was later helped to identify them at Njala University College. I also collected data on the sources of food items consumed on each study day, and asked women and men about the previous week's income and expenditures of money. Financial questions were highly sensitive, and this undoubtedly affected the accuracy of the data, but they nonetheless proved a useful basis for understanding patterns of resource access and allocation.

While I derived much information from casual conversations, various more formal interviews were also carried out, and these I tape-recorded. They included discussions of family history, kinship and marriage arrangements, and interviews with 'key informants' about specific topics of interest that arose in the course of the research. I carried out a number of surveys, including a complete census of the ages, marital status, and natal origins of residents of Madina. Other surveys covered:

(a) Residential house occupation (men and women, November 1987)
(b) Kitchen sharing arrangements (women, December 1987)
(c) Rice farm-household membership and farming plans (farm-household heads, February 1988)
(d) Plantation management (men and some women, October 1988)
(e) Vegetable gardens and individual swamps (women and young men, July 1988)
(f) Fuelwood species preferences and gathering patterns (women, April, July and November 1988)
(g) Strategies for obtaining palm oil (women, August 1988)
(h) Rice harvest labour patterns (women, November 1988)
(i) Cocoa and coffee acquisition (women and young men, November 1988).

Historical data were collected from a variety of sources before and during the 1987–88 fieldwork, including discussions with elderly people in Madina and other villages, the accounts of missionaries and anthropologists, colonial officers' reports and letters (mainly from the archives at Fourah Bay College, Freetown), and the work of historians of the region. Historically oriented ethnography presents methodological difficulties, including the tendency for the past to appear as overly aligned to present circumstances or theories, and as invariant and static compared with the variation and day-to-day dynamism discernible in present-day life. Ethnographic data of consistent detail and quality clearly cannot be obtained for the whole fifty-year time period. While these difficulties can only be recognised, not entirely overcome, as Guyer (1988) shows, the insights to be gained from historical analysis nevertheless justify attempting to make use of the sources that are available.

During the 1987–8 period in Sierra Leone I collected some information on wider aspects of socio-economic and forestry development and policy. I had the opportunity to supplement this in 1990 when I spent a month in Sierra Leone as a consultant for a British-based NGO. The work was to assess the NGO's current and future operations in the context of national socio-economic trends, and involved visiting rural development projects throughout the southern and eastern part of the country and interviewing government and aid agency staff, including those involved in conservation. I gained many important insights from these visits and interviews, and the concluding discussion of conservation and development approaches draws especially heavily on these.

My third visit, in 1991, was primarily to investigate interactions between Gola forest Mende and the numerous refugees who arrived in their communities in 1990 as a result of the civil war in Liberia. This research, documented elsewhere (Leach, 1992a), focused on the implications of refugee–host relations for forest-resource use and food security. The study itself gave a fascinating opportunity to see local resource-management practices and institutions operating under – and effectively coping with – a major 'shock'. Furthermore, during the four weeks I spent in Malema chiefdom I was able to discuss some of the findings from the 1987–8 research with villagers, follow up gender and forest-resource use issues and events over the intervening period, and carry out focused interviews relating to this book's concerns. Above all, for me this return village visit reinforced how change and continuity interplay in village life. I saw many differences between 1988 and 1991 – in who was doing exactly what, with whom, for which precise purpose or in response to which particular dilemma – but I also saw, again, the resilience of broad local concepts and socio-political relations.

APPENDIX II

Plant and Animal Names

CULTIVATED PLANTS
Field and garden crops

Common name	Botanical name	Mende name
Rice	*Oryza glaberrima/sativa*	Mba
Cassava	*Manihot utilissima*	Tanga
Sweet potato	*Ipomoea batatas*	Njowo
Yam	*Dioscorea spp.*	Mbole/nyamisi
Cocoyam	*Colocasia esculenta*	Kpoji
	Xanthosoma sagittifolium	Koko
Pumpkin	*Cucurbita pepo*	Towa
Lima beans	*Phaseolus lunatus*	Tɔwɔ
Egusi/melon seed	*Colocynthis citrullus*	Koja
Jakato	*Solanum melongena var.*	Kojo
Egg plant	*Solanum melongena*	Kɔbɔkɔbɔ
Onion	*Allium cepa*	Siba/yabasi
Pepper	*Capsicum sp.*	Pujɛ
Okra	*Hibiscus esculentus*	Bondɔ
Sour-sour	*Hibiscus sabdariffa*	Sato
Tomato	*Lycopersicon esculentum*	Kibɔngi
Millet	*Pennisetum leonis*	Kpɛlɛnyɔ
Maize	*Zea mays*	Nyɔ
Sesame/beniseed	*Sesamum indicum*	Mandɛ
Cotton	*Gossypium spp.*	Fande
Sorghum	*Sorghum spp.*	Kete
Pineapple	*Ananas cosmosus*	Nɛsi
Spinach	*Amaranthus spp.*	Hɔndi
Groundnut	*Arachis hypogaea*	Nikili
Cucumber	*Cucumis sativus*	Kɔkuba
Krin-krin	*Corchorus olitorius*	Ngengee

Tree crops

Common name	Botanical name	Mende name
Cocoa	*Theobroma cacao*	*Kakalo*
Coffee	*Coffea robusta*	*Kɔfi*
Kola	*Cola nitida*	*Tolo*
Banana	*Musa sapientum*	*Sɛlɛ*
Plantain	*Musa paradisiaca*	*Mana*
Breadfruit	*Artocarpus communis*	*Bɛfu*
Orange	*Citrus sinensis*	*Salo/lumbele*
Mango	*Mangifera indica*	*Maŋgo*
Avocado pear	*Persea americana*	*Pia*
Guava	*Psidium guajava*	*Goyaba*
Coconut	*Cocos nucifera*	*Kokonati*
Pawpaw	*Carica papaya*	*Fakali*
Oil palm	*Elaeis guineensis*	*Tɔkpɔ/mosanke*

WILD FOODS

Herbaceous plants

Botanical name	Mende name	Part of plant/use
Amaranthus sp.	*Ndɔgbɔ-hɔndi*	Leaf, in sauce
Piper umbellatum	*Poponda*	Leaf, in sauce
Solanum macrocarpon	*Peila*	Leaf, in sauce
Solanum anomalum	*Kete*	Fruit, in sauce
unidentified	*Hɔnikpui*	Leaf, in sauce
unidentified	*Sɔkɔta*	Leaf, in sauce
Crassocephalum crepidioides	*Kikpɔ*	Leaf, in sauce
Triumfetta cordifolia	*Gbohui*	Leaf, in sauce
Cassia sieberiana	*Kɔya*	Fruit, in sauce
Solanum verbascifolium	*Ndɔgbɔmaggi*	Berry, as stock cube substitute
Dioscorea spp.	*Ngawu*	'Bush yam': root as hunger food

Trees and creepers

Botanical name	Mende name	Use
Spondias mombin	*Gboji*	Fruit, snack/sale
Ancistrophyllum sp.	*Kavo*	Fruit, in sauce
Pterocarpus santalinoides	*Kpatoi*	Seed, as sauce
Coelocaryon sp.	*Kpei*	Seed, as sauce
Irvingia gabonensis	*Bɔbɔ*	Fruit, seed
Uapaca guineensis	*Kɔndi*	Fruit
Parinari excelsa	*Ndawa*	Fruit
Bussea occidentalis	*Hela*	Seeds, roasted
Pentaclethra macrophylla	*Fawa*	Seeds, oil
Rubiaceae	*Kafo*	Fruit
Phyllanthus mellerianus	*Hɔni-wulo*	Fruit
Sacoglottis gabonensis	*Kpɔwuli*	Fruit
Myrianthus spp.	*Fɔfɔi*	Fruit
Diospyros spp.	*Ndɔku-wuli*	Fruit
Pycnanthus angolensis	*Kpɔyɛi*	Oil-rich seed
Dialium guineense	*Ngolo-mambui*	Fruit

Fungi (*fali*)

Botanical name	Mende name	English translation
Schizophyllum commune	*Kɔma-vale*	'Upper back'
unidentified	*Jɛsia-vali*	'Walking about'
unidentified	*Hita-vali*	'Termite mound'
unidentified	*Kpagbani-vali*	'Flying insect'
Termitomyces sp.	*Kpɔkpɔ-howa*	—
unidentified	*Pɔ-vali*	—
Termitomyces striatus	*Ngolo*	—
unidentified	*Kpɔwɔ*	—

TIMBER AND BUILDING POLES

Botanical name	Mende name	Uses
Terminalia ivorensis	Baji	Timber/furniture
Chlorophora regia	Semei	Timber
Heritera utilis	Yawi	Timber
Bussea occidentalis	Hela	Timber
Tieghemella heckelii	Gofilei	Timber
Entandrophragma sp.	Jilei	Timber
Bridelia sp.	Kui	Building poles
Anisophyllea laurina	Kandi	Building poles
Dichrostachys sp.	Ndandei	Building poles
Diospyros sp.	Ndɔku-wuli	Building poles
Harungana madagascariensis	Yoŋgoei	Building poles
Afzelia africana	Kpɛdɛi	Building poles

HOUSEHOLD ITEMS, TOOLS AND FIBRES

Botanical name	Mende name	Uses
Funtumia africana	Bobo	Pestles, carving, spoons
Vitex micrantha	Fɛva	Pestles
Diospyros sp.	Ndɔku-wuli	Carving, traps, pestles
Hannoa klaineana	Gbovu	Pestles
Smeathmannia sp.	Ndavote	Pestles
Lophira alata	Hɔndu	Pestles
Nauclea diderrichii	Bundu	Pestles
Microdesmis puberula	Niki	Traps, fishing nets
Newbouldia laevis	Pomamagbo	Cutlass/hoe handles
Trichoscypha sp.	Kpomaluwo	Pestles
Rubiaceae (var.)	Kafo	Cutlass/axe handles
Anisophyllea laurina	Kandi	Traps
Ochna membranacea	Kpindi	Traps
Guttiferae (var.)	Sɔlɛ/njolei	Traps
Amphimas sp.	Njombo-wuli	Traps
Chlorophora regia	Semei	Mortars
Dichrostachys sp.	Ndandei	Cutlass/axe handles
Myrianthus sp.	Fɔfɔ	Cutlass/axe handles
Mitragyna stipulosa	Mboi	Leaves for wrapping
unidentified	Koko	Leaves as string
Holarrhena floribunda	Nuku	Spoons
Musanga cecropioides	Ngovu	Kitchen ladder, drums
Terminalia ivorensis	Baji	Mortars
Pycnanthus angolensis	Kpɔyɛi	Drums
Eremospatha spp. (rattan)	Balu	Tying, baskets, mats
Elaeis guineensis (oil palm)	Tɔkpɔ	Fibres, thatch, traps
Raphia hookeri	Nduvu	Fibres, thatch, mats
Raphia palma-pinus	Keli	Thatch, mats, baskets

FUELWOOD

Botanical name	Mende name
Macaranga sp.	Ndɛvɛi
Phyllanthus discoideus	Tijoi
Xylopia aethiopica	Hɛwɛi
Vitex micrantha	Fɛva
Uapaca guineensis	Kɔndi
Funtumia sp.	Bobo
Terminalia ivorensis	Baji
Blighia sp.	Yokomei
Amphimas pterocarpioides	Njombo-wuli
Diospyros sp.	Ndɔku-wuli
Chidlowia sanguinea	Nduvu-wuli
Parianari excelsa	Ndawei
Hymenocardia sp.	Fagbajoi

ANIMALS

Animals eaten as bushmeat: non-primate

Mende name	Common name	Scientific name
Hele	Forest elephant	Loxodonta africana cyclotis
Male	Pygmy hippopotamus	Choeropsis l. libericus
Kɔli	Leopard	Panthera pardus leopardus
Tewu	Bush cow (buffalo)	Syncerus nanus
Heke	Bongo	Tragelaphus euryceros
Ndɔpɔ	Bushbuck	Tragelaphus scriptus
Hene	Zebra duiker	Cephalophus zebra
Tɛwɛ	Black duiker	Cephalophus niger
Kpɛndi	Bay duiker	Cephalophus dorsalis
Tuawo	Maxwell's duiker	Cephalophus maxwelli
Hagbe	Royal antelope	Neotragus pygmaeus
Ndonde	Bush pig	Potamoerus porcus
Kuwulo	African civet	Viverra civetta
Mɔni	Forest genet	Genetta pardina
Kanya	Pangolin	Manis tricuspis
Sɛnje	Porcupine	Atherurus africanus
Bofi	Giant forest squirrel	Protoxerus strangeri
Bovi	Red-legged squirrel	Heliosciurus rufobrachium
Sewulo	Cane rat	Thyronomis swinderianus

Primates

Mende name	Common name	Scientific name
Lɔgbɔ	Campbell's monkey	*Cercopithecus c. campbelli*
Kele	Diana monkey	*Cercopithecus d. diana*
Nduwa	Red colobus	*Procolobus badia badia*
Towo	Sooty mangabey	*Cercocebus sp.*
Tuwa	Black and white colobus	*Colobus p. polykomos*
Kpingbili	Olive colobus	*Procolobus berus*
Hokpalakole	Spot-nosed monkey	*Cercopithecus p. petaurista*
Ngolo	Chimpanzee	*Pan troglodytes verus*

Fish

Mende name	Common name	Scientific name
Ngɔkɛi	—	*Tilapia sp.*
Tɛku	—	*Epiplatys sp.*
Pele	—	unidentified
Mbɔli	—	*Hemichromis fasciatus*
Kaŋa	—	*Etenopoma kingsleiyae*
Bɛbɛ	—	*Momyrid sp.*
Ndegbe	Catfish	*Clarias sp.*
Hale	Catfish	*Clarias sp.*
Kata	Catfish	*Heterobranchus sp.*
Lɔmbulɔmbu	—	unidentified
Gbɔi	—	unidentified
Bɔdui	—	unidentified
Ngaku	Crab	*Crustacea*

SOURCES AND IDENTIFICATION

Mende names and local uses of plants and animals were recorded during fieldwork. Tree species were identified with the aid of Savill and Fox (1967). Herbaceous plant species were identified using Deighton (1957), and the kind assistance of staff at the National Herbarium, Njala University College. Animal species were identified from Davies (1987) and Haltenorth and Diller (1977). Dr Sillah of the Department of Biological Sciences, Njala University College was extremely helpful in pinpointing the scientific names of local fish species.

NOTES AND REFERENCES

INTRODUCTION

1. This study was funded by the Economic and Social Committee on Overseas Research (ESCOR) of the Overseas Development Administration (ODA).
2. The organisation of the research and the methods it used are described more fully in Appendix I.

CHAPTER 1

1. This book treats Cameroon as part of the West African forest zone, even though it is sometimes grouped as a Central African country. In ecological and species terms south-west Cameroonian forests clearly belong with those of West Africa (Martin, 1991).
2. For convenience I use the popular term 'rainforest' in this book rather than the more ecologically correct 'tropical moist forest'.
3. Many ecologists consider that on the grounds of biogeography and faunal distribution these formations should be divided further, into Upper Guinean west (Sierra Leone, Liberia, Côte d'Ivoire); Upper Guinean east (Côte d'Ivoire, Ghana) and south west Nigerian (Nigeria, Cameroon and Congo).
4. 'Natural' (also primary or old growth) forest has been defined as forest where trees have not been felled within the last 250 years (IUCN/WWF/UNEP, 1991: 126).
5. Here defined as depletion of crown cover to less than ten per cent.
6. This book cannot deal with the origins and ideologies of colonial conservation concern in Africa, fascinating as they are; these are discussed for example by Millington (1987) in relation to Sierra Leone, and by Adams (1990), Bienart (1989), Grove (1987) and MacKenzie (1988).
7. The ecological effects of logging depend heavily on how it is done. Some practices – involving selective felling and careful machinery use – can actually improve the forest according to certain economic and ecological criteria (Poore, 1989).
8. Adams (1990) provides a useful discussion of the roots and growth of global environmentalism. Significant markers included the establishment of the International Biological Programme (1964), the Man and the Biosphere Programme (1968), and the United Nations Conference on the Human Environment in Stockholm (1972).
9. These are only two among many definitions of 'sustainable development'. For

discussions of the intellectual and practical controversy surrounding this concept, see Adams (1990) and Redclift (1987).

10. In many parts of the tropical forest world, such idealisations have become closely entwined with politically motivated debates and justifications for the rights and status of 'indigenous peoples'. Regardless of the often laudable aims to which such politically motivated concepts are put, it is important that they do not misdirect analysis of rural forest societies.

CHAPTER 2

1. This is necessarily selective. Potentially there are as many ways of theorising the relationship between gender and the environment as there are strands of feminism and strands of environmentalism.
2. See also Lynggard and Moberg, 1990; Rodda, 1991; Sontheimer, 1991.
3. My treatment of ecofeminism is highly selective, and not all ecofeminists would necessarily subscribe to the views presented here. A more comprehensive picture of ecofeminist debates from a variety of feminist viewpoints can be gleaned from Diamond and Orenstein (1990) and Plant (1989); Plumwood (1986) provides a useful overview.
4. I am using the term 'closer to nature' in the same ill-defined way as most ecofeminist authors. The spatial metaphor 'closer to' variously seems to become a political metaphor ('allied with'), a kinship metaphor ('belonging to'), or a biological metaphor ('part of').
5. For discussion of the issue of essentialism in feminist theory, see Fuss (1989).
6. Some anthropological formulations consider that binary oppositions such as nature:culture are basic to all human thought at an unconscious level. Avoiding the extensive debate on this issue, the present discussion treats the issue at the level of consciously held 'folk models', assuming (as Ortner implies) that such constructs are relatively accessible parts of people's self-awareness.
7. Shiva (1989) argues that Hindu cosmology viewed nature as Prakriti, both activity and diversity, and 'an expression of Shakti, the feminine and creative principle of the cosmos' which 'in conjunction with the masculine principle (Purusha) . . . creates the world'.
8. Even those ecofeminist arguments which recognise the need to differentiate women by age, ethnicity, level of wealth, etc. (e.g. King, 1989) do not pursue the implications of this for their basic analysis.
9. I cannot do justice to this extensive literature here. Conceptual and methodological issues are discussed, for example, by Guyer (1981), Guyer and Peters (1987), Evans (1991) and Harris (1984). Leach (1991b) and Mackintosh (1991) are among many West African case studies showing the inadequacy of 'household' models.

CHAPTER 3

1. Mende is classified along with Gbande, Kpelle, Loko and Loma as a south-west Mande language (Greenberg, 1966).
2. Gola is classified as a West Atlantic or Mel language, along with several other languages currently spoken in Sierra Leone and adjacent Liberia (Temne, Kissi, Limba and Sherbro/Bullom).
3. The precise dates and reasons for the spread of the Mende language in Sierra Leone are uncertain and disputed. Some historians link it to the 'Mane invasions' in the mid-sixteenth century (Rodney, 1967 and 1970; see also Hair, 1962), but others believe it to be a more recent, eighteenth- or nineteenth-century phenomenon.

4. For instance, certain aspects of marriage and social organisation around Gola North are more easily interpreted with reference to Gola ethnography (e.g. D'Azevedo, 1962a and 1962b) than to other Mende areas.

5. About 90 per cent of Madina villagers consider themselves Muslim, and about 10 per cent Christian. These world religions coexist and interact with resilient Mende ideas concerning God (ŋgɛwɔ), spirits and medicine (Reeck, 1976).

6. At the same time, this study's focus on natural resource management and everyday forest life should supplement previous ethnographers' concerns with more obviously socially salient life processes and events.

7. For example, on general aspects of Mende social and political organisation, see Little (1967). On gender see Hoffer (1972 and 1975), MacCormack (1975 and 1979), Bledsoe (1984) and Boone (1986). On aspects of 'Mende religion', see Harris and Sawyer (1968), Jedrej (1976a and b) and Gittins (1987).

8. There is a large literature on Poro and Sande. See, for example, Boone (1986), Bledsoe (1980a and 1984), Jedrej (1976a and 1980), Little (1949, 1965 and 1966), D'Azevedo (1980) and MacCormack (1975 and 1979).

9. *Hale* plays a central role in Mende life. While I adopt Little's (1967) shorthand 'medicine' in later chapters, *hale* is better glossed more broadly as 'esoteric' or 'special' power. Gittins' (1987: 103) definition of *hale* as 'metaphysical' seems doubtful, since Mende think of *hale* as physical power. It is often explicitly or implicitly recognised as a specific manifestation of the power of ŋgɛwɔ (God), which people can obtain through various forms of sacrifice.

CHAPTER 4

1. Rice is essential for social life. Not only is it central to cultural notions of dietary adequacy, considered as the only real food (*mɛhɛ vuli*), it is also integral to processes that bind and legitimate social relations and can in this sense be envisaged as a kind of 'social glue' (Linares, 1985). Rice is shared to express friendship and love; it is central to political hospitality, funerals and initiations.

2. This book discusses such spirits in relation to day-to-day resource-using activities. Further details, beliefs, stories and ceremonies connected with them are documented by Gittins (1987), Harris (1954) and Harris and Sawyerr (1968).

3. These ancestral spirits are usually distinguished as *kekeni* and *mamadani*, the spirits of those who died within living memory, rather than of *ndebla*, those who died long ago.

4. For example, she might be laughed at, or feared as someone with anti-social tendencies, such as possession of a witch spirit (*hɔna*).

5. In such circumstances the woman is considered merely a temporary custodian of the land. Control is expected to revert to male hands when this becomes feasible, although in practice lineage segments (and land control) sometimes remain under female leadership for several generations, passing from a mother to her daughter, for instance. One of the (six or seven) landholding families in Madina in 1988 was headed by a woman.

6. Murphy and Bledsoe (1987) provide a detailed account of settlement, land relations and links between kinship and territory in a Kpelle chiefdom, where the processes have been broadly similar to those in the Gola forest area. Abraham (1978) discusses the part played by warfare in these processes, and the ways the British colonial administration interpreted and restructured fluid precolonial political relations.

7. The term *mawɛɛ* seems to have originated during the turbulent warfare times of

early forest settlement, to refer to the entire group of male and female dependents and 'slaves' whom a warrior protected and accommodated (Little 1948a). The main social features were retained after the decline of warfare and slavery at the end of the nineteenth century.

8. For example, an elderly woman, her daughter and her granddaughter, all single, could not farm in 1988 because the two older women were ill, the youngest was pregnant, and male labour and cash were scarce. All three women were fit by November but had no rice to harvest. Asked how they would manage, the eldest woman explained that 'we must find a lot of rice this year'.

9. Chapter 8 discusses Mende attitudes to extra-marital affairs, and their economic importance to women, in more detail.

10. Women are also involved in tree crop cultivation, but in tasks that fall mainly in the dry season.

11. I have no data for 1989. The varied total numbers of farm-households each year reflect the year-to-year organisational rearrangements discussed earlier, as well as in- and out-migration.

CHAPTER 5

1. Coffee (*Coffea liberica*) is indigenous to the forests of the Mano river basin, but the main cultivar in Sierra Leone is the *robusta* variety from the Zaire basin (Gwynne-Jones, 1975).

2. Patron–client relations which bind farmers to sell to particular traders often lead farmers to accept what outside analysts would consider unduly low prices for their produce. Farmgate prices are also depressed because 'official' prices are announced too late in the season, and because sub-agents are involved (Bolder *et al.*, 1980; Peperkamp, 1984).

3. Die-outs are customarily replaced with new seedlings, so old tree farms still produce despite the 20–25 year limit on the productive lifespan of individual trees.

4. It is argued that such possibilities on forest land controlled by the state have underlain much of the expansion of smallholder cocoa production in Côte d'Ivoire, and to widespread deforestation associated with it (Hecht, 1983: 33).

5. Women in polygynous societies often have several husbands in the course of their lifetimes (serial polyandry) since it is common for young women to marry much older men, and to remarry when such husbands die.

6. The issue of financial transfers between husbands and wives is considered in more detail in chapter 8.

7. For example, one wife took a few pans of cocoa every time her husband and other members of a labour group left her breaking cocoa pods to carry produce back to the village. She concealed her accumulated pile of cocoa under banana leaves in the adjacent swamp, and fetched it the next day. Another three co-wives each contributed their small amounts of coffee amassed during respectively assigned tasks to a bag hidden in their sleeping house, sharing the profits from its sale at the end of the season.

CHAPTER 6

1. It seems more useful to focus, as Mende do, on the functions served by forest products than exhaustively to list species and their uses (cf. Falconer, 1990: 86). Accordingly, only a few examples of species are included in this chapter. More comprehensive lists by use category are given in Appendix II, and by Davies and Richards (1991). Savill and Fox (1967) identify Mende uses of Sierra Leonean tree species, although not all the uses they list were found in Madina.

2. Such exchange networks, which are of central importance to women's management of the day-to-day food economy, are discussed in more detail in Chapter 8.

3. Women purify palm oil by boiling it to make *ngulɔgbandi*, 'warmed oil'. This is used to render the skin moist and glistening, counteracting the dryness that signals old age and infertility.

4. 'Black soap' or 'country soap' (*Mende bawei*) combines palm oil with an alkali (*libi*) obtained from burned cocoa or *Pentaclethra* husks or other plant materials, through a preparation process requiring special female skills, into a sticky black substance with healing properties.

5. In their multifunctionality and polivalency, such plants are in some ways similar to staple food crops with a long history of cultivation (cf. Linares, 1985).

6. In (men's) ideal terms, co-wives share a kitchen, but wives often prefer to cook and to store their produce and tools separately. An influential senior wife can sometimes insist that her husband build her a separate kitchen; other wives sometimes have them built by their brothers or sons.

7. Fishing nets are feminine symbols, and weaving them is integral to the socio-culturally important activity of women's fishing, as Chapter 7 will show.

8. The national forest estate in 1980 covered a total of 2,853 km^2 of reserved forest and 118 km^2 of protected forest.

9. Such a linked division of labour and product rights was also common in other parts of pre-colonial West Africa (Martin, 1988).

10. By contrast Martin reports that men in south east Nigeria took over the oil industry but did not take over the kernel industry, reflecting 'the fact that women's property rights in the nuts were firmly anchored in local conventions' (1988: 47). She suggests that this was partly because men were unwilling to take over the work involved in cracking the nuts.

11. Whether husbands are obliged to *provide* palm oil for their wives – such as by purchase – is quite another question, considered in Chapter 8.

12. This integration also makes it difficult, not to say inappropriate, to analyse the relative proportions of time spent by villagers in gathering and agricultural activities.

13. The two uses can conflict both because palms do not bear fruit while being tapped, and because over-zealous wine-tapping, when too much is taken each day over a period longer than about three months, destroys the palm's oil-bearing potential for the future.

14. For example, in several villages, the town chief and descent-group heads designated a special area of bush from which refugees could collect palm fruit.

CHAPTER 7

1. For example the son of a well-known hunter in Misila related the following story: 'My father used to turn himself into an elephant and hunt among them. One day a bull elephant charged him and nearly killed him. His medicine had failed, and the elephant had seen through his transformation. When he reached town and told my mother, she simply said, "You had a very lucky escape." She meant that she had been with her lover while he was out.'

2. Hunters use the following story to explain 'why there are no teachers among the *kamajɛisia*' (i.e. why all are equal): 'A group of *kamajɛisia* encountered a *ndɔgbɔjusu* (deep bush devil) while walking, well spread out, along a forest path. The *ndɔgbɔjusu* asked the first "Where is your teacher?" and the *kamajɔ* replied, "Coming behind", and continued freely on his way. Each in turn replied in the same way. Once the last had passed there were no teachers, and no hunters for the *ndɔgbɔjusu* to disturb'.

CHAPTER 8

1. Economic reforms undertaken by the Sierra Leone government in 1990–1 as part of moves towards IMF-recommended 'Structural Adjustment' included marketing liberalisation, intended to result in increased producer prices to tree-crop farmers. Some farmers received higher prices from traders in 1991 than in the previous season. But such reforms, even if generally effective, are unlikely to counter the decline in world market prices.
2. In 1988 several thousand Malema chiefdom residents and strangers flocked to a diamond-digging site in the forest near Bandajuma. The following year, diamonds were discovered at Kotuma in the adjacent Jawi chiefdom and many diggers moved there.
3. For example, during 1990 Malema chiefdom residents faced repeated demands to contribute money and rice to support a government-installed regent chief, pending the election of a new paramount chief.
4. This may include fostered children. Child fosterage is common among Mende who consider it as a means both to assist children's progress and to create and consolidate social and political relationships between adults (cf. Bledsoe, 1990; Bledsoe and Isiugo-Abanihe, 1989).

CHAPTER 9

1. This was established in 1967 within the Forestry Division of the Ministry of Agriculture.
2. I am grateful to Dianne Rocheleau, who clarified this for me through her illumination of a similar example of women's 'soil conservation' in Kenya.

GLOSSARY

This glossary includes most of the Mende words cited in the text as single terms, but not those words cited only within sentences or phrases.

Tone notation:

high tone	´
low tone	(unmarked)
rising tone	ˇ
falling tone	^

Mende	English
bâa	Respect, price
bugbe	Cutlass
bului	Low-lying, run-off plot at foot of soil catena
bundi	Pit for washing palm fruit
fáli	To scatter (general), to broadcast seed
famálo	Greeting present
fandé	Cotton, thread
fɛ̂	Cooking pot
gadi	Vegetable plot, tree crop garden
gbɔ́	Help, assist, assistance
gbɔɛɛ	'Strong' fallow farmbush, c. 11–14years old
hakpá	Vegetable, sauce of boiled leaves and palm oil
hálé	Medicine/power
hálé nyámu	'Bad' medicine; i.e. used with destructive intent
hindâ	Place, affair, business
hîŋ	To plant
hîndo	Man, male
hinî	Husband
hɔ́ná	Witch spirit
hɔ́námɔ	Witch, i.e. person with witch spirit in their belly
hótá	Stranger, guest
hótá-kɛɛ	Stranger-father, host
hoú	Hold, take hold of

hɔ́hɔ́	Trap for fish or squirrels
huáŋ	Animal, meat
hugbatê	Arrange, take care, look after family property
húgbatêmɔ	Caretaker/manager
húmá	To steal, stealing, theft
jína	Non-ancestral/bush or forest spirit
káká	Area, piece, circle
kalɛ	Fence across a stream in which traps are set
kâa lopo	'Learning boy', apprentice, school child
káli	Hoe
kamajɔ́	Trained hunter who uses medicines
kamantí	Casting net for fishing
kénya	Maternal uncle
kɛké	Father, paternal uncle, respectful address to a man
kɛkéni	Ancestors (recently dead)
kísi	Kitchen
kókó	Fence around a farm
kondâ	Mortar
kondi-gulâ	Cotton country cloth
kɔ́	To give, give food to, a gift
kɔ	War, fight
kɔ-maha	War-chief
kɔ́li	To pick (e.g. fruit, coffee)
kɔ́li	Greed, meanness
kɔ́mbi	Company, society, labour group
kɔ́mí-wulɔ	Honey
kɔ́ndɔ́	Food prepared for workers
kɔti ˙	Stone, gravelly soil
kpaa	Rice farm
kpaa wa	Big/household rice farm
kpaa mumu	Small/individual rice farm
kpándê	Gun
kpatê	Wealth, prosperity
kpayá	Strength, power
kpété	Inland valley swamp, swamp rice farm
kpɛ́	Chase, hunt
kpiti	'Grass' outside a farm
kpɛwɔ	Tree-level trap for squirrels and monkeys
kpowâ	Farm hut
kpɔkɔ́	Evening
kpúwu	Rice barn
kúgbé	Warrior, group leader
kúgbé	Group of hired farm workers
kulâ	Cloth
kŭu	Local kin group: group of patrikin and residential affiliates occupying a section of a village
láválé	Speaker
lema	To forget

măgbatê	To prepare, a gift kept for someone
mahá	Chief, leader
máké	Training, train, raise a child
mamá	Grandmother, elderly woman, term of address
mamáda/maáda	Grandfather, elderly man, term of address
mamadáni	Ancestors (recently dead)
manî	Trap
mawéé	Past: residential/farming group. Present: (i) group of people who seek protection of same patron in town business; (ii) residential household; (iii) farm-household
mawéémɔ	*Mawεε* head
mbăa	Companion, age-mate, co-wife
mbalá	Sheep
mbálé	Hoop used to climb palm trees
mbawoma	Farm-site after rice harvest
mbembé	Scoop-fishing net
mbondâ	Family: consanguines, affines and residential affiliates
mbúmbú	Fish trap
mě	Eat, misappropriate
mεhê	Food
motihun	Farm-site after burning
navó	Money
ndaháiŋ	Meat/fish
ndakpâ	Young man, male age mate
ndáwúlɔ́	Palm-kernel oil
ndebla	Ancestors (long dead)
ndéhu	Patrilineage
ndéhunbla	Group of patrikin at core of *kuu*
ndéwe, ndée	Brother, sister, cousin
ndíámɔ́	Friend, lover
ndíí	Heart, seat of emotions
ndó	Child
ndoahú	Difference, boundary
ndóé	To brush, cut bush
ndoeke	Farm-site after initial brushing
ndólí	Fish hook
ndomá	Love, favourite
ndɔ́	Palm wine
ndɔgbɔ́	Bush
ndɔgbɔhínti	'Strong' fallow farmbush, *c.* 15–30 years old
ndɔgbɔjúsu	Deep bush 'devil'
ndɔ́lɔ	Country, ground, world
ndɔ́lɔ mahá	Paramount chief
ndɔlé	Hunger, hungry season
ndɔwɔ́	Weekly market
nεέ	Tongue, clitoris
ngafâ	Spirit
ngĕnda	Morning
ngengé	Work, job

ngetê	Pestle
ngevô	Dry season
ŋgɛwɔ́	God
ngílí	To cook
ngolâ	High forest, >30–40 years old
ngolagbaa	Farm made in high forest
ngɔɔ	Elder brother/sister, respectful term of address to a person older than the speaker
ngúlɔ́	Oil
ngulu	Tree, weed
ngúlɔ́gbɔu	Red palm-fruit oil
ngúndé	Fireplace
njagbe	Sister's child
njalói	Water spirit
nje	Mother (*yie* – term of address to an older woman)
njé	Goat
njɔpɔ́	Young fallow farmbush, normally <10 years old
nú	Person
númu wa	Big person, patron
nú wova	Old person
njoyô	To send a gift, gift sent to someone
nyahâ	Woman, wife
nyahâmagbangoe	Post-menopausal woman
nyahâ wá	Senior wife, big woman
nyahâ wúlo	Junior wife
nyăpo	Young woman
nyɛ́	Fish
pawa	To pay, payment
pélɛ́	House
pélɛ́ wá	Women's sleeping house
píyɛ́	Basket to hold fish
poé, póe gbua	Extra-marital sex
pokpaa	Farm-site after tree felling
pówó	Loose talk, sex talk
pɔ́	To fell trees
Pɔ́ɔ́	Poro, men's secret society
pujâ	To dig with a hoe
puu	Europe, European, Westernised
sáini	To nurse/try out, an experiment
sámbá	Broad, open basket
Sande	Sande, women's secret society
sawa	Rule, law, commandment
sɛ́mɛ́	Barri, court house, open-sided building for public meetings
tă	Town
tă mahá	Town chief
ta yenge	Community labour
tawu	Fish poison
téé	Cut, harvest rice

Bell, R., 1987. 'Conservation with a human face: conflict and reconciliation in African land use planning', in *Conservation in Africa: People, Policies and Practice*, D. Anderson and R. Grove (eds), 79–101. Cambridge: Cambridge University Press.

Bellman, B., 1984. *The Language of Secrecy: Symbols and Metaphors in Poro Ritual.* New Brunswick: Rutgers University Press.

Berkes, F. (ed.), 1989. *Common Property Resources: Ecology and Community-based Sustainable Development.* London: Belhaven Press.

Berry, S., 1975. *Cocoa, Custom and Socio-economic Change in Rural Western Nigeria.* Oxford: Clarendon Press.

—— 1988. 'Property rights and rural resource management: the case of tree crops in West Africa', *Cahiers des Sciences Humaines* (ORSTOM) 24 (1), 3–16.

—— 1989. 'Social institutions and access to resources', *Africa* 59 (1), 41–55.

Bienart, W., 1989. 'Introduction: the politics of colonial conservation', *Journal of Southern African Studies* 15 (2), 143–62.

Bledsoe, C., 1980a. 'Stratification and Sande politics', *Ethnologische Zeitschrift Zürich* 1, 133–42.

—— 1980b. *Women and Marriage in Kpelle Society.* Stanford: Stanford University Press.

—— 1984. 'The political use of Sande ideology and symbolism', *American Ethnologist*, 455–72.

—— 1987. 'The politics of polygyny in Mende education and child fosterage transactions', in *Gender-hierarchies*, B. D. Miller (ed.).

—— 1990. '"No success without struggle": social mobility and hardship for foster children in Sierra Leone', *Man* (NS) 25, 70–88.

Bledsoe, C. and Goubaud, M., 1985. 'The reinterpretation of western pharmaceuticals among the Mende of Sierra Leone', *Social Science and Medicine* 21 (3), 275–82.

Bledsoe, C. and Isiugo-Abanihe, U. C., 1989. 'Strategies of child fosterage among Mende "grannies" in Sierra Leone', in *African Reproduction and Social Organization*, R. Lesthaeghe (ed.). Berkeley: University of California Press.

Bledsoe, C. and Robey, K. M., 1986. 'Arabic literacy and secrecy among the Mende of Sierra Leone', *Man* (NS) 21, 202–26.

Bolder, R., Huisman, P., den Otter, W., Peperkamp E., and Stevens, J., 1980. *The Production and Marketing of Export Crops by Small Farmers in Sierra Leone.* Unpublished manuscript, Nijmegen.

Boone, S. A., 1986. *Radiance from the Waters: Ideals of Feminine Beauty in Mende Art.* New Haven: Yale University Press.

Boserup, E., 1970. *Women's Role in Economic Development.* London: Allen & Unwin.

Bradley, P. N., 1990. 'If I had known the discussion was to be about kuni I wouldn't have wasted my time in coming', in *Agroforestry for Sustainable Production: Economic Implications*, R. T. Prinsley (ed.). London: Commonwealth Science Council, 123–46.

—— 1991. *Woodfuel, Women and Woodlots: Volume 1, The Foundations of a Woodfuel Development Strategy for East Africa.* London and Basingstoke: Macmillan.

Bromley, D. W. and Cernea, M. M., 1989. 'The management of common property natural resources: some conceptual and operational fallacies', *World Bank Discussion Paper* 57. Washington DC: World Bank.

Bruce, J. and Fortmann, L., 1989. 'Agroforestry: tenure and incentives', *Land Tenure Centre Paper* 135, University of Wisconsin-Madison.

Bukh, J., 1979. *The Village Woman in Ghana.* Uppsala: Scandinavian Institute of African Studies.

Cashman, K., 1991. 'Systems of knowledge as systems of domination: the limits of established meaning', *Agriculture and Human Values* 8 (1 and 2).

Cernea, M., 1989. 'User groups as producers in participatory afforestation strategies', *World Bank Discussion Paper* 70. Washington DC: World Bank.

Chambers, R., 1987. 'Sustainable rural livelihoods: a strategy for people, environment and development', *IDS Commissioned Study* No.7. Brighton: Institute of Development Studies.

Chambers, R. and Leach, M., 1989. 'Trees as savings and security for the rural poor', *World Development* 17 (3), 329–42.

Chambers, R., Conroy, C. and Leach, M. (1992). 'Trees as savings and security for the rural poor', *IIED Gatekeeper*. London: IIED.

Chambers, R. Pacey, A. and Thrupp, L. A. (eds), 1989. *Farmer First: Farmer Innovation and Agricultural Research*. London: IT Publications.

Chimedza, R., 1989. 'Women, natural resource management and household food security: an overview', in *Women's Role in Natural Resource Management in Africa*, E. Rathgeber (ed.), 73–86. Canada: IDRC.

Christophersen, K. A., Karch, G. E. and Arnould, E., 1990. *Economic Incentives for Natural Resources Management*. Natural Resources Management Support Project. Washington: AID

Clad, J. C., 1985. 'Conservation and indigenous peoples: a study of convergent interests', in *Culture and Conservation*, J. McNeely and D. Pitt (eds), 45–62. London and Sydney: Croom Helm.

Clarke, J. I. (ed.), 1969. *Sierra Leone in Maps*. London: Hodder & Stoughton.

Cleaver, K., 1992. 'Deforestation in the western and central African forest: the agricultural and demographic causes, and some solutions', in 'Conservation of West and Central African Rainforests', *World Bank Environment Paper* No.1, K. Cleaver *et al.*(eds), 65–78. Washington DC: World Bank.

Cline-Cole, R. A., 1984. 'Towards an understanding of man-firewood relations in Freetown (Sierra Leone)', *Geoforum* 15 (4), 583–94.

Coulthard, N., 1990. 'RSPB has a new project in Africa: Sierra Leone, the Gola Rain Forest', *Birds Magazine*, Winter, 18–20.

Crosby, K. H., 1937. 'Polygamy in Mende country', *Africa* 10 (3), 249–64.

Cunningham, M. K., 1991. 'Mende kinship reconsidered: a critique of the patrilineal/patrilocal assumptions in Mende ethnography', paper presented at the American Anthropological Association 90th Meeting, Chicago, 20–24 November 1991.

Dalziel, J., 1937. *The Useful Plants of West Tropical Africa*. London: Crown Agents.

Dankelman, I. and Davidson, J., 1988. *Women and Environment in the Third World: Alliance for the Future*. London: Earthscan Publications.

Davidson, J., 1990. 'Gender and environment: ideas for action and research', paper presented at Conference on Environment, Development and Economic Research, ODI, London 27–28 March 1990.

Davies, G., 1987. *The Gola Forest Reserves, Sierra Leone: Wildlife Conservation and Forest Management*. Cambridge and Switzerland: IUCN.

—— 1990. *Survey of Agro-forestry Potential of Indigenous Trees in Sierra Leone*. Report to GTZ, Bo-Pujehun Rural Development Project.

Davies, A. G. and Leach, M. (1991). 'Indigenous cocoa plantation management and rainforest conservation in Sierra Leone'. Unpublished manuscript.

Davies, S., Leach, M. and David, R., 1991. 'Food security and the environment: conflict or complementarity?', *IDS Discussion Paper* 285. Brighton: Institute of Development Studies.

Davies, G. and Richards, P., 1991. 'Rain Forest in Mende life: resources and subsistence strategies in rural communities around the Gola North forest reserve (Sierra Leone)', report to ESCOR, UK Overseas Development Administration.

Davison, J. (ed.), 1988. *Agriculture, Women and Land: the African Experience*. Boulder and London: Westview Press.

D'Azevedo, W. L., 1962a. 'Uses of the past in Gola discourse', *Journal of African History* 11, 11–34.

—— 1962b. 'Common principles of variant kinship structures among the Gola of western Liberia', *American Anthropologist* 64, 505–20.

—— 1962c. 'Some historical problems in the delineation of a Central West Atlantic Region', *Annals, New York Academy of Sciences* 96, 513–38.

—— 1980. 'Gola Poro and Sande: primal tasks in social custodianship', *Ethnologische Zeitschrift Zürich* 1, 13–24.

Deighton, F. C., 1957. *Vernacular Botanical Vocabulary for Sierra Leone*. London: Crown Agents.

De Klemm, C., 1985. 'Culture and conservation: some thoughts for the future', in *Culture and Conservation*, J. McNeely and D. Pitt (eds), 239–58. London and Sydney: Croom Helm.

Devitt, P., 1989. *Korup Project Socio-economic Survey*. Gland, Switzerland: WWF.

Diamond, I. and Orenstein, G. F. (eds), 1990. *Reweaving the World: the Emergence of Ecofeminism*. San Francisco: Sierra Club Books.

Dries, I., 1989. 'Development of wetlands in Sierra Leone: farmers' rationality opposed to government policy', in *The People's Role in Wetland Management: Proceedings of the International Conference on Wetlands*, Leiden, The Netherlands, 5–8 June.

Dupire, M., 1960. 'Planteurs, autochtones et étrangères en basse Côte d'Ivoire orientale', *Etudes Eburnéennes* 8, 7–38.

Durning, A., 1988. 'Poverty and the environment: reversing the downward spiral', *Worldwatch Paper* 92. Washington DC: Worldwatch Institute.

Ellen, R. F., 1986. 'What Black Elk left unsaid: on the illusory images of Green primitivism', *Anthropology Today* 2 (6), 8–12.

Engel, A., Karimu, J. *et al.*, 1984. 'Promoting Smallholder Cropping Systems in Sierra Leone: an Assessment of Traditional Cropping Systems and Recommendations for the Bo-Pujehun Rural Development Project', unpublished paper, Technical University, Berlin.

Evans, A., 1991. 'Gender issues in rural household economics', *IDS Bulletin* 22 (1), 51–9. Brighton: Institute of Development Studies.

Falconer, J., 1990. 'The major significance of "minor" forest products: local people's uses and values of forests in the west African humid forest zone', *Community Forestry Note* 6. Rome: FAO.

FAO, 1985. *The Tropical Forestry Action Plan*. FAO, World Bank, UNDP. Rome: FAO.

FAO, 1987. *Restoring the Balance: Women and Forest Resources*. Rome: FAO.

FAO, 1988. *An Interim Report on the State of Forest Resources in the Developing Countries*. Rome: FAO.

FAO, 1989. *Women in Community Forestry: a Field Guide for Project Design and Implementation*. Rome: FAO.

FAO, 1990. *Interim Report on Forest Resources Assessment 1990*. Committee on Forestry, tenth session, 24–28 September 1990, Rome.

Flint, M., 1991. *Biological Diversity and Developing Countries: Issues and Options*. Synthesis paper for Overseas Development Administration. London: ODA.

Fortmann, L., 1985. 'The tree tenure factor in agroforestry with particular reference to Africa', *Agroforestry Systems* 2, 229–51.

Fortmann, L. and Bruce, J. (eds), 1988. *Whose Trees? Proprietary Dimensions of Forestry*. Boulder and London: Westview Press.

Fortmann, L. and Riddell, J., 1985. *Trees and Tenure: an Annotated Bibliography for Agroforesters and Others*. ICRAF, Nairobi and Land Tenure Centre, University of Wisconsin.

Fortmann, L. and Rocheleau, D., 1985. 'Women and agroforestry: four myths and three case studies', *Agroforestry Systems* 2, 253–72.

Francis, P. and Atta-Krah (n.d.). 'Institutions, Resources and Land Management in Southern Nigeria'. Unpublished manuscript.

Fuss, D., 1989. *Essentially Speaking: Feminism, Nature and Difference*. New York: Routledge.

Fyfe, C., 1962. *A History of Sierra Leone*. Oxford: Oxford University Press.

Gittins, A. J., 1987. *Mende Religion: Aspects of Belief and Thought in Sierra Leone*. Styler Verlag: Wort und Werk.

Goba, J., 1984. 'Coffee and Cocoa Land Use in Mattru on the Rail: a Case Study of the Development of Cash Crops in a Section Town of Tikonko Chiefdom, Bo District', BA dissertation, Njala University College, University of Sierra Leone.

Goody, J. (ed.), 1958. *The Developmental Cycle in Domestic Groups*. Cambridge: Cambridge University Press.

Gordon, O. L. A., Kater, G. and Schwarr, D. C., 1979. 'Vegetation and land use in Sierra Leone', *UNDP/FAO Technical Report* No. 2. AG:DP/SIL/73/002.

Government of Sierra Leone, 1989. *Unified Action Programme for Increased Rice Production by Small-scale Farmers*. Ministry of Agriculture, Natural Resources and Forestry, and FAO. Field Document TCP/SIL/8952. Rome: FAO.

Gradwohl, J. and Greenberg, R., 1988. *Saving the Tropical Forests*. London: Earthscan Publications.

Greenberg, J. H., 1966. *The Languages of Africa*. Bloomington: Indiana University Press.

Grove, R., 1987. 'Early themes in African conservation: the Cape in the nineteenth century', in *Conservation in Africa: People, Policies and Practice*, D. Anderson and R. Grove (eds.), 21–39. Cambridge: Cambridge University Press.

Guyer, J., 1980. 'Food, cocoa and the division of labour by sex in two West African societies', *Comparative Studies in Society and History* 22 (3), 355–73.

—— 1981. 'Household and community in African studies', *African Studies Review* 24 (2/3), 87–137.

—— 1984a. *Family and Farm in Southern Cameroon*. Boston: Boston University African Studies Centre.

—— 1984b. 'Naturalism in models of African production', *Man* (NS) 19, 371–88.

—— 1986. 'Intra-household processes and farming systems research: perspectives from anthropology', in *Understanding Africa's Rural Households and Farming Systems*, J. Moock (ed.), 92–104. Boulder and London: Westview Press.

—— 1988. 'The multiplication of labour: historical methods in the study of gender and agricultural change in modern Africa', *Current Anthropology* 29 (2), 247–59.

Guyer, J. and Peters, P., 1987. 'Introduction', in *Conceptualising the household: issues of theory and policy in Africa*, special issue of *Development and Change*, 18 (2), 197–214.

Gwynne-Jones, D. R. G., 1975. *The Geography of Sierra Leone*. UK: Longman.

Hair, P. E. H., 1962. 'An account of the Liberian hinterland c. 1780', *Sierra Leone Studies* 16, 218-66.

Haltenorth, T. and Diller, H., 1977. *A Field Guide to the Mammals of Africa*. London: Collins.

Hannan-Andersson, C., 1990. *Consultancy on the Women and Natural Resources Management (WNRM) Programme in IUCN*. Consultancy report, Stockholm.

Hardin, G., 1968. 'The tragedy of the commons', *Science* 162, 1243–8.

Harris, O., 1984. 'Households as natural units', in *Of Marriage and the Market*, K. Young *et al.* (eds), 49–68. London: Routledge & Kegan Paul.

Harris, O. and Young, K., 1981. 'Engendered structures: some problems in the analysis of reproduction', in *The Anthropology of Pre-capitalist Societies*, J. Kahn and J. Llobera (eds), 109–47. London: Macmillan.

Harris, W. T., 1954. 'Ceremonies and stories connected with trees, rivers and hills in the Protectorate of Sierra Leone', *Sierra Leone Studies* 2, 91–7.

Harris, W. T. and Sawyerr, H., 1968. *The Springs of Mende Belief and Conduct*. Freetown: Sierra Leone University Press.

Hazell, P. and Magrath, W., 1992. 'Summary of World Bank forestry policy', in K. Cleaver *et al.* (eds), 'Conservation of West and Central African Rainforests'. *World Bank Environment Paper* No. 1, 10–20. Washington DC: World Bank.

Hecht, R. M., 1983. 'The Ivory Coast economic "miracle": what benefits for peasant farmers', *Journal of Modern African Studies* 21, 25–53.

Hecht, S. B., Anderson, A. B. and May, P., 1988. 'The subsidy from nature: shifting cultivation, successional palm forests and rural development', *Human Organisation* 47 (1), 25–35.

Hill, M., 1984. 'Where to begin? the place of the hunter founders in Mende histories', *Anthropos* 79, 653–6.

Hill, P., 1956. *The Gold Coast Cocoa Farmer*. Oxford: Oxford University Press.

—— 1963. *Migrant Cocoa Farmers of Southern Ghana*. Cambridge: Cambridge University Press.

Hoeksema, J., 1989. 'Women and social forestry', *BOS Document* 10, Amsterdam.

Hoffer, C., 1972. 'Mende and Sherbro women in high office', *Canadian Journal of African Studies* 6 (2), 151–64.

—— 1974. 'Madam Yoko: ruler of the Kpa Mende confederacy', in *Woman, Culture and Society*, M. Z. Rosaldo and L. Lamphere (eds), 173–88. Stanford: Stanford University Press.

—— 1975. 'Bundu: political implications of female solidarity in a secret society', in *Being Female: Reproduction, Power, and Change*, D. Raphael (ed.), 155–63. The Hague and Paris: Mouton.

Hofstra, S., 1937. 'The social significance of the oil palm in the life of the Mendi', *Internationales Archiv. für Ethnographie* 34, 105–18.

Hoskins, M., 1983. 'Rural Women, Forest Outputs and Forestry Projects', draft paper for FAO Forestry Department, Rome.

Hough, J., 1988. 'Obstacles to effective management of conflicts between national parks and surrounding communities in developing countries', *Environmental Conservation* 15 (2), 129–36.

ILO, 1990. *Alleviating Unemployment and Poverty under Adjustment – Issues and Strategies for Sierra Leone*. Report on ILO/JASPA Employment Advisory Mission. Addis Ababa: ILO.

Innes, G., 1969. *A Mende-English Dictionary*. Cambridge: Cambridge University Press.

—— 1971. *A Practical Introduction to Mende*. London: School of Oriental and African Studies.

IUCN/WWF/UNEP, 1980. *World Conservation Strategy: Living Resource Conservation for Sustainable Development*. Gland, Switzerland.

—— 1991. *Caring for the Earth: a Strategy for Sustainable Living*. Gland, Switzerland.

Jackson, M., 1977. *The Kuranko: Dimensions of Social Reality in a West African Society*. London: C. Hurst.

Jeanrenaud, S., 1990. 'A Study of Forest Use, Agricultural Practices, and Perceptions of the Rainforest: Etinde Rainforest, South West Cameroon', draft report to Overseas Development Administration.

Jedrej, M. C., 1976a. 'Medicine, fetish and secret society in a West African culture', *Africa* 46, 247–57.

—— 1976b. 'An analytic note on the land and spirits of the Sewa Mende', *Africa* 44, 38–45.

—— 1980. 'Structural aspects of a West African secret society', *Ethnologische Zeitschrift Zürich* 1, 133–42.

Johnny, M., 1985. 'Informal credit for integrated rural development in Sierra Leone,' *Studien zur Integrierten Landlichen Entwicklung* No. 6. Hamburg: Weltarchiv.

Johnny, M., Karimu, J. and Richards, P., 1981. 'Upland and swamp rice farming systems in Sierra Leone: the social context of technological change', *Africa* 51, 596–620.

Kamara, J. N., 1986. *Firewood Energy in Sierra Leone: Production, Marketing and Household Use Patterns*. Hamburg: Verlag Weltarchiv.

Karimu, J., 1981. 'Strategies for Peasant Farmer Development: an Evaluation of a Rural Development Project in Northern Sierra Leone', unpublished PhD thesis, University of London.

King, Y., 1989. 'The ecology of feminism and the feminism of ecology', in *Healing the Wounds: the Promise of Ecofeminism*, J. Plant, (ed.), 18–28. Philadelphia: New Society Publishers.

Klomberg, A. and van Riessen, A., 1983. 'Marginalisation of Export Crop Producing Households, Exemplified by the Position of Women, Food Crop Production and Marketing Conditions: Upper Bambara Chiefdom, Sierra Leone as a Case Study', MA dissertation, Nijmegen.

Konneh, A. M., 1988. 'Problems of Cocoa Marketing Involving Sierra Leone Produce Marketing Board Farmers in Dea Chiefdom, Kailahun District', BA dissertation, Njala University College, University of Sierra Leone.

La Fontaine, J., 1981. 'The domestication of the savage male', *Man* 16 (3), 333–49.

Lahai, A. M., 1971. 'Tribal Education of the Mende of Dasse Chiefdom, Moyamba District, Southern Province, Sierra Leone', BA thesis, Fourah Bay College, University of Sierra Leone.

Leach, G. and Mearns, R., 1988. *Beyond the Woodfuel Crisis: People, Land and Trees in Africa*. London: Earthscan Publications.

Leach, M., 1990. 'Images of Propriety: the Reciprocal Constitution of Gender and Resource Use in the Life of a Sierra Leonean Forest Village', PhD thesis, University of London.

—— 1991a. 'Social organisation and agricultural innovation: women's vegetable production in eastern Sierra Leone', in *Proceedings of a Workshop on 'Peasant Household Systems: Partners in the Process of Development'*, H. de Haen (ed.), 186–208. DSE: Germany.

—— 1991b. 'Locating gendered experience: an anthropologist's view from a Sierra Leonean village', *IDS Bulletin* 22 (1), 44–50. Brighton: Institute of Development Studies.

—— 1991c. 'Engendered environments: understanding natural resource management in the West African forest zone', *IDS Bulletin* 22(4), 17–24. Brighton: Institute of Development Studies.

—— 1991d. 'Women's use of forest resources in Sierra Leone', in *Women and the Environment*, A. Rodda (ed.), 126–8. London and New Jersey: Zed Books.

—— 1991e. 'Shifting social and ecological mosaics in Mende forest farming', paper presented at the 90th annual meeting of the American Anthropological Association, invited session on 'The ecology and economy of food crop production in sub-Saharan West Africa'.

—— 1992a. 'Dealing with displacement: refugee-host relations, food and forest resources in Sierra Leonean Mende communities during the Liberian influx, 1990–91', *IDS Research Report* No. 22. Brighton: Institute of Development Studies.

—— 1992b. 'Gender and the environment: traps or opportunities?', *Development in Practice: An Oxfam Journal*. March 1992, 12–22.

—— 1992c. '"Women's crops in women's spaces": gender relations in Mende rice farming', in *Bush Base: Forest Farm, Culture, Environment and Development*, E. Croll and D. Parkin (eds), 76–96. London: Routledge.

Leonard, H. J. *et al.*, 1989. *Environment and the Poor: Development Strategies for a Common Agenda*. US-Third World Policy Perspectives, No. 11. Washington DC: Overseas Development Council.

Linares. O., 1976. '"Garden hunting" in the American tropics', *Human Ecology* Vol. 4, No. 4, 331–49.

—— 1981. 'From tidal swamp to inland valley: on the social organisation of wet rice cultivation among the Diola of Senegal', *Africa* 51, 557–95.

—— 1985. 'Cash crops and gender constructs: the Jola of Senegal', *Ethnology* 24, 83–94.

—— 1992. *Power, Prayer and Production: the Diola of Senegal*. Cambridge: Cambridge University Press.

Little, K., 1948a. 'The Mende farming household', *Sociological Review* 40, 37–55.

—— 1948b. 'Land and labour among the Mende', *African Affairs* 47 (186), 23–30.

—— 1949. 'The role of secret societies in cultural specialisation', *American Anthropologist* 51, 199–212.

—— 1951. 'The Mende rice farm and its cost', *Zaire* 5 (4) 227–73, 371–80.

—— 1965. 'The political role of the Poro, part 1', *Africa* 35, 349–65.

—— 1966. 'The political role of the Poro, part 2', *Africa* 36, 62–71.

—— 1967. *The Mende of Sierra Leone: a West African People in Transition*. London: Routledge & Kegan Paul.

Little, P. and Brokensha, D. W., 1987. 'Local institutions, tenure and resource management in Africa', in *Conservation in Africa: People, Policies and Practice*, D. Anderson and R. Grove (eds), 193–210. Cambridge: Cambridge University Press.

Lynggard, T. and Moberg, M. (eds), 1990. *Women and Sustainable Development*. Report from the Women's Forum, Bergen, Norway, 14–15 May 1990.

McCay, B. J. and Acheson, J., 1987. *The Question of the Commons: the Culture and Ecology of Communal Resources*. Tucson: University of Arizona Press.

MacCormack, C., 1975. 'Sande women and political power in Sierra Leone', *West African Journal of Sociology and Political Science* 1 (1), 42–50.

—— 1979. 'Sande: the public face of a secret society', in *The New Religions of Africa*, B. Jules-Rosette (ed.), 27–37. New Jersey: Ablex Publishing.

—— 1980. 'Proto-social to adult: a Sherbro transformation', in *Nature, Culture and Gender*, C. MacCormack and M. Strathern (eds), 1–24. Cambridge: Cambridge University Press.

MacCormack, C. and Strathern, M. (eds), 1980. *Nature, Culture and Gender*. Cambridge: Cambridge University Press.

MacFoy, C., 1983. *Medicinal Plant Survey of Sierra Leone*. Department of Botany, Fourah Bay College, Freetown.

MacFoy, C. and Sama, A., 1983. 'Medicinal plants of Pujehun District, Sierra Leone', *Journal of Ethnopharmacology* 8, 215–23.

MacIntire, J. *et al.*, 1985. *An Economic Analysis of Alley Farming with Small Ruminants*. Ibadan: ILCA.

MacKenzie, J., 1988. *The Empire of Nature*. Manchester: Manchester University Press.

Mackintosh, M., 1991. *Gender, Class and Rural Transition: Agribusiness and the Food Crisis in Senegal*. London: Zed Books.

McNeely, J. A. and Pitt, D. (eds), 1985. *Culture and Conservation: the Human Dimension in Environmental Planning*. London and Sydney: Croom Helm.

McNeely, J. A., Miller, K. R., Reid, W. V., Mittermeier, R. A. and Werner, T. B., 1990. *Conserving the World's Biological Diversity*. Gland, Switzerland and Washington: IUCN, WRI, Conservation International, WWF-US, World Bank.

Malcolm, J. M., 1939. 'Mende warfare', *Sierra Leone Studies* (OS) 21, 47–52.

Martin, C., 1991. *The Rainforests of West Africa: Ecology – Threats – Conservation*. Basel, Boston and Berlin: Birkhauser Verlag.

Martin, S., 1988. *Palm Oil and Protest: an Economic History of the Ngwa Region, South Eastern Nigeria, 1800–1980*. Cambridge: Cambridge University Press.

Mathias-Mundy, E., Muchena, O., McKiernan, G. and Mundy, P., 1990. 'Indigenous Technical Knowledge of Private Tree Management', final draft report submitted to FAO, Rome.

Meillassoux, C., 1975. *Femmes, Greniers et Capitaux* (English version 1981: *Maidens, Meal and Money*. Cambridge: Cambridge University Press).

Merchant, C., 1983. *The Death of Nature: Women, Ecology and the Scientific Revolution*. San Francisco: Harper and Row.

Mies, M., 1986. *Patriarchy and Accumulation on a World Scale*. London: Zed Books.

Miller, K. and Tangley, L., 1991. *Trees of Life: Saving Tropical Forests and their Biological Wealth*. World Resources Institute Guide to the Environment. Boston: Beacon Press.

Millington, A., 1987. 'Environmental degradation, soil conservation and agricultural policies in Sierra Leone, 1895–1984', in *Conservation in Africa: People, Policies and Practice*, D. Anderson and R. Grove (eds), 229–48. Cambridge: Cambridge University Press.

Minah, E. M., 1981. 'Agricultural commercialisation and farmer resistance to change: a case of coffee cultivation in Kpaka Chiefdom, Pujehun District', BA dissertation, Njala University College, University of Sierra Leone.

Molnar, A. and Schreiber, G., 1989. 'Women and Forestry: Operational Issues'. *Policy, Planning and Research Working Paper* No. 184. Women in Development Division, Population and Human Resources Department, The World Bank. Washington DC: World Bank.

Moock, J. (ed.), 1986. *Understanding Africa's Rural Households and Farming Systems*. Boulder and London: Westview Press.

Moore, H., 1988. *Feminism and Anthropology*. Cambridge: Polity Press.

Moser, C., 1991. 'Gender planning in the Third World: meeting practical and strategic gender needs', in *Changing Perceptions: Writings on Gender and Development*, T. Wallace (ed.) with C. March, 158–71. Oxford: Oxfam.

Munasinghe, M. and Wells, M., 1992. 'Protection of natural habitats and sustainable development of local communities', in 'Conservation of West and Central African Rainforests', K. Cleaver *et al.* (eds). *World Bank Environment Paper* No. 1, 161–8. Washington DC: World Bank.

Munyakho, D. K. (ed.), 1985. *Women and the Environmental Crisis: a Report of the Proceedings of the Workshops on Women, Environment and Development*, 10–20 July, Nairobi, Kenya. NGO Forum. Nairobi: Environment Liaison Centre.

Murphy, W. P., 1980. 'Secret knowledge as property and power in Kpelle society: elders versus youth', *Africa* 50 (2), 193–207.

—— 1981. 'The rhetorical management of dangerous knowledge in Kpelle brokerage', *American Ethnologist* 8, 667–85.

Murphy, W. P. and Bledsoe, C., 1987. 'Kinship and territory in the history of a Kpelle chiefdom (Liberia)', in *The African Frontier: the Reproduction of Traditional African Societies*, I. Kopytoff (ed.), 123–47. Bloomington and Indianapolis: Indiana University Press.

Myers, N., 1984. *The Primary Source: Tropical Forests and our Future*. Ontario: General Publications.

—— 1989. *Deforestation Rates in Tropical Forests and their Climatic Implications*. London: Friends of the Earth.

National Research Council, 1986. *Proceedings of the Conference on Common Property Resource Management*. Washington DC: National Academy Press.

Nowicki, P., 1985. 'Culture, ecology and "management" of natural resources, or knowing when not to meddle', in *Culture and Conservation*, J. A. McNeely and D. Pitt (eds), 269–82. London and Sydney: Croom Helm.

Nyerges, E., 1989. 'Coppice swidden fallows in tropical deciduous forest: biological, technological and socio-cultural determinants of the secondary succession', *Human Ecology* 17, 379–400.

OECD/DAC, 1989. *Focus on the Future: Women and Environment*, report of the OECD's Development Assistance Committee (DAC) Expert Group on Women in Development Seminar, Paris, May 1989.

Okafor, J. C., 1981. 'Woody Plants of Nutritional Importance in Traditional Farming Systems of the Nigerian Humid Tropics', PhD Thesis, University of Ibadan, Nigeria.

Okali, C., 1983. *Cocoa and Kinship in Ghana*. London: Kegan Paul for the International African Institute.

Okali, C. and Berry, S. (n.d.). 'Alley farming in West Africa in comparative perspective', *Discussion Paper* No. 11, African Studies Center, Boston University.

Oppong, C., 1983. 'Introduction', in *Female and Male in West Africa*, C. Oppong (ed.), 72–75. London: Allen & Unwin.

Ortner, S. B., 1974. 'Is female to male as nature is to culture?', in *Woman, Culture and Society*, M. Z. Rosaldo and L. Lamphere (eds), 67–88. Stanford: Stanford University Press.

Ortner, S. B. and Whitehead, H., 1981. 'Introduction: accounting for sexual meanings', in *Sexual Meanings: the Cultural Construction of Gender and Sexuality*, S. B. Ortner and H. Whitehead (eds), 1–28. New York: Cambridge University Press.

Ostrom, E., 1990. *Governing the Commons: the Evolution of Institutions for Collective Action*. Cambridge: Cambridge University Press.

Paulme, D., 1954. *Les Gens du Riz*. Paris: Librairie Plon.

Pearce, D., Barbier, E. B. and Markandya, A., 1989. *Blueprint for a Green Economy*. London: Earthscan Publications.

—— 1990. *Sustainable Development: Economics and Environment in the Third World*. London: Edward Elgar.

Pearse, A., 1909. Report of a tour made by Major A. Pearse, R.A.M.C. from Freetown to Monrovia through the Protectorate of Sierra Leone and Liberia, 23 February–19 April, Native Affairs Department Letterbook, Sierra Leone Government Archives.

Peperkamp, G., 1984. 'Spatial constraints and the functioning of a marketing system, exemplified by the marketing of cocoa and coffee in Sierra Leone', *Tidschrift voor Economische en Sociale Geographie* (Amsterdam) 75 (3), 186–95.

Person, Y., 1961. 'Les Kissi et leurs statuettes de pierre dans le cadre de l'histoire ouest-africaine', *Bull. IFAN* (B), 23 (1).

Persoon, G., 1989. 'Respect for nature among forest people', *BOS Newsletter* 18 (8), 11–27.

Peters, C., Gentry, A. and Mendelsohn, R., 1989. 'Valuation of an Amazonian rainforest', *Nature* 339, 655–6.

Plant, J. (ed.), 1989. *Healing the Wounds: the Promise of Ecofeminism.* Philadelphia: New Society Publishers.

Plumwood, V., 1986. 'Ecofeminism: an overview and discussion of positions and arguments', *Australian Journal of Philosophy*, 64, 120–38.

Poore, D., 1989. *No Timber without Trees: Sustainability in the Tropical Forest.* London: Earthscan Publications.

Pretty, J. and Sandbrook, R., 1991. 'Operationalising Sustainable Development at the Community Level: Primary Environmental Care', paper presented to DAC Working Party on Development Assistance and the Environment, October 1991. London: IIED.

Rathgeber, E. (ed.), 1989. *Women's Role in Natural Resource Management in Africa.* IDRC Manuscript Report 238e. Canada: IDRC.

Redclift, M., 1987. *Sustainable Development: Exploring the Contradictions.* London and New York: Methuen.

Reeck, D., 1976. *Deep Mende: Religious Interactions in a Changing African Rural Society.* Leiden: E. J. Brill.

Repetto, R. and Gillis, M. (eds), 1988. *Public Policies and the Misuse of Forest Resources.* New York: Cambridge University Press.

Republic of Cameroon, 1990. *The Korup Project: Plan for Developing the Korup National Park and its Support Zone.* World Wide Fund for Nature, Commission of the European Communities and Natural Resources Institute.

Richards, P., 1985. *Indigenous Agricultural Revolution: Ecology and Food Production in West Africa.* London: Hutchinson.

—— 1986. *Coping with Hunger: Hazard and Experiment in an African Rice Farming System.* London: Allen & Unwin.

—— 1988. 'The Sierra Leone Department of Agriculture, 1912–1960: lessons for today?', in *History and Socio-economic Development in Sierra Leone*, C. M. Fyle (ed.), 148–78. Freetown: SLADEA.

—— 1990. 'Local strategies for coping with hunger: northern Nigeria and central Sierra Leone compared', *African Affairs* 89, 265–75.

—— 1992. 'Saving the rain forest: contested futures in conservation', in *Contemporary Futures: Perspectives from Social Anthropology*, S. Wallman (ed.). London: Routledge.

Roberts, P., 1988. 'Rural women's access to labour in West Africa', in *Patriarchy and Class: African Women in the Home and the Workforce*, S. B. Stichter and J. L. Parpart (eds), 97–114. Boulder and London: Westview Press.

Robertson, A. F., 1983. 'Abusa, the structural history of an economic contract', *Journal of Development Studies* 18 (4), 447–8.

Rocheleau, D., 1987. 'A land user perspective for agroforestry research and action', in *Agroforestry: Realities, Possibilities and Potentials*, H. Gholz (ed.). Dordrecht: Martinus Nijhoff.

—— 1988. 'Women, trees and tenure', in *Whose Trees? Proprietary Dimensions of Forestry*, L. Fortmann and J. Bruce (eds). Boulder and London: Westview Press.

—— 1990. 'Gender Complementarity and Conflict in Sustainable Forestry Development: a Multiple User Approach', paper presented to IUFRO World Congress Quinquennial, 5–11 August 1990, Montreal.

Rodda, A. (ed.), 1991. *Women and the Environment*. London: Zed Books.

Rodney, W., 1967. 'A reconsideration of the Mane invasions of Sierra Leone', *Journal of African History* 8 (2), 219–46.

—— 1970. *A History of the Upper Guinea Coast 1545–1800*. London and New York: Monthly Review Press.

Rogers, S. C., 1975. 'Female forms of power and the myth of male dominance: model of female/male interaction in peasant society', *American Ethnologist* 2, 727–57.

Ruitenbeek, H. J., 1990. 'Economic Analysis of Tropical Forest Conservation Initiatives: Examples from West Africa', commissioned Paper for WWF, Surrey, UK.

Salleh, A. K., 1984. 'Deeper than deep ecology: the ecofeminist connection', *Environmental Ethics*, Vol. 16, Winter.

Savill, P. S and Fox, J. E. D., 1967. *Trees of Sierra Leone*. Freetown: Government of Sierra Leone.

Serageldin, I., 1990. *Saving Africa's Rainforests*. Washington: World Bank, Africa Region.

Shepherd, G., 1990. *Communal Management of Forests in the Semi-arid and Sub-humid Zones of Africa*. Report prepared for FAO Forestry Department. London: ODI.

Shiva, V., 1989. *Staying Alive: Women, Ecology and Development*. London: Zed Books.

SIDA, 1990. *Striking a Balance: Gender Awareness in Swedish Development Cooperation*. Stockholm: Swedish International Development Agency.

Singh, K. D. *et al.*, 1990. *A Model Approach to Studies of Deforestation*. DEFR 3. Rome: FAO.

Skutsch, M., 1986. 'Participation of women in social forestry programmes: problems and solutions', *BOS Newsletter* 5 (1), 9–18.

Sommer, A., 1976. 'Attempt at an assesssment of the world's tropical moist forests', *Unasylva* 28, 5–24.

Sontheimer, S. (ed.), 1991. *Women and the Environment: a Reader*. London: Earthscan Publications.

Strathern, M., 1980. 'No nature, no culture: the Hagen case', in *Nature, Culture and Gender*, C. MacCormack and M. Strathern (eds), 174–222. Cambridge: Cambridge University Press.

—— 1987. 'Introduction', in *Dealing with Inequality: Analysing Gender Relations in Melanesia and Beyond*, M. Strathern (ed.), 1–32. Cambridge: Cambridge University Press.

Thompson, H. S. S., 1991. 'Status and Conservation of Threatened Bird Species in the Gola Forest, Sierra Leone'. Regional Seminar on Environmental Management and Rural Development, Sierra Leone, 11–12 April 1991.

Todd, S. K., 1971. 'Gift Situations among the Mende', MA dissertation, Fourah Bay College, University of Sierra Leone.

Unwin, A. H., 1909. *Report on the Forests and Forestry Problems in Sierra Leone*. Waterlow, London, for the Government of Sierra Leone.

Van den Breemer, J. P., 1989. 'Farmers' perception of society and environment, and their land use: the case of the Aouan in Ivory Coast', *BOS Newsletter* 8 (18), 28–44.

Waldock, E. A., Capstick, E. S. and Browning, A. S., 1951. *Soil Conservation and Land Use in Sierra Leone*. Freetown: Government Printer.

WCED, 1987. *Our Common Future*. Report of the World Commission on Environment and Development. Oxford: Oxford University Press.

Wells, M., Brandon, K. and Hannah, L., 1992. *People and Parks: Linking Protected Area Management with Local Communities*. World Bank, World Wildlife Fund and USAID, Washington DC.

Whitehead, A., 1984. 'I'm hungry, Mum: the politics of domestic budgeting', in *Of Marriage and the Market*, K. Young *et al.* (eds). London: Routledge Kegan Paul.

—— 1990. 'Food crisis and gender conflict in the African countryside', in *The Food Question: Profits versus People?*, H. Bernstein *et al.* (eds). London: Earthscan Publications.

Winterbottom, R., 1990. *Taking Stock: the Tropical Forestry Action Plan after Five Years*. Washington DC: World Resources Institute.

Wood, P., 1991. 'Education in a Rain Forest Conservation Programme'. Regional Seminar on Environmental Management and Rural Development, Sierra Leone, 11–12 April 1991.

WWF, 1990. *Cross River National Park Oban Division: Plan for Developing the Park and its Support Zone*. WWF with ODNRI for the Federal Republic of Nigeria and the Cross River State Government.

Zon, R. and Sparhawk, W. N., 1923. *Forest Resources of the World*, Vol. II. London: McGraw-Hill Book Company Inc.

INDEX

Page numbers which are in italics denote tables, diagrams and plates.